Pitman
Office Handbook

Pat Smith, B.A.
Lester B. Pearson Collegiate Institute
Scarborough, Ontario

Pamela J. Hay-Ellis, B.A.
Woodbridge High School
Woodbridge, Ontario

Margaret A. McConnell, B.A.
Elmvale District High School
Elmvale, Ontario

Copp Clark Pitman
A division of Copp Clark Limited
Toronto

ISBN 0-7730-4282-2

Cover/Lorraine Huebner Hulme
Design/Lorraine Huebner Hulme
Technical Illustrations/Peggy Heath
Typesetting/Lithocomp Limited
Printing/The Hunter Rose Company Ltd.
Binding/The Hunter Rose Company Ltd.

Acknowledgements

Many sources and people were consulted in the compilation of this handbook; too
many—unfortunately—to list here. However, the authors would like to express
their thanks to the following people and organizations whose contributions were
of such tremendous assistance to them: Air Canada; Bay Travel; Bell Canada;
CNCP Telecommunications; Canada Customs; Canada Post; Canadian Imperial
Bank of Commerce; Margaret Daniel, Albert Campbell Collegiate Institute;
Gestetner (Canada) Ltd.; Government of Canada, Canadian General Standards
Board; Government of Canada, Dept. of Industry, Trade & Commerce, Small
Business Secretariat; Government of Ontario, Department of Labour; Gray Coach
Lines Ltd.; Betty Klein, Woodbridge High School; Moore Business Forms; Pitney
Bowes Inc.; Charmaine Reynolds; Jean Sharman; David M. Stewart Ltd.;
3M Company; UPS; Via Rail; Xerox Corporation.

Canadian Cataloguing in Publication Data

Smith, Pat.
    Pitman office handbook

Includes index.
ISBN 0-7730-4282-2

1. Office practice — Handbooks, manuals, etc.
I. Hay-Ellis, Pamela J. II. McConnell, Margaret A.
III. Title.

HF5547.S64   651.3'02'02   C82-094098-4

Copp Clark Pitman
517 Wellington Street West
Toronto, Ontario M5V 1G1

Printed and bound in Canada

Preface

Office workers are very special people. Theirs is a demanding and ever-changing role. The office worker has procedures to follow, skills to master, decisions to make, processes to understand, and new challenges to meet; and all this must be accomplished while he or she works harmoniously with others. No mean feat!

The *Pitman Office Handbook* is the "how" book for office workers. It provides instant, practical help in such traditional tasks as writing and typing letters or reports in styles currently favoured in business, making travel arrangements, planning meetings, keeping records, and handling the petty cash. As well, this book enlightens office personnel about such non-traditional topics as word processing, the uses of the computer, "electronic mail," the selection of courier services, conducting a job interview, and the right cutlery to use at dinner. A glance at the table of contents will indicate just how wide-ranging and current is the coverage of this reference source.

To make the book easy to use, the presentation is alphabetic; the information is in concise, point-form arrangement with many heads and subheads; each entry has its own locator code; and the language is easy to read.

Not only will this be an invaluable aid to the worker *on* the job, but it will be an excellent basic text for students in secondary and post secondary institutions learning *how to do* the job.

The conventional business procedures text is large, expensive, and highly descriptive. The *Pitman Office Handbook* offers an exciting new concept; it has the advantages of being small, inexpensive, and succinct. To complete the learning package, a separate teacher's manual/student study guide is available which contains review questions, quizzes, test material, research problems, and a host of original and challenging activities which will permit the teacher to develop a stimulating and effective business procedures program.

How to Find Information in Your Handbook

Find the particular topic you are interested in in the alphabetic index at the end of the book. Beside the index entry will be a page number and a locator code. Find the page indicated, then look at the left-hand side of the page for the locator code, and there will be the information you seek.

Example Itinerary **236**-TA19 (236 is the page;
            TA19 is the locator code on that page)

Table of Contents

Unit 1—Banking and Financial Management   1

Banking: *Types of Accounts*—Current Account, Personal Chequing Account, Savings Accounts, Joint Account; *Making Deposits; Making Withdrawals; Writing Cheques; Endorsing Cheques*—Blank Endorsement, Full Endorsement, Restrictive Endorsement; *Special Types of Cheques*—Certified Cheques, Stopped Cheques, Post-Dated Cheques, Stale-Dated Cheques, N.S.F. Cheques, Cancelled Cheques, Dishonoured (Irregular) Cheques; *The Bank Reconciliation Statement; Other Key Banking Services*—Cash Dispensers (Automatic Tellers), Collections, Credit Cards, Drafts, Financial Advice, Foreign Currency, Letters of Credit, Loans, Money Orders, Package Service, Safety Deposit Boxes, Term Deposits, Traveller's Cheques. **Operating a Petty Cash Fund. Payroll:** *Calculation of Gross Earnings; Preparing the Payroll; Payroll Deductions*—Compulsory Deductions, Voluntary Deductions; *Vacation Pay; Severance Pay; Making Payroll Payment; Employers' Legal Obligations*—Remittance of Collected Funds to Revenue Canada, Workmen's Compensation, T4 (Withholding Statement), Separation Certificate. **Accounting:** *Accounting Records*—Source Documents, Journals, The Ledger, An Account, Trial Balance; *Financial Statements*—The Income Statement, The Balance Sheet.

Unit 2—Communications and Language Skills   21

The Technicalities of Language: *The Right Words*—Clichés to Avoid, Frequently Confused Words, Frequently Misspelled Words, Misused Words, One Word or Two?, Words With Accompanying Prepositions; *Correct Sentence Structure*—Sentence Construction Hints, Sentence Flaws to Avoid; *Punctuation*—Apostrophe, Colon, Comma, Dash, Exclamation Mark, Hyphen, Parentheses and Brackets, Period, Question Mark, Quotation Marks, Semi-Colon, Underscore; *Style Mechanics*—Abbreviations, Capitalization, Numbers, Plurals, Word Division. **The Expression of Language:** *Written Expression of Language*—Basic Writing Tips, Letter Samples (Acknowledgement, Apology, Collection, Complaint, Congratulatory, Enquiry, Form or Circular, Gratitude, Introduction, Order, Payment, Recommendation, Reservations, Response to Job Application, Response to Donation Request, Sales, Sympathy), Forms of Address, Salutations and Complimentary Closings, Memorandums, Press or News Releases, Reports and Manuscripts; *Oral Expression of Language*—Introducing a Speaker, Thanking a Speaker, Making a Speech or Oral Report, Speaking Before Large Groups, How to Dictate; *Grammatical Terms.*

Unit 3—Data Processing   79

Computer Components; The Steps Involved in Processing Data Through the Computer; Input Devices; Central Processing Unit (CPU)—Primary Storage (Memory) Unit, Arithmetic/Logic Unit, Control Unit; *Problem Solving (Programming)*—Computer Languages; *Output Devices; Secondary (Auxiliary) Data Storage; Communicating Facilities (Data Transmission); Word Processing; Computer Facilities for the Small Office*—Service Bureau, Time Sharing; *Data Processing Personnel; Computer Terms.*

Boxed Tabulations; *Tabulation—Typing*—Spacing, Headings, Numbers, Tabulations with Long Edge of Paper Inserted First, Production Tips for Tabulations. **Corrections and Revisions:** *Making Corrections*—Realigning, Spreading, Squeezing (Crowding), Proofreading Tips, Proofreading (Correction) Marks. **Style Practices:** *Typing Metric Expressions*—Symbols, Numbers, Numeric Times and Dates; *Spacing Rules*. **Typed Communications:** *Charts and Graphs*—Line Graph, Vertical Bar Graph, Horizontal Bar Graph, Pictogram, Pie Chart; *Envelopes*—Large Envelopes, Addresses Typed on Continuous Form Labels, Chain Feeding Envelopes; *Folding Correspondence*—Speedy Envelope Sealing and Hand Stamping; *Financial Statements; Forms; Legal Documents*— Typing Preprinted Legal Forms, Typing Entire Legal Documents, Endorsements; *Letters*—Basic Letter Styles, Basic Punctuation Styles, Letter Placement, Mailing Notations, Special Notations, Date, Inside Address, Attention Line, Salutation, Subject Line, Body, Complimentary Closing, Company Name in Closing, Identification Line, Reference Initials, Enclosure Notation, Carbon Copy Notation, Postscript, Headings on Multiple Page Letters, Displayed Information, Additional Business Letter Styles, Form Letters, Letters on Small Stationery, Tips on Rapid Letter Production; *Memorandums; Post Cards; Reports, Essays, Manuscripts*— Title Page, Preface, Table of Contents, Placement (Margins and Starting Lines), Spacing, Headings, Numbering Systems, Ending the Pages, Numbering the Pages, Displayed Information, Illustrations, Quoted Material, Footnotes and Endnotes, Bibliography, Index, Typing Guide Sheet for Reports and Manuscripts; *Transcription Tips*—Taking Dictation in Shorthand, Transcribing. **Typewriter Care:** *Regular Care; Periodic Care.* **Typewriter Selection:** *Carriage Length; Type Size; Type Faces; Self-Correcting Typewriters; Word Processors; Electronic Typewriters.*

Unit 1

Banking and Financial Management

Since money plays a significant role in most business activities, the efficient office worker must be able to perform or at least comprehend the routine tasks associated with money management: banking; keeping a petty cash account; where small businesses are involved, handling the office payroll; and understanding basic accounting functions.

Banking

B1 Legally, only chartered banks operating under the *Bank Act* may call themselves banks. However, other financial institutions such as trust companies, provincial savings banks, credit unions, and caisses populaires offer services similar to those of banks. The information provided here relates to both banks and the other financial institutions.

B2 Types of Accounts

Current Account
(Business Chequing Account)

B3 This account is used by businesses for making deposits and payments.

- No interest is paid.
- Unlimited cheques may be written.

- Regular bank statements, plus cancelled cheques and debit or credit memoranda (explanations of special transactions) are returned to the account holder.
- Monthly service charge is calculated according to the number of transactions and the balance in the account.
- Cash withdrawals are made by cheque.

Personal Chequing Account

B4

This account is used by individuals for making deposits and payments.

- No interest is paid.
- Cash withdrawals must be made by cheque.
- Service charges depend on the number of cheques written. Some institutions waive service charges if a specified monthly balance is maintained.
- Bank statement and cancelled cheques are provided monthly.

Note: Some financial institutions also offer a Daily Interest Bearing Chequing Account, a personal chequing account on which a low interest rate is paid.

Savings Accounts

B5

Chequing Savings Account

This is used by individuals who wish to earn interest on their deposits and who write few cheques.

- Interest is paid but is lower than that paid for a non-chequing savings account.
- Interest is usually calculated on the minimum half yearly balance and is paid each April 30 and October 31. (Interest is paid only on sums on deposit for complete calendar months.)
- Cheques may be written on these accounts, but the cancelled cheques are not returned.
- A service charge is usually made for cheques processed, but certain banks permit some free cheques depending on the balance carried.
- A savings pass book is issued which provides a record of all transactions.

Non-Chequing Savings Account (True Savings)

This account is used by individuals wishing to earn interest on their deposits.

- It earns a higher rate of interest than that paid on a chequing/savings account.
- Interest is calculated on the minimum monthly balance and is paid each April 30 and October 31. (Interest is paid only on sums on deposit for complete calendar months.)

- No cheques may be written.
- A savings pass book is issued in which all transactions are recorded.

Daily Interest Bearing Account

This is essentially a savings account and is used by individuals wishing to earn interest on deposits made too late to earn the full month's interest payable on other savings accounts. Because the interest rate is calculated daily, the rate is usually lower than that paid on a true savings account.

Joint Account

This term is used when an account is shared by two or more persons and may apply to any type of account. Each person may use the account on his or her own signature, unless arrangements with the bank specify that two or more signatures are necessary for transactions.

Making Deposits

Deposit slips for all accounts are similar in format and are designed to indicate to the bank which account should be credited, who is making the deposit, the amount of the deposit, and if some of the money is to be withdrawn.

If a deposit is to be made to a savings account, provide the teller with the account pass book.

Current Account deposit slips come in book form and consist of deposit slips with copy paper behind each one. When a deposit is made, the bank retains the original and stamps the copy, which remains in the book as the customer's record.

Completed deposit slip

To speed up the processing of your deposit:

- Fill out the deposit slip carefully.
- Arrange bills with the smallest denomination on top and place a rubber band around them.
- If there are enough of each coin denomination, roll them in coin wrappers.
- Endorse each cheque properly. (See this unit, B10.)

Making Withdrawals

B8   Where withdrawals are to be made from a savings or chequing/savings account, use the withdrawal slip provided by the bank. Withdrawals from current and personal chequing accounts must be made by cheque.

Writing Cheques

B9   Cheques may be written for any amount up to the amount held on deposit in the account. They may be prepared by hand, typewriter, cheque protector machine, or computer.

- Complete the cheque stub or account record book first.
- Use ink if you prepare the cheque by hand.
- Be sure to insert the correct date.
- Correctly spell the full name of the payee. Titles such as Mr., Miss, Dr., Rev. are unnecessary.
- Write the amount in figures close enough to the printed $ sign so that it cannot be altered.
- Write the amount in words, making sure it is the same amount as the figures indicate. (Express cents as fractions of a dollar.) Begin at the extreme left and fill in any unused part with a line so that there is no space for changes.
- Do not erase. Either prepare a new cheque or properly correct and initial the incorrect one. Do not destroy an unused cheque; write "Void" in large letters across the face of it and the stub, and retain it in the files.
- Ensure the cheque is properly signed.

Completed cheque

Voucher cheque

Endorsing Cheques

B10

Before a cheque can be cashed or deposited it must be properly endorsed. This means that the payee signs his or her name on the reverse side of the cheque or, in the case of a company, uses a rubber stamp. The endorsement does three things:

- relieves the bank of responsibility should the cheque be dishonoured
- acts as a receipt for the cash
- serves as identification of the payee

There are three types of endorsements.

Blank Endorsement

B11

This is used if the payee cashes or deposits a cheque.

- Endorse the cheque exactly as the name appears on the face of the cheque.
- Endorse the cheque only at the bank, just before cashing or depositing it, because the blank endorsement enables anyone presenting the cheque to cash it.

Note: If the payee's name is incorrectly spelled on the face of the cheque, endorse the cheque twice—once as shown on the cheque and then correctly. This is called a *double endorsement.*

Full Endorsement

B12

This is used if the payee wishes to transfer ownership of the cheque to another person. Endorse the cheque with the wording "Pay to the order of (new payee)" and sign it as shown on the face. The new payee may then cash, deposit, or transfer ownership of the cheque again.

Restrictive Endorsement

B13

This is used when it is necessary to protect a cheque against loss or theft. Endorse the cheque with the wording "For deposit only to the account of.....," and sign it as shown on the face. The endorsement may either be written or rubber stamped.

Blank endorsement	Full endorsement	Restrictive endorsement
Mike Belza	*Pay to the order of A. Frendinette M. Belza*	*For deposit only to Ac. 04-0167 for M. Belza M. Belza*
Double endorsement *Mike Belzar Mike Belza*		

Endorsement styles

B14 Special Types of Cheques

Certified Cheques

B15 These are used when a personal cheque is not acceptable.

- Prepare a cheque in the regular way and present it to the bank teller.
- The teller will stamp "Certified" on the face of the cheque and return it to you.
- The bank will immediately deduct the amount of the cheque from the account and transfer it to a special account so that payment is assured when the cheque is presented.

Stopped Cheques

B16 This bank service is used when for some reason — theft, loss, error in preparation — you do not want the bank to make payment on a cheque you have issued.

- Phone the bank immediately to explain why stopping payment is necessary and give complete details of the cheque.
- Write a confirming letter to the bank or fill in a stop-payment form.
- Do not issue a replacement cheque until the bank confirms payment has been stopped on the first one.

Post-Dated Cheques

B17 These cheques are issued for some date in the future. Banks recommend that they not be used because they are easily forgotten, and the money may not be available in the account when they are actually presented.

Stale-Dated Cheques

B18 In the eyes of the bank, cheques have a life span of six months. Stale-dated cheques are over six months old and will not be accepted.

N.S.F. Cheques

B19   N.S.F. means *not sufficient funds*. Cheques stamped with these letters are returned to the payee when the maker's account lacks enough money to meet the amount. It is up to the payee, not the bank, to follow up on the problem.

Cancelled Cheques

B20   These are cheques on which all transactions have been completed. They are returned to the maker with his/her regular statement.

Dishonoured (Irregular) Cheques

B21   This term is used when a cheque is not accepted by the bank for some reason, e.g., amounts in words and figures do not agree; the cheque is undated and/or unsigned.

The Bank Reconciliation Statement

B22   The balance on the statement sent to you by the bank will usually differ from the balance shown in your records. There may be several reasons for this difference:

- The bank has not yet recorded all the deposits you have made.
- All cheques issued have not yet been cleared by the bank for payment (outstanding cheques).
- The bank has added on interest or other payments (credit memos).
- The bank has deducted service charges (debit memos) or an N.S.F. cheque.
- An error has been made.

Follow these steps to reconcile the discrepancy between the bank's balance and yours. Then prepare a Bank Reconciliation Statement which verifies the accuracy of both balances. To do this, you must first:

- Compare the amounts of cancelled cheques and other documents with the amounts shown on the statement. Call the bank immediately if there are any discrepancies.
- List the numbers and amounts of all outstanding cheques. Be sure to include any from the previous reconciliation statement still not cleared through the bank.
- Compare the deposits shown on the bank statement against those in your records.
- List any deposits not shown on the bank statement (late deposits).

- Prepare the actual Bank Reconciliation Statement as follows:
  a. Note the bank statement balance.
     Add the total of late deposits.
     Subtract the total of the outstanding cheques.
     Balance will be the Adjusted Bank Balance.
  b. Note the balance in your cheque record book (or cash account) for the end of the month.
     Add any credit memos shown on the bank statement.
     Subtract any debit memos or N.S.F. cheques shown on the bank statement.
     Balance will be the adjusted amount of your records (Adjusted Cheque Book Balance).

The Adjusted Bank Balance and the Adjusted Cheque Book Balance will now be the same.

```
                    J. Young Landscaping Company

                    Bank Reconciliation Statement

                             19-- 10 31


  Bank Statement Balance                              $1 042.00
  Plus Late Deposit                                      350.00
                                                       1 392.00
  Less Outstanding Cheques
            Cheque 102                  $   5.10
            Cheque 107                     24.80
            Cheque 110                    110.46
            Cheque 116                     51.07
                                                         191.43
  Adjusted Bank Balance                               $1 200.57


  Cheque Book Balance                                 $1 224.32
  Plus Credit Memo--Bond Interest                        41.00
                                                       1 265.32
  Less Outstanding Charges
            N.S.F. Cheque--Daley Co.    $32.50
            Service Charge                4.25
            Loan Interest                28.00
                                                          64.75
  Adjusted Cheque Book Balance                        $1 200.57
```

Bank Reconciliation Statement

B23 Other Key Banking Services

Cash Dispensers (Automatic Tellers)

B24   These permit withdrawals and deposits 24 hours a day. The user is issued a special card and a confidential code number.

Collections

B25   Banks offer collection services for businesses by many means. These include commercial drafts and discounted promissory notes.

Commercial Drafts

Once the buyer and seller have come to a financial agreement, the creditor originates the draft, indicating that presentation of the draft will be made on a particular date. On that day, collection is made from the debtor's bank and the amount (less collection charges) is added to the creditor's bank account.

Discounted Notes

If the holder of a promissory note needs the funds before the date specified on the note, the bank may discount the note, i.e., give the creditor the value of the note, less a discount (the bank charge for redeeming the note earlier than the due date). The bank then collects the proceeds of the promissory note from the debtor.

Credit Cards

B26 Participating banks issue either Visa or Master Charge cards. These cards may be used to purchase goods and services or to obtain cash advances. Such cash advances are treated as loans and interest is charged on a daily basis. Accounts may be paid in full or in part. If payment is in part, the unpaid balance is automatically carried to the next statement and interest is charged. Credit card cheques may be drawn on the holder's credit card account. The money drawn against this account is treated as a loan on which daily interest is charged.

Drafts

B27 These are documents issued by one bank which instruct another bank to pay a specified sum to the person or company named.

Commercial draft: (See this unit, B25.)

Domestic draft: for use in Canada only and issued in unlimited amounts.

International draft: for use outside Canada and issued in domestic or foreign currency.

Financial Advice

B28 The bank will give financial advice on savings and investment programs, pension and annuity plans, home ownership plans, trust fund arrangements, *etc.*

Foreign Currency

B29 This may be bought and sold at most branches of any financial institution.

Letters of Credit

B30 A letter of credit gives instructions from one bank to another to pay up to a specified amount of money to the holder. Satisfactory identification is needed. Letters of credit may be used in Canada and abroad.

Loans

B31   These are available for many business and personal purposes. The contractual agreement to repay the loan is the *promissory note*, which shows the amount borrowed, the interest, and the due date.

Money Orders

B32   **Domestic:** issued in Canadian dollars for amounts up to $500. These may be redeemed at any branch of the issuing bank or deposited with any other Canadian financial institution.

International: issued in U.S. funds up to $500.

Overseas: issued in Canadian currency for transmission to points outside Canada.

Package Service

B33   This is designed for people who use a variety of banking services frequently. For one fixed service charge each month, the customer has free unlimited chequing privileges, buys drafts and traveller's cheques without a service charge, pays bills without a service charge, and receives a discount on a safety deposit box rental.

Safety Deposit Boxes

B34   These may be rented for the safekeeping of valuables.

Term Deposits

B35   A term deposit is a savings plan which permits high interest rates to be earned provided the sum is left on deposit for a preset period of time.

Traveller's Cheques

B36   Traveller's cheques are a safe method of carrying money for vacations or business trips, and are available in many currencies. If they are lost or stolen, your money will be replaced. The purchaser signs each cheque at the time of purchase and countersigns it when it is used.

Operating a Petty Cash Fund

B37   Petty cash (or imprest fund) is the amount of cash kept in the office to pay for small purchases or expenses such as taxi fares, odd stationery items, and mailing costs.

Follow these hints to operate your office fund successfully:

- Decide on a starting sum for the fund (usually enough to cover miscellaneous expenses for approximately one month).
- Give *one* person responsibility for operating the fund.
- Keep the cash and supporting records in a locked cash box or drawer during the day and in the vault overnight.
- Fill out a petty cash voucher (showing amount paid, date, purpose of expenditure, and signature of spender) for each amount paid out. Obtain receipts (invoices, sales slips) whenever possible and attach them to the voucher.
- Record each transaction. Use either a Petty Cash Book or loose sheets of cash paper kept in a binder.
- Replenish your fund before it gets too low. (The amount required to restore the fund to its original amount should be the sum of the vouchers.)
- Record the cash received in the Petty Cash Book.
- The cash box should always contain cash and/or vouchers totalling the exact amount of the fund.

PETTY CASH VOUCHER

Date __March 16, 19--__

Amount __$5.12__

Account to be charged __Office Expense__

Paid to __Drew Young__

For __Taxi fare (delivery of urgent package)__

Received payment __D. Young__
Signature

Petty Cash Voucher

Petty Cash Book for March, 19--

Date		Receipts	Payments
March 1	Balance	50.00	
March 2	Postage		2.00
March 3	Advertising		2.00
March 5	Taxi		4.50
March 6	Owner's Drawing		10.00
March 8	Meals		7.00
March 15	Advertising		3.83
March 16	Taxi fare		5.12
March 21	Special stationery		3.19
March 27	Telegram		2.00
		50.00	39.64
Apr. 1	Cash on hand	10.36	
Apr. 1	Cheque #171	39.64	

Petty Cash Book page

DEPPISCH COSMETICS

Petty Cash Requisition

REQUEST TO REPLENISH PETTY CASH FOR

PERIOD 19-- 03 01 to 19-- 03 31

Petty Cash Summary:

Advertising expense	$ 5.83
Office expense	9.62
Miscellaneous expense	14.19
J. Deppisch, Drawing	10.00
Total disbursements	39.64
Cash on hand	10.36
Amount of Petty Cash Fund	$50.00

__B. Farrar__
Petty Cashier

Petty cash requisition

Payroll

B38　In larger organizations the payroll is the responsibility of a payroll clerk — or even an entire department — and may be totally automated. In the smaller firm, the job may be done manually as part of an office worker's other duties.

Regardless of the number of employees and the extent of automation, the fundamentals of successful payroll operation are the same:

- Every employee should be paid on time.
- Payment must be accompanied by a statement explaining gross earnings, deductions, and net payment.
- Federal and provincial laws concerning payroll records and payment of collected funds must be followed.
- All payroll information must be kept confidential.

Calculation of Gross Earnings

B39   Earnings are usually calculated on one of the following bases.

Commissions: paid as a percentage of the dollar amount of sales. Employees may receive straight commission or a combination of salary and commission.

Piecework rates: earnings based on the number of units produced.

Salaries: incomes quoted for a specific period of time (weekly, monthly, or yearly) with equal payments being made each pay period.

Wages: earnings based on an hourly rate.

Employers are required by law to keep a record of the hours worked by all employees. In most cases, this work attendance record is some form of timecard or time sheet. This provides a record of the employee's arrival and departure times, or the time spent on a particular job. The employee's gross earnings are based on the total hours shown on the timecard. Most companies have rules for overtime and penalties for lateness.

Time Card							
Week Ended September 14					19--		
Social Insurance No. 603 456 667							
Name				Burns, Joseph			

Day	Morning In Out		Afternoon In Out		Extra In Out		Total Hours
M	7:58	12:01	12:59	5:01			8
T	7:56	12:01	12:58	5:02			8
W	8:03	12:00	12:58	5:01			7¾
T	7:58	12:01	12:59	5:01			8
F	7:59	12:01	12:57	5:00	5:57	7:02	8½
S	7:59	12:02					¼
S							

	Hours	Rate	Earnings
Regular Time	39¾	6.80	270.30
Overtime	5	10.20	51.00
Gross Pay			321.30

Time card

Preparing the Payroll

B40   *The Payroll Journal* (Summary or Register) is kept as a permanent record of all employees' hours, gross pay, deductions, and net pay. This form must be completed for each pay period.

The journal must balance:
- The sum of the Regular and Extra Earnings columns must equal the sum of the Gross Earnings column.
- The sum of the Total Deductions column must equal the total of all the separate Deductions columns.
- The sum of the Net Pay column must equal the sum of the Gross Pay column minus the Total Deductions column.

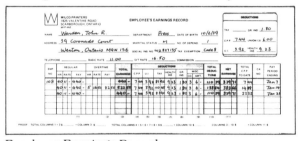

EMP. NO.	NAME OF EMPLOYEE	NET CL. CODE	REGULAR	OVERTIME	GROSS EARNINGS	CPP	UI	REG. PEN	TAXABLE EARNINGS	TAX	HEALTH	GROUP INS	CODE	OTHER	TOTAL DEDUCTIONS	NET EARNINGS
103	John Coleman	9	312.00	35.10	347.10	5.92	3.60	9.50	338.08	52.10	11.00	7.00			89.12	257.98
104	Bill Straham	1	304.50		304.50	5.11	3.60	9.50	286.29	57.40	5.50	7.00			88.61	215.89
105	Linda Sherman	10	372.00	40.80	312.80	5.29	3.60	9.50	294.41	39.65	11.00	7.00			76.04	256.76
106	Lesley Durran	1	324.00		324.00	5.47	3.60	9.50	305.43	64.15	5.50	7.00			95.22	228.78
107	Stan Houser	9	272.00	61.20	333.30	5.65	3.60	9.50	314.45	48.75	11.00	7.00			85.50	247.70
108	Tracey St James	1	272.00	30.60	302.60	5.11	3.60	9.50	284.39	57.90	5.50	7.00			88.61	213.99
	Totals		1756.50	167.70	1924.20	32.55	21.60	57.00		320.45	49.50	42.00			523.10	1401.10

Gross	$1924.20
Deductions	523.10
Net	1401.10

Payroll Journal page

An *Employee Earnings Record* must also be kept for each employee. This is a cumulative record of the employee's earnings and deductions for the whole year.

Employee Earnings Record

Payroll Deductions

B41   The employer withholds a portion of an employee's pay because of compulsory government and union regulations, and such other considerations as fringe benefit schemes.

Compulsory Deductions

B42   **Pension**

Employees between 18 and 65 in all provinces except Quebec must contribute to the Canada Pension Plan. Quebec employees must contribute to the Quebec Pension Plan, which is administered by that province. The amount of the

Canada Pension Plan or Quebec Pension Plan contribution is shown in tables available from Revenue Canada, Taxation.

Unemployment Insurance

Deductions for unemployment insurance are compulsory for employees under 65 who are employed for more than a prescribed number of hours or a specific weekly sum. (The currently prescribed number of hours or weekly sum may be obtained by contacting the Unemployment Insurance Commission.) Deductions are made according to a schedule issued annually by Revenue Canada, Taxation. The employer records payments made, weeks worked, and unemployment insurance contributions.

Income Tax

Deductions for income tax must be made for all employees except those whose yearly taxable income falls below the minimum taxable income. These deductions must be made in accordance with tables issued annually for each province by Revenue Canada, Taxation. New employees must complete an Employee's Tax Deduction Declaration (TD1), a claim for personal exemptions which provides the employer with a *net claim code* for the employee.

Provincial Health Insurance

In some provinces it is compulsory for employers to deduct health insurance premiums. Sometimes the employer pays part or all of the premium as a taxable fringe benefit.

Voluntary Deductions

B43   The following is a list of other deductions that might be made. Such deductions may only be made with the employee's permission.

Private pension plan contributions	Group life insurance premiums
Extended health care	Bond purchases
Dental health care	Charitable contributions
Professional association fees	Stock purchases

These amounts are collected and then remitted by the company to the agency concerned.

Vacation Pay

B44   In most provinces it is mandatory for certain classes of workers to receive vacation pay. This is usually handled by issuing the regular pay cheque for the vacation period on the pay day before the holiday commences. The employee is paid for the most recent pay period worked plus a payment for the earned holiday period.

If an employee who has not earned the full year's vacation entitlement leaves employment without taking the earned holiday, that employee is entitled to vacation pay of a percentage of the annual salary. Provincial legislation determines the percentage.

Severance Pay

B45
If an employee is discharged, the employer should give notice in writing. The discharged person is entitled to receive severance pay according to his/her length of service. The severance pay entitlement is dictated by the Employment Standards Act of each province.

Making Payroll Payment

B46
Payment may be made by *cheque*, by *transferring the funds* to a particular bank or to the employee's bank, or in *cash*.

Payment by cheque or transfer of funds eliminates handling large sums of cash and cuts down on the danger of theft. Payroll cheques are usually issued on a separate bank account. To transfer funds to this account, a regular cheque for the amount of the total payroll is issued and deposited in the special payroll account. This account is easy to reconcile because when all the cheques are cashed, the balance will be zero.

Attached to each cheque is a voucher which shows gross pay, deductions, and net pay.

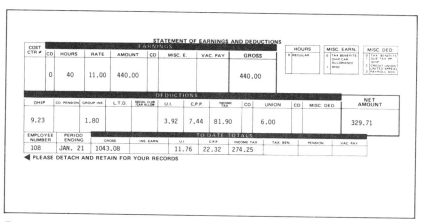

Earnings statement

Payment by cash requires that a cheque is issued on the firm's regular bank account for the total of the Net Earnings column of the Payroll Journal for that pay period; and also that the bank is supplied with a Payroll Currency Requisition form. This is a breakdown of each employee's earnings according to the denominations of both bills and coins.

Each employee should be provided with a pay envelope which should include a statement showing the employee's earnings, deductions, and net pay. When the envelopes are distributed, the employee's signature as proof of payment should be obtained.

B47 Employers' Legal Obligations

Remittance of Collected Funds to Revenue Canada

B48 Each month a remittance must be made to the Receiver General of Canada which includes the combined employee deductions for income tax, Canada or Quebec Pension Plan and unemployment insurance, as well as the company's share of Canada or Quebec Pension Plan and unemployment insurance.

Workmen's Compensation

B49 All provinces require *employers* to contribute to a workmen's compensation fund. The amount is based on the annual payroll, the type of industry, and the company's safety record. Details of amounts payable and payment dates may be obtained from the Workmen's Compensation Board.

T4 (Withholding Statement)

B50 By February 28 each year, employers must provide each employee with a T4 form, which shows the employee's gross earnings and any taxable benefits (such as an employer-provided automobile) for the preceding year, and contributions withheld for Canada or Quebec Pension Plan,

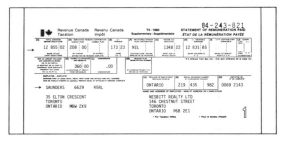

Completed T4 form

unemployment insurance, income tax, and any other deductions (such as union dues and charitable donations). One copy of the form must be sent to the District Taxation Office as part of the annual T4-T4A Return and two copies to the employee.

Separation Certificate

B51 An employee leaving employment must be given a separation certificate (Record of Employment form). The person named must present this document to the local Canada Employment Centre in order to collect unemployment insurance benefits.

Accounting

B52 Accounting in a business involves the recording of all financial transactions (purchases, sales, returns, money received, and money paid out) and the preparation of financial statements. While the accounting function in most organizations is automated and is the concern of specialists in the field, *every* office worker should at least be familiar with the terms and processes involved.

B53   Accounting Records

Source Documents

B54 The accounting process starts with a basic business record known as a *source document*. Invoices, credit invoices, cheques, purchase orders, cash register tapes, and timecards, are all examples of source documents. Where an automated accounting system is involved, the source document information must be translated into a form that can be used by the data processing equipment, e.g., magnetic tape or disk.

Journals

B55 Information from a source document is recorded in a journal (a daily record) which for manual or mechanical accounting systems may be in loose leaf, book, or card form. The journal entry shows the accounts affected by the transaction and provides a brief explanation of the transaction. Very small businesses may use only one journal; larger ones may use some or all of the following special journals.

Cash Receipts Journal: to record cash received in currency, cheques, money orders, or other cash substitutes.

Cash Payments (or Disbursements) Journal: to record payments made by cash or cheque.

Purchases Journal: to record purchases made on credit.

Sales Journal: to record sales made on credit.

General Journal: to record transactions not already recorded in one of the other journals.

Some very small businesses amalgamate these journals into one combination or *synoptic* journal.

The Ledger

B56 The information recorded in a journal is *posted* (transferred) to separate, individual accounts. A group of related accounts (e.g., accounts payable, accounts receivable) is referred to as a *ledger.*

An Account

B57 An account is a record of all transactions which have affected revenue; a particular client; or a specific asset, expense, or liability. Each account has three columns—debit, credit, and balance. Increases in asset and expense accounts are recorded in the debit column and decreases in the credit column. Increases in liability and revenue accounts are recorded in the credit column and decreases in the debit column. The difference between the total debits and total credits is the account *balance.*

Monthly *statements of account* are sent to customers who owe money. The statement shows the opening balance, purchases, returns, payments, and closing balance for the month. (See Unit 6, FO22.)

Some organizations use a journalless-ledgerless accounting system. In this case, documents related to a particular customer are simply filed and used to produce a statement of account on a particular day of the month. In a large, computerized accounting system, statements may be printed by the computer directly from information stored in the Accounts Receivable Ledger.

Trial Balance

B58 A trial balance is prepared as a check on the mathematical accuracy of the ledger. On the trial balance are listed the balances of all the separate accounts under the headings of debit and credit. The totals of the two columns must be identical. The information provided in the trial balance is used in the preparation of the Income Statement and the Balance Sheet.

Financial Statements

B59 The operating results and financial standing of a business are reported to shareholders, management, and others by means of financial statements. The two key statements are the Income Statement and the Balance Sheet. (The Income Statement might also be called the Profit and Loss Statement, Earnings Statement, Operating Statement, or Revenue and Expenditure Statement.)

The Income Statement

This is a summary of the revenue, expenses, and net income or net loss earned over a given period of time.

```
                        J. Savage Services

                         Income Statement

                 For the Month Ended December 31, 19--
                         Current Year              Previous Year
      Income
      Gross Sales ..................  $103 000
           Less Returns ...........      3 000

      Net Sales ...................            $100 000 (100%)  $85 000 (100%)


      Cost of Goods Sold
      Opening Inventory, Dec. 1 ....  $ 16 000
      Purchases ...................     54 000
      Cost of Goods for Sale ......     70 000
           Less Ending Inv., Dec. 31   10 000
      Cost of Goods Sold ..........               60 000
      Gross Profit ................             $ 40 000  (40%)  $35 000 (41.2%)


      Expenses
      Salaries Expense ............   $ 20 000
      Advertising Expense .........      5 000
      Depreciation Expense ........      2 000
      Miscellaneous Expense .......      2 000

           Total Operating Expenses              29 000

      Net Income ..................             $ 11 000 (11%)  $12 000 (14.1%)
```

Income Statement (comparative)

Net sales represents total sales minus returns and discounts. *Cost of goods sold* is arrived at by adding beginning inventory and purchases made during the period, and then deducting the ending inventory. *Gross profit* is the difference between cost price and selling price. The figure should be large enough to cover the expenses of the business and provide a reasonable profit. If gross profit is not large enough to cover expenses, an overall loss will result. *Operating expenses* are the expenses incurred in running the business, e.g., salaries, heat, light, telephone, *etc*.

Income Statements in Percentage Terms

Ratios that exist between the separate elements of the Income Statement provide worthwhile comparisons with previous years' performances and with competitors' prices (see illustration). Some firms have standard ratios that they aim to achieve each year. The standard ratio also proves useful in establishing prices for items where competitive prices are not significant factors.

The Balance Sheet

B61   The Balance Sheet is a picture of the financial standing of a business at a specific time. It summarizes the assets (owned items of value), liabilities (amounts owed by the business), and owners' equity (capital), which is the owners' claim against the assets. The "balance" in the title of the statement indicates that assets equal liabilities plus owners' equity (capital).

Current assets are assets used up or converted into cash within one year. Accounts receivable is the amount to be received by the company from customers supplied with goods or services on credit. Notes receivable indicates outstanding promissory notes (promises to repay a debt). Fixed assets are the virtually permanent assets of the firm. Current liabilities are debts that will be paid within one year. Accounts payable is the amount of money to be paid by the business to its creditors. Owner's equity represents the owner's claim on the assets of the company.

```
                        J. Savage Services
                          Balance Sheet
                      as at December 31, 19--


                              ASSETS

         Current Assets
         Cash .............................     $12 000
         Accounts Receivable ..................   45 000
         Notes Receivable .....................    3 000
         Inventory ............................   10 000
                                                             $ 70 000

         Fixed Assets
         Land .................................   $45 000
         Buildings ...............  $60 000
             Less Depreciation ....  10 000
                                                  50 000
                                                               95 000

         Total Assets ........................              $165 000

                            LIABILITIES

         Current Liabilities
         Accounts Payable .....................   $52 000

         Fixed Liabilities
         Long-term Debt .......................    10 000

         Total Liabilities ....................              $ 62 000

                          OWNER'S EQUITY

         J. Savage, Capital ...................   $92 000
         Net Income ...........................    11 000
                                                              103 000

         Total Liabilities and Owner's Equity ..            $165 000
```

Balance Sheet

Unit 2

Communications and Language Skills

To communicate successfully in business, you must be able to:

- speak well and write legibly
- use English that is simple and correct
- convey courtesy in the tone of your message

The first part of this unit is concerned with the technicalities of language; you will be provided with the information needed to help you:

- choose your words with precision
- structure your sentences properly
- punctuate accurately
- follow the conventions of style

The second part of this unit is concerned with producing written and oral communications; you will learn how to produce communications to fit most typical business situations.

Note: This unit is not designed to provide you with a detailed analysis of the English language but rather to help you solve the day-to-day problems which arise in the preparation of business communications. However, in the discussion of writing and language which follows, certain grammatical terms are used which may need some clarification. Brief definitions of the terms used are provided in a glossary at the end of this unit.

The Technicalities of Language

The Right Words

C1
Writing for business situations is no different from writing for other situations: there is a message to communicate and an audience to communicate to. The writer's task is to eliminate any possible barriers in this process of communication so that the message is *received and understood*.

Keep your words simple, and use them with precision and care. Avoid clichés, slang, and jargon. Stay away from overused and dated expressions. Be very careful to steer clear of ambiguities, redundancies, and inaccuracies.

If in doubt, search it out! The dictionary, the thesaurus, and a handbook of English usage will prove invaluable reference books. (See Unit 8, I6.)

Clichés to Avoid

C2
To be effective, business correspondence should be straightforward, as brief as possible, and easy to understand. Do not use clichés or hackneyed, old-fashioned words in the hope that they will make a good impression on the reader. Let one word do the work of three or four.

Avoid	Use	Example
(We) acknowledge receipt of	Thank you	Thank you for your letter...
(We) are in receipt of	We have received, thank you	We have received your order No....
At all times	Always	We always enjoy our business association with you.
At an early date	Soon, immediately	We expect to have an answer soon.
At this point in time, or at this time	Now, at present	Your representative is here now.
Due to the fact that	Because, since, as	Because the workers are on strike...
Encounter difficulty	Have trouble, need help	If you need help, please call us.
Enclosed please find, enclosed herewith	We enclose, enclosed is	We enclose a cheque for...
In due course	As soon as, when	My client will pay as soon as she is able.

Avoid	Use	Example
In re	Regarding, about	Your suggestion regarding the annual bonus...
In the event that	In case, if	If it rains, the games...
In the amount of	For	Your cheque for $10 arrived...
In the near future	Soon, shortly	You can expect to hear from us shortly.
In view of the fact that	Because, since	They had to agree because he was their president.
May we anticipate an early reply?	May we expect	May we expect to hear from you soon?
Of the opinion that	Think	They think this is a good time to buy.

Frequently Confused Words

C3

The complexity of the English language sometimes causes confusion because of words which sound alike but have different meanings. Consult the following chart if you are in doubt about the correct word to choose.

Word	Meaning	Usage Example
accept	to receive	Please accept this present from us.
except	not including	Everyone except Julio was invited.
adverse	hostile	Shouting at a customer has an adverse effect on business.
averse	opposed	Politicians are averse to being blunt.
advice (n.)	counsel	Their advice was freely given.
advise (v.)	to recommend	Please advise me of the best action to take.
		The lawyer was eager to advise the client.
affect (v.)	to move or to touch (mind), to assume	Love will affect a child positively.
		He affected an air of confidence.
effect (n.)	consequence	Meeting the Pope had a profound effect on Ginette.
effect (v.)	to accomplish	We will do everything we can to effect prompt delivery.
alternate	one of two choices	She took the scenic route; we took the alternate one.
alternative	choice of several	When four roads meet, the driver has three alternatives; he can turn right, or left, or go straight on.

Word	Meaning	Usage Example
assistance	help, aid	Give your assistance to those nurses.
assistants	helpers	The managers and their assistants were present.
cite	to quote (in support of)	The witness was asked to cite an example.
sight	view	What a wonderful sight the ocean was!
site	location	The new site for our home has been chosen.
coarse	rough, common	The unfinished table has a coarse surface.
course	path, way	Every ship's captain must plot a safe course.
	division of a meal	We ate the seven-course meal slowly.
	outline of a subject to be learned	The teacher prepared the course of study for Grade 11 English.
complement	to fill up or complete	Use alyssum to complement the flower arrangement.
compliment	polite expression of praise	It is kind to pay a compliment.
council (n.)	administrative body	The North York Council meets this week.
counsel (n. or v.)	guidance	Ask for counsel from someone with experience.
	to advise	Parents should counsel their children wisely.
decent	respectable	Returning a lost article is the decent action to take.
descent	decline, down-ward motion	The elevator's descent from the tenth to the ground floor was fast.
dissent (n. or v.)	disagree (ment)	The dissent between players caused their team to lose.
defer to	to respect the opinion of	It is customary for young people to defer to older people.
	to postpone	Shall we defer the meeting until next week?
differ	to be unlike	Their opinions differed, so they reached a compromise.
defective	faulty	The defective computer was returned to the store.
deficient	incomplete	This office is deficient — it has no typewriter.

Word	Meaning	Usage Example
desert	to abandon	The ruler was deserted by his followers.
	barren land	Sand is everywhere in the desert.
dessert	sweet course	Dessert after dinner will be baked alaska.
eligible	fit to be chosen	Your training makes you eligible for this job.
illegible	unreadable	That doctor's writing is illegible.
emigrant	person leaving country	Sanjay is an emigrant from Kenya.
immigrant	person entering country	Joe Chan is an immigrant to Canada.
eminent	distinguished	The Queen of England is an eminent lady.
imminent	about to happen	They were told a hurricane was imminent.
formally	according to form, rule	Please dress formally for the Prime Minister's dinner.
formerly	previously	His mother's family was formerly from Poland.
foreword	preface	A book often contains a foreword.
forward	in front	Please go forward ten paces.
hear	to listen	Birdsong is pleasant to hear.
here	in this place	Bring the files here, please.
incite	to stir up	The union leader incited the workers to riot.
insight	penetration with under-standing	A year in India will give you an insight into some Asian cultures.
its	possessive form of *it*	The lion protects its young.
it's	contraction for *it is*	It's the end of the year on December 31.
last	final	The last train left at 2:30 p.m.
latest	most recent	What is the latest news on world food supplies?
later	farther on in time	The later we dine, the more we will eat.
latter	second of two	Sue and Carol came together; the latter drove.
loose	free	Because his shoe was loose, it fell off.

Word	Meaning	Usage Example
lose	to be deprived of	They may lose their place if they are not here soon.
moral	concerned with distinction between right and wrong	Children's moral behaviour is patterned after adults' behaviour.
morale	mental condition or attitude	The morale in our office is very high under the new manager.
overdo	to go too far	If you overdo the exercise, you will be ill.
overdue	late, past the due time	The March payment is long overdue.
passed	past tense of *to pass*	Every student passed the exam.
past	beyond in time or place	It is now long past midnight.
personal	one's own	Each member is entitled to a personal opinion.
personnel	body of workers	All our personnel are happy.
peruse	to examine carefully	Please peruse the report and give me your opinion.
pursue	to follow with intent to catch	The tiger pursued the deer.
precede	to go before	A precedes B in the alphabet.
proceed	to go on	Let us proceed with the meeting.
principal	chief, major	The principal cause of car accidents is careless driving.
principle	fundamental truth, personal code of conduct	Accounting principles require considerable study. Albert Schweitzer's high principles brought him world renown.
stationary	unmoving	A statue is stationary.
stationery	writing materials	Most firms have printed stationery.
their	possessive form of *they*	Their house is very large.
there	in that place	Take this cake over there, please, Jill.
they're	contraction for *they are*	They're late for the meeting.
weather	atmospheric conditions	The weather forecast called for rain.

Word	Meaning	Usage Example
whether	which of two alternatives	I do not know whether or not the relatives are coming.
whose	possessive form of *who*	Whose hat is this?
who's	contraction for *who is*	The one who's first gets the prize.
your	possessive form of *you*	Make sure you take your own pen.
you're	contraction for *you are*	When you're in Spain, speak Spanish.

Frequently Misspelled Words

C4   The words listed here frequently pose spelling problems to writers. If you have difficulties with spelling, consult a dictionary often, refer to this section, or compose your own list of troublesome words.

absence	catalog(ue)	dissatisfied	height
accidentally	category	dividend	hors d'oeuvre
accommodate	champagne	efficiency	hundredth
achievement	changeable	eighth	hypocrisy
acquaintance	chauffeur	embarrass	inasmuch as
acquiesce	column	en route	incidentally
acquisition	commitment	etiquette	indictment
advantageous	committee	exaggerate	indispensable
advisable	concede	exceed	intercede
all right	congratulate	excise	irrelevant
amortize	conscience	exercise	itinerary
analysis	conscientious	exhaustible	leisure
analyze	conscious	extension	liaison
apparently	convenience	facsimile	licence or
argument	correspondence	fascinating	license (v.)
arrears	courteous	February	lien
ascertain	courtesy	foreign	lieutenant
assessment	criticism	forty	lightning
attitude	debt	fourteen	loose (adj.)
bachelor	deceive	friend	lose (v.)
bankruptcy	defendant	fulfill	lying
beginning	definitely	gauge	maintenance
believe	dependant (n.)	government	meantime
beneficiary	dependent (adj.)	grammar	mileage
bulletin	desirable	grateful	miscellaneous
business	development	grievance	mischievous
calendar	dilemma	guarantee	mortgage
campaign	disappoint	handkerchief	necessary
carriage	discreet	harass	neighbour

neither	preferable	restaurant	synonym
nickel	prejudice	rhythm	tariff
ninety	prerogative	schedule	technique
ninth	privilege	seize	temperament
noticeable	procedure	separate	thoroughly
occasion(ally)	proceed	similar	unanimous
occurred	professor	simultaneous	usable
occurrence	promissory	sincerely	or useable
omission	pronunciation	skillful	vacuum
omitted	psychiatric	sponsor	vice versa
oversight	psychology	subpoena	warehouse
pamphlet	pursue	substantial	Wednesday
parallel	questionnaire	subtle	weird
permissible	queue	subtlety	whether
perseverance	receipt	subtly	wholly
personnel	receive	succeed	wield
persuade	recognize	suing	withhold
phase	recommend	supersede	woollen
possession	reference	surprise	writing
precede	resistance	susceptible	yield

Misused Words

C5   Certain words and phrases are frequently misused. Below is a list of the most commonly misused expressions and their acceptable forms.

among and **between**
Use *between* when two items are referred to; *among* for more than two.

> The argument is only between you and me.
> Please sort out the problem among all of you.

and etc. and **etc.**
etc. means "and the rest" or "and so forth"; therefore *and* is redundant.

> Corn, beans, *etc.*, are common vegetables.

anyplace and **anywhere**
Use *anywhere* only.

> Is there a restaurant anywhere near here?

anyways and **anyway**
There is no such word as *anyways*.

> He had to be present anyway.

bring and **take**
Use *bring* to this place (here); and *take* to that place (there).

> Will you bring the cake when you come?
> Take these books home with you when you go.

can and **may**

Can implies capability; *may* signifies a request or probability.

> An athlete can usually run fast.
> May my friends join me in the contest?
> The Games may take place in Canada.

come and **go**

Use *come* when implying "here"; *go* when meaning "there."

> The P.M. is expecting twenty guests to come for lunch.
> I am going to Africa for my holidays.

every which way and **in all directions**

Every which way is slang.

> The traffic seemed to be moving in all directions at the same time.

fix and **repair**

These words have different meanings.

> Please repair the television as quickly as possible.
> **But**
> Let's fix the date for Wednesday.

good and **well**

The adjective *good* must modify a noun; *well* is used as an adverb or an adjective.

> She did a good job.
> He did well.
> I am well.

in regards to and **in regard to**

In regard to is correct.

> Call me in regard to the picnic.

lay and **lie**

Lay means to place and requires a direct object; *lie* means to recline and can stand alone.

> Edith was asked to lay the documents on the desk.
> Robert had to lie down every afternoon while recuperating from his illness.

real and **really**

Real is an adjective which describes a noun; *really* is an adverb.

> She ran a really fine race.
> He is wearing a real diamond.

seeing as how and **since**

Seeing as how is slang.

> Since you like chocolates, here is a large box for you.

shall and **will**

In formal English, to indicate:

future: use *shall* in the first person (I shall, we shall);
will in the second and third person (you will, he will,
they will).

> We shall submit the report tomorrow

determination: use *will* in the first person (I will, we will);
shall in the second and third persons (you shall, he shall,
they shall).

> We will strike if agreement is not reached.

Note: In modern usage, *will* is increasingly used in all
persons to express both future and determination.

> I expect I will have a good trip. (future)
> I will complete this report if it kills me. (determination)

some place and **somewhere**

Some place is incorrect.

> I left my glasses somewhere.

than and **then**

Use *than* for making comparisons; use *then* when referring
to time.

> The tall boy is much stronger than the short one.
> First came the caviar; then came the pheasant.

there is and **there are**

Is refers to a singular noun; *are* refers to a plural one.

> There is only one Queen of England.
> There are many books to be sold.

who and **which** (relative pronouns)

Who refers to a person; *which,* to a thing.

> The man *who* delivered the computer was very polite.
> The telephone, *which* is near the door, is within easy
> reach.

One Word or Two?

C6

If you are in doubt, refer to the list below.

all ready (all prepared): They are all ready to go.
already (adv.) (past the time): It is already too late for lunch.

all right (acceptable, satisfactory): Everyone agreed that the
office layout was all right. (Alright: incorrect spelling of *all
right.*)

all together (in unison): The choir should sing all together.
altogether (adv.) (entirely): Your holiday was altogether too
expensive.

any time (adj. and n.) (used with a specific time in mind): If you
have any time next week, please call.

anytime (adv.) (used when no specific time is intended): You are welcome here anytime.

any way: Is there any way in which we can help?

anyway (adv.) (in any case): Anyway, the game had already been won. (There is no such word as anyways.)

every day (each day): It is good to practise every day.

everyday (adj.) (daily): Coffee break is an everyday occurrence.

may be: The children may be going out this afternoon.

maybe (adv.) (perhaps): Maybe the children will go out soon.

no body: There was no body to be found in that murder case.

nobody (pronoun) (no one): Nobody came to the party.

some time (adj. and n.) (used with a specific time in mind): Snow usually falls some time in January.

sometime (adv.) (used when no specific time is intended): He promised to call her sometime.

sometimes (adv.) (on occasion): Sometimes it's difficult to sit up straight.

Words With Accompanying Prepositions

C7   Certain words in English must be accompanied by a particular preposition. For example:

accompanied *by*	She was accompanied by her mother.
according *to*	According to the news, the damage was great.
capable *of*	Jock is capable of doing that job well.
comply *with*	If you agree, please comply with my request promptly.
concur *in* (something)	Everyone did not concur in that decision.
concur *with* (people)	The president concurred with the manager.
conform *to*	The building does not conform to specifications.
different *from* (not *to* or *than*)	Bill is quite different from Ned.
plan *to* (not *on*)	Let us plan to stay slim while on vacation.
superior *to* (not *than*)	One twin is superior in intelligence to the other.
surrounded *by*	That farmhouse is surrounded by fields.
try *to*	Please try to see it my way.

Correct Sentence Structure

C8   Sentences may be long or short, simple or complex. However, regardless of length or complexity, they must always be grammatically sound.

Sentence Construction Hints

C9   **Select your words with care**. Use words only in their exact, precise meanings. Avoid wordiness.

> *Wordy*: The customer was mad because when he returned the merchandise the clerk was rude and she refused to give him a refund.
> *Better*: When the customer returned the merchandise, he was annoyed at the clerk's rudeness and refusal to refund the money.

Be grammatically consistent. Avoid disagreements in number, tense, or mood.

> *Inconsistency in number: Each person* is responsible for *their* own assignment.
> *Correction: Each person* is responsible for *his/her* own assignment.

> *Inconsistency in tense:* The architect *designed* the city hall, and then the Council *rejects* it.
> *Correction:* The architect *designed* the city hall, and then the Council *rejected* it.

> *Inconsistency in mood:* We *would* appreciate it if you *can* come early.
> *Correction:* We *would* appreciate it if you *could* come early.

Use parallel (balanced) structure to make your writing flow smoothly.

> *Not parallel:* Do you think writing or a messenger would be faster? (Here, writing is a participle; messenger is a noun.)
> *Correction:* Do you think the mail or a messenger would be faster? (Here, mail and messenger are both nouns.)

Position modifiers properly. Closely related parts of a sentence should be placed close together to avoid ambiguity.

> *Improperly placed modifier:* Having been fined for jay walking, the judge told the mail carrier to step down.
> *Correction:* The judge told the mail carrier who had been fined for jay walking to step down.

Use the active voice as much as possible to give your words energy.

> *Weak*: His name will be seen in lights. (passive voice)
> *Better*: He will see his name in lights. (active voice)

Avoid excessive co-ordination (too many "ands" and "buts").

> *Too many "ands"*: I attended a meeting, and she stood up and took her time, and started a long monologue on her new invention.

Correction: I attended a meeting, during which she stood up slowly and began a long monologue on her new invention.

Place the part to be stressed at the beginning.

Stress improperly placed: They do more work than a human being in the same time, and they threaten many jobs, but computers calculate rapidly and we must use them.

Correction: We must use computers, in spite of their threat to many jobs, because they can calculate so rapidly.

Sentence Flaws to Avoid

C10 Sentence fragment (incomplete thought)

* Although the singer is good.
  Correction: The singer is good.

Comma fault (do not separate subject from verb unless a non-restrictive clause is used)

* The woman with the broken leg, could not walk.
  Correction: The woman with the broken leg could not walk. (See also this unit, C14.)

Shifted constructions

* Because of an oil shortage and we are losing money, the plant will have to shut down.
  Correction: Because of an oil shortage and a loss of money, the plant will have to shut down.
  Or
  Because we are suffering from an oil shortage and are losing money, we will have to shut down.

Pronoun-antecedent non agreement (pronoun must agree with antecedent in number and gender)

* *Everyone* was given *their* own office.
  Correction: *Everyone* was given *his/her* own office.

Subject-verb non agreement (in number)

* His *contribution* to the school's funds *were* extremely high.
  Correction: His *contribution* to the school's funds *was* extremely high.

* The *president*, as well as her staff, *have* arrived.
  Correction: The *president*, as well as her staff, *has* arrived.

Incorrect case (nominative, objective, or possessive?)

* We do not approve of *them arriving* late.
  Correction: We do not approve of *their arriving* late.

Note: a noun or pronoun preceding a gerund (e.g., arriving), is written in the possessive case.

- *Me and my brother* are going shopping.
  Correction: My brother and I are going shopping.

Adjective and adverb confusion

- He did a *real* good job.
  Correction: He did a *really* good job.

- Kathy played *good* yesterday.
  Correction: Kathy played a *good game* yesterday.
  Or
  Kathy played *well* yesterday.

Punctuation

C11 Punctuation marks are designed to give a sentence meaning and expression by showing the relationships among its various parts.

Note: If you have difficulty in choosing the appropriate punctuation for a sentence, it may be that your sentence has been improperly constructed. Revise the sentence into a form that you know is correct.

Apostrophe (')

C12 **Contractions**

When a letter or number is omitted, use an apostrophe: don't, doesn't, 'tis, I'll, Hallowe'en, '45, you're

You're sure Hallowe'en falls on October 31?
The class of '75 was a large one.

Plurals

Although plurals of many isolated letters or words are formed by adding *s* only (see this unit, C28), the apostrophe is used before the *s* in cases where confusion might result with the addition of *s* only.

Please dot all the i's.
One can never earn too many A's.

Possessives

To form the singular possessive, add an apostrophe plus *s* ('s).

Singular	Possessive
boy	boy's
woman	woman's
witness	witness's
secretary	secretary's
Joan Haslam	Joan Haslam's
Charles	Charles's

The boy's coat and the woman's shoes were dirty.
Joan Haslam's responsibility is to pay the secretary's salary.
You are invited to Charles's party tonight.

Note: Where the addition of apostrophe plus s would add a new syllable that would make pronunciation difficult, add the apostrophe only.

Jesus	Jesus'
goodness	goodness'

To form the plural possessive, add an apostrophe if the plural noun ends in s (s'); add an apostrophe plus s ('s) if it does not.

Plural	Possessive
boys	*boys'
women	women's
witnesses	*witnesses'
children	children's
gentlemen	gentlemen's

Boys' coats and women's shoes are on special this week.
The two witnesses' testimony continued all day.
The children's bulletin board was blank.

*The s after the apostrophe is omitted in most plural words ending in s to make pronunciation easier. The words noted above are examples.

Individual Ownership

Phil's and Maya's marks were good last term.

Apostrophes in both names make it clear that Phil had a high mark and Maya had a high mark, but they did not get the same mark.

Joint Ownership

John and Sarah's apartment is spacious.

The apostrophe in the latter name tells you that the apartment is shared by John and Sarah.

Expressions relating to time or measure employ the possessive.

Could I have a dollar's worth of peanuts, please?
Justin will be home in two month's time.
She was released with one week's pay.

Colon (:)

C13 **Direct Quotations**

Introduce a quotation of more than three lines with a colon.

When you are feeling downhearted, remember these lines from the poem "Smile":

We know the distance to the sun,
   The size and weight of earth.
But no one's ever told us yet
   How much a smile is worth.

Introductory Statement Followed by Lists or Series

Use a colon to introduce a list.

   The agenda is as follows: ...
   They brought the following: ...
   We still need these dishes for the staff party: stroganoff, rice, salad, and broccoli.

Comma (,)

C14   The comma is the most common punctuation mark and is often misused and overworked. Apply common sense to your writing by asking yourself if there *is* need for a pause where you have placed the comma. Remember, "When in doubt, leave it out!"

Adjectives

When two or more adjectives precede a noun, or when several adjectives follow the noun they are describing, use the comma.

   He is a punctual, efficient employee.
   That employee, punctual and efficient, deserves a raise.

But when the first adjective qualifies the second, omit the comma.

   a large, red hat
   a bright red hat

Compound Sentences

When two independent clauses are joined by a conjunction and have *different* subjects, use a comma. (An exception is permitted if the sentence is very short and the conjunction is "and.")

   Subject 1
   |Our old office manager|demanded a very high standard of work, but|the new one|is more interested in quantity than quality. **Subject 2**

   Exception: Our old office manager demanded high standards and the new one does not.

When two independent clauses are joined by a conjunction and *share* the same subject, no comma is necessary.

   One Subject
   |Our old office manager|demanded high standards and also insisted upon a high production rate.

Correspondence

Dates

Separate the day from the year by a comma unless using the international date method.

> September 1, 19--
> 19-- 09 01

Place Names

Place commas after the street address and the town or city.

> 130 Franklin Street, Brandon, Manitoba
> Calgary, Alberta, is a large city.

Note: In French addresses only, also separate the number from the street (e.g. 250, rue Printemps).

Names and Titles

Separate the name from the title by means of a comma.

> Mr. J. Barry, Jr.
> R. Newsome, Sales Manager

Non-Restrictive (Non-Essential) Clauses and Words or Phrases in Apposition

Non-restrictive clauses and phrases are expressions which are not essential to the meaning of the word they modify but add information. They need a comma at the beginning and end to separate them from the remainder of the sentence.

> The rain, which falls constantly in April, makes grass grow.

But

> Only the rain which falls in April makes our grass grow.

Words or phrases in apposition explain something about the subject. They, too, require a comma at beginning and end.

> The woman, hat in hand, came in from the rain.
> Fred, an Irishman, was an excellent football player.

Use a comma on either side of the phrases beginning: as well as, together with, in spite of, or, like, such as.

> The man, as well as his wife, is coming to dinner.
> Actors in Montreal, like those in Toronto, work hard.

Note: Restrictive clauses and phrases do not require commas because they are essential to the meaning of the sentence.

> The man who held the smoking gun was the obvious killer.
> The acid rain which fell around Sudbury damaged the crops.

Note: Do not be trapped into using a comma between the

subject and the verb unless these are separated by a non-restrictive clause.

> *Incorrect*: The small boy with curly hair, played the tuba.
> *Correct*: The small boy with curly hair played the tuba.
> **Or**
> The small boy, who had curly hair, played the tuba.

Omission of Words

Insert a comma to indicate that one or more words have been omitted.

> He travelled the scenic route; she, the most direct one.

Here, *travelled* is implied after *she.*

Parenthetical Expressions

Parenthetical expressions are words which are not necessary to the meaning of a sentence but give added emphasis to it. These may occur at the beginning or in the middle of a sentence.

At the Beginning of a Sentence (Introductory)

Place a comma after an introductory word, phrase, or clause.

> *Yes,* Edgar is expected tonight.
> *In the circumstances,* it was the best decision.
> *When the rain stopped,* we all went out for dinner.

Within a Sentence

Place the parenthetical word(s) within commas.

> Everyone knew, *of course,* that Edna would be captain.
> The oldest person was, *however,* very dissatisfied.
> England is, *without doubt,* a beautiful country.

The following words and phrases are common introductory and parenthetical expressions which should be set off with commas.

accordingly	however	of course
also	in fact	otherwise
as a matter of fact	in my opinion	personally
besides	in other words	therefore
consequently	in the meantime	thus
finally	meanwhile	well
first, first of all	moreover	without a doubt
for example	needless to say	yet
fortunately	nevertheless	
further, furthermore	obviously	

Series

Insert a comma after all words, phrases, and clauses in a series.

> Her favourite colours are green, purple, and orange.
> The visitors were expected to behave politely, to ask questions, and to return to the hotel by noon.

Dash (—)

C15

A dash is a separating device. Use it to enlarge upon a point or to give emphasis to a statement.

> He went west—Calgary, Edmonton, and Vancouver—for his holidays.
> Roger lost a tough battle—and I don't blame him for being disappointed.
> The teacher—I'm pleased to say—gave them extra help.
> Kate plays excellent tennis—she has lost only one match out of twenty this month.

Exclamation Mark (!)

C16

Use an exclamation mark to indicate surprise, enthusiasm, strong emotion, or a command.

> Happy Birthday, Canada!
> Stop, thief!

Use the exclamation mark after the interjections *Ah* and *Oh*.

> Ah! What low prices.
> Oh! How beautiful.

When a single exclamatory word is used as a sentence, use the exclamation mark.

> Help!
> Wait!

Hyphen (-)

C17

Use a hyphen to join words or syllables.

Compound Adjectives and Words

When two or more words are used in combination immediately preceding the noun they modify, join them with a hyphen to form a compound adjective.

> They went away for a four-day holiday.
> My car has an eight-cylinder engine.
> Her brother is a good-looking man.

When each adjective separately describes the subject, use a comma.

> Her brother is a big, strong man.

Fractions

When fractions are spelled out, use a hyphen.

> Two-thirds of the residents are employed downtown.

Numbers

Use a hyphen when the spelled-out number consists of two or more words.

> The band consisted of twenty-nine musicians.

Prefixes

Many prefixes require the use of a hyphen after them.

> A post-mortem is required when a person dies from unknown causes.
> Many entertainers have a mid-Atlantic accent.
> The ex-Prime Minister is a colourful man.

Parentheses () and Brackets []

C18

Parentheses

These are used with parenthetical expressions (i.e., explanatory material) incidental to the context. The expression is made by the author of the sentence.

> Grammar (essential to every student) is high on the priority list.

They are also used to give references.

> Letter styles (Chapter 3) was the next topic covered.

Brackets

These are used to set off inserted matter that is incidental to the context. The insertion is made by someone other than the author, e.g., an editor's comments or explanations.

> In 1938, he [Best] was involved in Canada's most exciting medical research undertaking.

Period (.)

C19

Use a period after a sentence, an abbreviation, and with figures in various contexts.

The sun came up very early that day.	a.m.
	Ph.D.
Mr. S. Eby	$17.75
St. Cecilia's Church	1.82 per cent
U.S.S.R.	2:55 p.m.
C.N.I.B.	6.667

Note: If an abbreviation closes a sentence, only one period is needed at the end of that sentence.

> The goods should have been shipped C.O.D.

Use a period instead of a question mark when you are making more of a demand than a request.

Would you kindly forward your cheque at once.
(*Compare with*: Did you receive the cheque we sent?)

Question Mark (?)

C20

Use a question mark:

- after a direct question

    How much does it cost?

- to express doubt (place the question mark in parentheses and use after the doubtful term)

    He was born in 1947(?).

Do *not* use a question mark:

- after an indirect question

    I asked him how much it cost.

- after a request (see this unit, C19)

    Will you please find out the cost.

Quotation Marks (" ")

C21

These are used in two ways:

Direct Quotes

The man cried, "Stop, thief!" and then fired.
He said, "Stop, or I'll shoot."
Did he say, "Stop, or I'll shoot"? No, he did not.
"If you don't stop," he said, "I'll shoot."

Titles

Parts of magazines, parts of books, articles, essays, sermons, speeches, *etc.*, and poems are indicated by quotation marks.

The poem, "Ode on a Grecian Urn," by Keats, is famous.
When you read Chapter 5, "Punctuation," study the section entitled "Comma."

Note: Use single quotation marks for the second quote when a quote within a quote must be indicated.

She said, "I heard him say, 'Come to dinner.'"

Semi-Colon (;)

C22

The semi-colon has two main uses.

Compound Sentences

If a comma is used in either of the two independent clauses, use a semi-colon before the conjunction.

It was a hot, dry summer; and we were concerned about the water supply.

Separate independent but related clauses, which are not connected by a conjunction, with a semi-colon.

> The wind was high; the sea was rough.

Series

Use a semi-colon for clarity when a comma is inadequate.

> Most of the executives were present: Hugh Fine, President, Ottawa; Elizabeth Jacques, Treasurer, Three Rivers; Todd Taylor, Secretary, Edmonton; and James Zabig, Vice-President, Halifax.

Underscore (__)

C23   Use the underscore (underline) in handwritten or typewritten material to indicate titles of books, plays, works of art, magazines, newspapers, words which need emphasis, and foreign expressions.

> Hard Times is a fine novel by Charles Dickens.
> The last issue of Macleans contained an interesting article.
> Have you seen Michelangelo's sculpture, the Pietà?
> Please tell Bill that this order is rush.

Style Mechanics

C24   Concern with detail is important in the writer's craft. Rules on abbreviation styles, capitalization principles, numeral usage, and guidelines for word division are outlined below.

Abbreviations

C25   Generally, abbreviations should be avoided because it is possible they may be misinterpreted or misunderstood. However, they are acceptable in statistical or tabulated matter.

- Use only commonly accepted abbreviations that cannot be misunderstood.
- Use capitals only if the word being abbreviated is capitalized.

> Nov.   *etc.*   Mon.   ibid.

Note: Most abbreviations consisting only of initial letters are capitalized, e.g., J.P., I.O.U.

- For companies, agencies, unions, societies, use only the abbreviations shown in the legally registered title, i.e., the abbreviations in the organization's letterhead.
- Use the ampersand (&) *only in company names*, never in text matter.

> Braithwaite & Singh   Zimmer & Co., Ltd.

- Abbreviate months or days of the week in tabular material only where space is very limited.

Addresses
- Abbreviate only when essential, never in the body of a letter or other text. (See Unit 18, TT46 and Unit 19, U3 and U4.)

Business Terms
The following standard abbreviations are frequently used in such business communications as forms and tables.

acct., a/c	account
ad val., A/V	ad valorem—according to value
ASAP	as soon as possible
assoc., assn.	association
b.l., B/L	bill of lading
B/S	bill of sale
C	hundred
c.i.f., CIF	cost, insurance, freight
CL, c.l.	carload
c.o., c/o	in care of
Co.	Company
c.o.d., C.O.D.	cash on delivery
Corp.	Corporation
cr.	credit
dept.	department
do.	ditto
dr.	debit
E. and O.E.	errors and omissions excepted
e.o.m., EOM	end of month
et al.	and others
FIFO	first-in, first-out
f.o.b., FOB	free on board
fwd.	forward, forwarded
Inc.	Incorporated
inv.	invoice
l.c.l., LCL	less than carload
LIFO	last-in, first-out
Ltd.	Limited
M	thousand
mdse.	merchandise
Messrs.	Messieurs (plural of Mr.)
mfg.	manufacturing
mgr.	manager
misc.	miscellaneous
Mlle	Mademoiselle
Mme	Madame
MS	manuscript
N.B.	nota bene (note well)
n/c, NC	no charge

NSF	not sufficient funds
No., Nos.	number(s)
n/30	net in 30 days
os, O/S	out of stock
pkg.	package
P.S.	post script
qty.	quantity
R.R.	Rural Route or railroad
vol.	volume
W.B.	waybill

Dates and Times

- If the abbreviations B.C. or A.D. are to be shown, use them only when dates are in numerals.
- Use a.m. and p.m. (upper or lower case — lower case preferred) when hours are shown as numerals (not to be used when 24-hour clock is used).

> A.D. 1948, 11:45 p.m., 13:30

Measurements

Metric, see Unit 19, U11.

Places

Provinces, see Unit 19, U3.
States, see Unit 19, U4.

Compass points (in technical material only).
Abbreviate using capital letters.

> N   NE   W   SW   NNW   SSE *etc.*

Publication Terms

Some usual abbreviations follow.

Ch., Chap.	Chapter	p., pp.	page(s)
Div.	Division	sec.	section
Fig., Figs.	Figure(s)	v., vs.	verse(s)
l., ll.	line(s)	Vol., Vols.	Volume(s)

Titles After Names

Some usual abbreviations follow.

> Jr., Sr., M.A., B.A., M.D.
>
> R.K. Kahn, Ph.D.
>
> Dr. R. Farmer, Jr.

See Unit 19, U2 for listing of Academic degrees.

Titles Before Names

Some usual abbreviations follow.

Mr., Mrs., Ms., Messrs., Mmes, Dr., Rev. (when first name is used).

> Rev. Charles Parnell, or The Reverend Parnell but never Rev. Parnell.

Capitalization

Although the conventions of capitalization are common knowledge, there are many specific uses of capital letters for emphasis or clarification of an idea. The general rule is to capitalize proper nouns, and words which begin a sentence. Other uses are given in this section.

Note: A simple, basic guide to correct capitalization is this: When being specific, capitalize; when being general, do not capitalize.

- Our Prime Minister is a good statesman. (You are referring to a specific person.)
  There was a heated discussion between two prime ministers. (No specific prime minister is in mind.)
- Vancouver's City Hall is an example of fine architecture. (specific building)
  Every sizable town should have a city hall. (general reference)
- Our Sales Manager is popular. (specific person)
  I saw an advertisement for a sales manager. (general reference)
- I think Unit 3 is the most interesting. (specific)
  Every unit in this book is long. (general)

Academic Field

Capitalize as follows:

Courses: Linguistics I, Spanish 307Y, Biology 23
Degrees: B.A., Ph.D., M.Sc., LL.B.
Titles: Professor William Chiu, Dr. Yvonne Borden

Note: Language names are always capitalized.

Carl enjoyed French and Japanese, but he did not like accounting or science.

Advertising Trade Marks

Capitalize trade marks.

Shake and Bake, Tide, Dove, Electrohome

Astronomical Bodies

Capitalize astronomical bodies.

The Great Bear, The Milky Way, Venus

Note: When sun, moon or earth are used with other astronomical bodies, they should be capitalized.

Festivals and Holidays

Capitalize festivals and holidays.

Civic Holiday   St. Jean Baptiste
Yom Kippur   Ramadan

Geographic Terms

Compass points should be capitalized only when a specific place is intended.

> The Joneses went out West for their holiday.
> He drove west from Kenora.
> The golf courses in South Carolina are lovely.
> How far south do you plan to drive?

Governments and Political References

Capitalize as follows:

Bodies:

> The Department of External Affairs
> The Saskatchewan Legislature
> Royal Canadian Mounted Police
> Supreme Court of Canada

Acts, Treaties:

> Statute of Westminster
> Bill of Rights

Titles:

> The Governor-General of Canada
> The Minister of Industry, Trade and Commerce

Institutions

Capitalize names of institutions.

> Mount Allison University
> Canadian National Institute for the Blind
> Beth Tzedec Synagogue

Monuments and Parks

Capitalize names of monuments and parks.

> Stanley Park
> Les Tuilleries
> Trafalgar Square

Nationalities, Languages, Races

Capitalize nationalities, languages and races of people.

> Asian   Black
> French   Latin
> Chinese   Caucasian

Organizations

Capitalize names of organizations.

> Canadian Broadcasting Corporation
> The Surf and Turf Club

Note: Minor words *of, the, and, etc.,* in a name are not capitalized.

> Girl Guides of Canada

Places

Names of continents, countries, nationalities, bodies of water, provinces, cities, valleys, mountains, regions and localities should be capitalized.

The Mackenzie River	Canadians
Mont Tremblant	Essex County
Lake of the Woods	Lake Athabaska
Barbados	The Okanagan Valley

Publications

Capitalize all the important words in titles of plays, books, articles, newspapers, magazines, operas, pictures, long poems.

The Cherry Orchard
The Importance of Being Earnest
Macbeth

Punctuation Marks

Capitalize the first letter after the following:

Colon when an independent clause follows.

Canada is beautiful: The lakes, mountains, and beaches are popular with tourists.

Period, Question Mark, Exclamation Mark

Please come. If you insist.
Are you coming? No, thanks.
Do come! It is not possible.

Quotation marks when a complete sentence is quoted.

The visiting dignitary said, "It's my pleasure to be here."
But
The visitor's "pleasure to be here" was coloured by bad weather.

Religious References

Capitalize words with religious significance.

The Koran	God
Buddhism	Good Friday
Judaism	The Nicene Creed

Titles

Capitalize as follows:

I asked Mom to help me with my work.
But
My mother enjoys cooking.
This call is for Miss Dominique Goulet.
The Mayor of Charlottetown
The Reverend Jim Battye

Numbers

C27 Figures or words? Figures are preferred for most business situations because they are easier to read. If in doubt, follow these general guidelines.

Use Figures

Situation	Example
numbers above 10	Send 15 radios.
a series of numbers	Send 15 radios, 2 television sets, 4 tapes.
with abbreviations or symbols	3 kg, 2 cm, 6 p.m., #42
money	
a series of round amounts	$25, $43, $82
a series of amounts including cents	$23.95, $43.00, $9.50
a series of amounts in cents only	17¢, 28¢, 79¢
house or building number	15 King Street, Apartment 804 (spell out One King Street)
street names above 10	402-40th Street
dates	1984 02 29, or February 29, 1984, or 29th February, 1984
percentages	We saved 20 per cent.
mixed numbers	His mass increased 1½ times.
clock time	2:30 p.m., or 14:30
exact unit of time	The trip took 1 year, 7 months, 10 days.
decimals	0.50 L, 7.3 million
exact age	She will be 2 years, 3 months old on Tuesday.
ratios	5:2, or 5 to 2
business forms, documents, serial or size numbers	Invoice No. 468 (or #468), Order No. 2071, Policy No. 168-2948, Lot No. 9, size 8 shoes
temperature	The temperature rose to 20°C today.
measures and measurements	49° (49 degrees), 2 t, 30 km, 22 cm × 27 cm

Use Words

Situation	Example
numbers under 10	They sent five sets.
street names under 10	240 Fifth Avenue
numbers beginning a sentence	Eighteen children came.
date (formal usage)	November eighth, nineteen hundred...
unit of time	He stayed for six months.
round numbers	Two thousand years, thirteen hundred soldiers

Situation	Example
fractions standing alone	Only three-quarters of the group attended the party.
legal documents and formal correspondence	Two thousand dollars; nineteen hundred and sixty...
age and anniversary	Else is eighteen today.
	It's their fifteenth anniversary.

Note: When two numbers are used consecutively, spell out the lower number, e.g., Buy twelve 20-cent stamps, please.

Plurals

C28

Abbreviations, Letters, Numbers, Words: Form the plural by adding *s*.

ands and buts	the 1900s
in twos and threes	the pros and cons
the 5 Cs	YMCAs

If the plural form is not clear with the simple addition of *s*, use 's to remove confusion.

37 B.A.'s and 42 B.Sc.'s
There are two a's in my name.

Hyphenated Words: As a rule, pluralize the principal word.

officer-in-charge; officers-in-charge
man-of-war; men-of-war

If no noun is contained in the compound word, add *s* to the end of it.

pick-me-up; pick-me-ups

Nouns: Generally, form the plural by adding *s*.

desk desks; employer employers; fuse fuses

Exceptions to the above rule are as follows:

- Words ending in *s*, *ch*, *sh*, *x*, or *z*, add *es*.

business businesses; arch arches;
appendix appendixes

- For nouns ending in *y* preceded by a consonant, change the *y* to *i* and add *es*.

city cities; community communities

- Nouns ending in *y* preceded by a vowel add *s* to the singular form to become plural.

attorney attorneys; monkey monkeys; tray trays

- Some nouns have irregular plural endings.

man men; foot feet; mouse mice

- Some nouns remain the same in the plural.

sheep sheep; fish fish; series series

Word Division

C29

Before you contemplate word division, remember that it is better to avoid it. If you absolutely must divide a word, follow these guidelines.

- Consult your dictionary if you are in doubt about the correct division.
- Make the reader's task easy by giving a strong indication of the entire word.
- Have no more than two successive lines ending with a division.

Never Divide

- words of one syllable or words pronounced as one syllable

    brought   stopped   healed

- proper names

    Jonathan   Portugal   Micheline

- short words (fewer than six letters)

    after   alone

- contractions or abbreviations

    haven't   Ph.D.

- the last word in a paragraph or on a page
- where only one or two characters would be separated

    mount*ed*   large*ly*   *ob*lique   read*y*

- numbers (unless they are *very* long)

    $2147.75

Where to Divide Words

Always divide words between syllables. Specifically:

- as close to the centre as possible

    communi-cation

- after prefixes

    contra-dict

- before suffixes

    lov-able

- between double consonants when the root word does not contain double consonants

    run-ning   occur-rence

    But
    stall-ing   bluff-ing

- after the vowel where there is a one-letter syllable followed by a consonant

    regu-late   sepa-rate

- between the vowels where there are two one-letter syllables

    radi-ator   anxi-ety

- at the hyphen when the term is already hyphenated

    self-control

Where to Divide Related Expressions

Avoid dividing parts of a related expression; but if division is essential, choose the logical breaking point.

Dates: May 24, 19--   *Break after*: May 24,

Money (very large amounts only): $2 million   *Break after*: $2

Names: Professor B. Cormier   *Break after*: Professor B.

Numbers: 24 000 500   *Break after*: 24 000

Addresses: 37 Bayview Avenue   *Break after*: 37 Bayview

The Expression of Language

The most effective communications are well organized, clear, concise, courteous, factually accurate, and positively worded. The purpose of this section is to show you how to produce written and oral communications which meet these criteria.

Note: Instructions for the following writing situations are presented in other parts of this book.

Advertisements, see Unit 12, P5.
Formal Acceptances, see Unit 15, S7.
Job Applications, see Unit 9, J6.
Minutes, see Unit 11, MC9.
Telegrams, see Unit 16, T29.

C30   Written Expression of Language

Basic Writing Tips

C31   **Get Off to the Right Start**

- Collect all the facts and documents you need.
- Make an outline of the points you wish to cover.
- Underline important facts on a letter to which you are replying.
- Make notes in the margin of a letter to which you are replying.

Follow the Five Cs

Produce written work that is coherent, clear, concise, courteous, and correct.

- coherent: progresses logically, after starting with a clear statement of purpose
- clear: is written in simple, easy-to-follow, unambiguous language
- concise: is short and to the point
- courteous: contains frequent use of "you," and is written in a tactful, friendly style which indicates concern for the reader
- correct: states place, date, time, and other facts accurately, and displays correct spelling, punctuation, and grammar

Dear Mr. Meilleur:

You are invited to a meeting of all our representatives to be held in our Head Office in Calgary on Tuesday, December 10, 19-- at 09:00.

As you will see from the attached agenda, we are planning an expansion of the business over the next five years. Your suggestions, either before or during the meeting, will be most welcome.

Please let us know whether you expect to attend the meeting, and whether or not you will require any hotel accommodation.

Sincerely yours,

Use a Logical Development

Introduction

Start in a pleasing way with a clear statement of the purpose of your communication. If you do this, the reader does not have to wonder why you are writing.

Expansion

- Develop the introduction by giving further details (background, anticipated outcome, *etc.*).
- Tailor your language to that of the reader (e.g., do not assume that everyone will be familiar with the specialized vocabulary of your particular business).
- Give precise information to avoid confusion.

Ending

- Find a friendly way of closing the letter.
- Ask for action if this is appropriate.
- Do not *thank in advance* because it is an imposition on the reader to assume that he/she will fulfill your request.

Short is Better Than Long

A one-page communication is more likely to be carefully read than a two-page one. One-paragraph letters are now acceptable in business. Brevity is a key to quick and effective communication.

The "You" Approach

Consider your reader. Don't bore him with I's or we's. Show him that your interest lies in him by putting yourself in his place when you write. **Make your reader feel important**. Be sincere and friendly.

Mean What You Say

Be honest in your writing. Stay away from *urgent, as soon as possible,* and similar terms unless you really mean them.

Handle the Negatives Positively

When you have bad news to impart (e.g., you must close a client's charge account), precede the negative statement with a positive one to soften the blow.

> We have enjoyed doing business with you for the past five years, but regret that because of slow payments this year we are forced to cancel our credit arrangements with you. We will, of course, be glad to accommodate you with cash purchases.

Appearances Count

An attractively typed letter makes a favourable impact. Be a good ambassador for your company.

Proofread Carefully

A document with mistakes tells the reader you do not care. Create a good impression by producing error-free correspondence.

Use Short Cuts Where Feasible

- Is a letter really necessary for less important correspondence? Instead of a formal letter in reply to a routine request, a compliment slip with the sender's name or business card will often fulfill the same function with a saving of time and money.

```
The Sylvia Harding Music Co.    4716 13 Street N.E.
Calgary, Alberta
T2E 6P1


                        Sylvia Harding
                        President


692-9213
```
Business card

```
┌─────────────────────────────────────────────┐
│  The Sylvia Harding Music Co.   4716 13 Street N.E.  │
│  Calgary. Alberta                            │
│  T2E 6P1                                     │
│                                              │
│                                              │
│            With the compliments of           │
│                  Sylvia Harding              │
│                  President                   │
│                                              │
└─────────────────────────────────────────────┘
```

Compliment slip

- Consider a telephone call instead of a letter.
- Perhaps a post card can deliver your message more cheaply. This method can be used for meeting announcements, order acknowledgements, or sales announcements, for example.
- If a very brief answer is required, reply on the bottom of the incoming letter, make a photocopy for your files, and return the original to the sender.
- Consider using a form letter rather than creating an original. (See this unit, C39.)

Letter Samples

C32   Effective business correspondence demonstrates courtesy, conciseness, clarity, completeness, and correctness. The sample letters in this section are offered as guides to achieving best results. For business etiquette practices regarding salutations and their appropriate complimentary closings see this unit, C50.

Acknowledgement Letter (in Someone's Absence)

C33   If your task is to handle someone's correspondence, and certain decisions must wait until that person is able to deal with them (e.g., upon returning from vacation), the polite thing to do is to write an acknowledgement.

Dear Ms. Belza:

    Thank you for your kind invitation to Mr. Reubens to make the keynote speech at the Kiwanis Club Annual Meeting on May 10, 19--.

    Mr. Reubens is away on a trip to the West at the moment. He will be returning next week and will contact you then.

                    Yours sincerely,

Apology Letter

C34 If something more formal than a telephone call is appropriate, write a note giving a reason for your regrets.

Dear Mr. Smillie:

Thank you very much for offering me the honour of speaking at the Old Manorians Annual Dinner on September 17.

It would have been a great pleasure for me to meet old colleagues and recount experiences, but unfortunately I will be away on a trip to the Orient for the entire month of September.

Please accept my apologies and offer my warm wishes to all the Old Manorians.

Cordially yours,

Collection Letter

C35 After several statements and reminder notices have been sent without effect, the time comes for you to demand payment for an overdue account by means of letters. Start with a lenient reminder letter:

Dear Professor Lazier:

We hope you are satisfied with the typewriter you bought from us three months ago.

At the time of purchase you made a down payment of $150, with a promise to pay the balance in 30 days. However, we have not heard from you.

If you are having a problem with the machine, please let us know; if not, we would appreciate a cheque for the outstanding $300 right away.

Yours truly,

If there is still no reply, send a more demanding note two weeks later:

Have you overlooked something? According to our records, your balance outstanding is still $300.

The amount due us is, as you know, nearly four months old. Since we also have to meet our financial commitments, we would appreciate it if you could complete your end of the bargain by putting a cheque in the mail today.

Please act now and preclude our taking any further action.

Yours truly,

If this firmer request brings no response, the following letter may work:

Since our numerous requests for payment of your outstanding account of $300 have not elicited even a partial settlement, we must inform you that unless you send us a cheque for the full amount due within one week, we will put your account in the hands of a collection agency.

We regret having to take this step, but you have given us no other choice.

Yours truly,

Complaint Letter

C36
If a verbal expression of dissatisfaction brings no results, turn to a firmly worded but courteous letter. Wait until you are calm before writing because anger works against you.

Dear Mr. Boehm:

Our July shipment of frames arrived on schedule, but unfortunately 100 of them were badly damaged.

We telephoned your shipping department twice last week and were told that the matter would be investigated immediately; however, we have not heard from them. Since we want to enter a claim for the damage promptly and order more frames to replace the broken ones, we would appreciate your immediate attention to our problem.

Please telephone Mr. Lopez before Friday so that he can proceed with the necessary paper work.

Yours truly,

Reply to Complaint Letter

Dear Mrs. Bobinski:

As requested in your letter of July 15 regarding damaged frames, I telephoned Mr. Lopez to clarify your problem.

I apologize for the delay in contacting you, but our shipping department — in spite of numerous efforts — had difficulty in obtaining the necessary details from the carrier to enable you to proceed. Mr. Lopez now has the information he needs to enter a claim with the transport company. He has also placed an order for 100 frames to replace the broken ones.

Thank you for your patience and courtesy. I hope our future dealings will be trouble free and mutually beneficial.

Yours sincerely,

Congratulatory Letter

C37   Make it short and sincere.

Dear Marcello:

    I was delighted to hear of your promotion to the position of Sales Manager of Elliott Galleries. After all your years of dedication and service, you certainly deserve this honour, as those of us who know you realize.

    Congratulations, Marcello! I hope you will be happy in your new post.

                    Most sincerely,

Reply to Congratulatory Letter

Dear Catherine:

    How kind of you to write a note about my recent promotion. Your good wishes certainly added to my delight at being promoted at Elliott Galleries.

    I look forward to a challenging and rewarding future.

                    Cordially yours,

Enquiry Letter

C38   When a telephone enquiry is not possible, send a written request for information. Be specific about the information you desire.

Gentlemen:

    Our class is conducting a survey to find out which types of letter and punctuation styles are currently popular with business firms in our community.

    To obtain this information, we are asking several companies to write to us using the letter style and punctuation style typical of their firms. It would be of great value to our class if you would take part in our survey.

    We would appreciate your replying to us on your company letterhead so that we can collect a file of these also.

    We look forward to hearing from you.

                    Yours truly,

Reply to Enquiry, Acknowledgement, or Receipt Letter

Dear Ms. DiFiore:

    Thank you for your letter of February 19.

    We are pleased to take part in your efforts to determine typical styles of business letters, and we hope you have a good response to your survey.

    Good luck in your endeavours!

                    Yours truly,

Form Letter (Circular Letter)

C39   When routine correspondence is mailed to a large number of
people (e.g., advertising a new product, introducing a new
sales person, announcing a change of location, asking
repeatedly for payment of an account), a most economical
method of handling this is by preprinting the body of a letter
on the letterhead and inserting date, inside address,
salutation, and other pertinent information at the time of
mailing.

Dear
    Enclosed is our cheque for $ which represents the
proceeds of your loan. The attached statement shows the
terms of your contract.
    Your monthly payments are $, payable on the   of
each month, and the first payment will be due on
It is wise for you to meet your payments on time in order to
maintain your good credit rating.
    Thank you for bringing your financial requirements to
our company.
                         Very truly yours,

Gratitude or Thank-You Letter

C40   Avoid gushing phrases, but show your genuine appreciation.

For a Present

Dear Armand:
    It was so thoughtful of you to send me the Picasso print
for my birthday. Shaun will have it framed for me this
weekend, and it will then hang in splendour in my office.
    Thank you very much. Perhaps the next time you are in
town you will stop by for lunch and let me show you your
beautiful gift in its new setting.
                         Kindest regards,

For a Favour

Dear Lison:
    Thank you very much for the tickets to the final round of
the Canadian Open last week. What a thrilling experience it
was to see the pros in real life! I know that you went out of
your way to get the tickets.
    Your thoughtfulness was very much appreciated.
                         Cordially,

To a Speaker

Dear Dr. Liontos:

   It was a pleasure to meet you at our annual board meeting and to hear your thoughts on technology in this decade.

   I know I voice the opinion of all our members when I say a sincere thank you for coming to address our organization. We are all grateful for your interest.

                                   Cordially yours,

Introduction Letter

C41   A letter introducing a person may either be mailed directly to the addressee or delivered to the addressee by the person being introduced. It should clearly state its purpose.

Dear Dr. Shaefer:

   I am glad to introduce my friend, Professor Morley Mazier, whose work in mechanical engineering is probably familiar to you. He is keen to visit your research laboratory and to discuss a matter he believes will interest you greatly.

   I hope your meeting will prove mutually beneficial.

                                   Yours sincerely,

Or

   I am pleased to introduce to you Max Von Eben, my colleague of the past five years.

   Max and his family have decided to move West for business reasons, and it occurred to me that you and he might derive some mutual benefit from a meeting. I would be very grateful for any assistance or guidance you could offer Max.

                                   Sincerely,

Order Letter

C42   When a preprinted order form is not available, send a simple, detailed letter to make your request.

Gentlemen:

   Would you please send the following items to our branch at 16 Sheppard Avenue, Shubenacadie, N.S. immediately.

Qty.	Description	Unit Price	Total
1000	No. 204 T Hinges, Copper Plate	$1.00	$1 000.00
500	No. 72 Corner Braces, Copper Plate	1.25	625.00
		Total	$1 625.00

   A flurry of orders recently has depleted our supplies and we would, therefore, appreciate your assistance in rushing this shipment to us.

                                   Very truly yours,

Payment Letter

C43   If a letter is required to accompany a payment, give an explanation of the payment.

Gentlemen:

Enclosed is our cheque in payment of Invoice No. 473.

The amount of $784 on the cheque is equivalent to the invoice total of $800 less your 2% discount if payment is made within 10 days.

Yours truly,

Recommendation Letter

C44   On occasion you may be asked to write a letter of reference for an employee or co-worker. Keep it short, positive, and honest.

Dear Miss Wang:

I am very pleased to recommend Glenn Asano to you as a prospective office manager.

Glenn has worked with our organization for four years as a clerk typist, bookkeeper, payroll clerk, and, finally, office supervisor. He has been a loyal and conscientious worker; and his eagerness to improve, combined with his friendly personality, has made him very popular.

Our loss will be your gain. I know Glenn will be an asset to your company, and I wish him every success.

Yours sincerely,

If you do not have an addressee's name, use this expression in place of a salutation: **To Whom It May Concern**.

Reservations Letter

C45   Although most reservations for convention facilities or hotel accommodation are made by telephone, a letter is sometimes necessary to confirm the details of the reservation. Remember to give full details and to address the letter to the reservations manager at the hotel.

Dear Sir:

Please reserve a three-room suite for September 17 and 18, 19-- for our annual conference of sales managers.

One room should be suitable for informal social meetings, one for product displays, and one for formal meetings for 15 to 20 people.

The conference will open with a social gathering at 3 p.m. on September 17 and close with a brief business meeting at 10 a.m. on the 18th.

An early confirmation of this booking will be appreciated.

Yours truly,

Response to Unsolicited Job Application

C46   Try not to discourage the writer. Be straightforward in a gentle way.

Dear Mr. Denobrega:

Thank you for submitting an application to join our organization. Unfortunately, we cannot help you at the moment because there are no openings in our accounting department.

If a position to suit you does become vacant, we will get in touch with you. In the meantime, good luck with your job hunting.

Yours sincerely,

Response to Request for Donation

C47   Whether your reply is affirmative or negative, be kind.

Affirmative Reply

Dear Ms. Blackburn:

In reply to your request for a donation towards prizes at the "Games for the Handicapped," I am pleased to enclose a cheque for $250 from our company. On behalf of the manager and staff, I wish you and your organizers every success.

Yours sincerely,

Negative Reply

Dear Ms. Blackburn:

Thank you for inviting us to participate in your annual "Games for the Handicapped" by means of a donation toward prizes.

Unfortunately, we cannot assist you because it is our policy to make one major donation yearly to the United Way.

Please accept our regrets and our good wishes for a successful evening.

Yours sincerely,

Sales Letter

C48   Since the purpose of this letter is to sell a product, be positive and use the *you* approach.

Dear Mr. McDonald:

How would you like to increase the efficiency of your office workers by 10 per cent this summer? Tests in 100 offices where Iceberg Air Conditioners were installed proved that worker efficiency improved 10 per cent.

Greater efficiency means larger profits for your organization; thus the Iceberg pays for itself in a short time. Spread the cost of the air conditioner over one, two, or three years if you wish. The money you spend to improve worker comfort and morale and thus increase productivity will be a wise investment.

Won't you call us today and let our engineer determine your office air conditioning needs? Every day without an Iceberg is costing you money.

Yours sincerely,

Covering Letter With Sales Information

Use this letter as a friendly encouragement to a prospective buyer. Make sure you close with a request for action.

Dear Mr. McDonald:

We are pleased to enclose a catalogue and price list of Iceberg Air Conditioners as requested by our engineer, Joe Ubelacker, following his visit to your company. It is Joe's opinion that the models marked with an asterisk are those most suited to your office needs.

If you have any questions after you have had an opportunity to look over the catalogue, please give us a call so that we can remove any doubts. We know you and your employees will be delighted with the performance of the Iceberg.

We are at your service, so call us now for immediate delivery.

Yours sincerely,

Sympathy or Condolence Letter

C49   Here again it is time to be brief but compassionate.

Dear Miss Jacques:

It was with much regret that I read today about your brother's sudden death. Everyone who knew him will feel the loss.

I realize I cannot offer much comfort, but please count on me to help if you need anything.

Most sincerely,

Reply to Sympathy

Dear Ms. Kordez:

Your thoughtful note and donation to the Cancer Society were very much appreciated by our family.

It is good to be back at the office again with plenty of work to occupy me, and I know that your kind thoughts will help sustain me through the weeks ahead.

Yours sincerely,

Forms of Address

C50   Although most written communication in business is an exchange between organizations, it is sometimes necessary to contact individuals outside industry or commerce. The correct method of addressing prominent people in all sectors is included in this section.

Business Titles

Female:

Miss   Misses
Ms.
Mrs.
Mademoiselle (Mlle): French for an unmarried woman
Mesdemoiselles (Mlles): French for two or more unmarried women
Madam (Mme): French for a married or mature woman
Mesdames (Mmes): French for two or more married or mature women

Male:

Mr.
Messieurs (Messrs.): used in English in addressing two or more men, and sometimes in addressing companies

Messrs. Smith and Weston
Messrs. Brack, Brack and Company

Monsieur (M.): French
Messieurs (MM.): French plural

For Forms of Address chart see pp. 63-67.

Forms of Address

Position	Address	Salutation	Complimentary Closing
Civic			
Mayor	His Worship the Mayor of... or Her Worship, Mayor Jane Doan	Dear Sir or Dear Mr. Mayor Dear Madam or Dear Mayor Doan	Yours very truly

Position	Address	Salutation	Complimentary Closing
Diplomatic			
Ambassador (Canadian) or High Com- missioner	C. Ronning, Esq. Canadian Ambassador to...	Dear Sir Dear Mr.	Very truly yours
Ambassador (foreign) or High Com- missioner	Her Excellency D. Raj Ambassador of...	Dear Madam Excellency	Respectfully
Education			
President of University	Joe L. Billings, LL.D. President, University of...	Dear Sir, Dear Dr. Billings, Dear Mr. President	Very truly yours
Chancellor of University	Mary L. Billings, Ph.D. Chancellor, University of...	Dear Madam Dear Chancellor	Very truly yours Yours sincerely
Dean of College/ Faculty	Joe R. Billings, Ph.D. Dean of...	Dear Sir, Dear Dean Billings, Dear Dr. Billings	Very truly yours
Professor of University	Mary L. Billings, Ph.D. University of...	Dear Madam or Dear Professor Billings	Very truly yours
Government			
Governor General	His Excellency The Right Honourable Joe Billings, *P.C., C.C.,	Sir or Dear Governor General	I have the honour to be, Sir, Your Excellency's obedient servant
Prime Minister	The Right Honourable Joe Billings, P.C., *M.P. Prime Minister of Canada	Sir	I am, Sir, Yours very truly

Position	Address	Salutation	Complimentary Closing
Lieutenant Governor	Her Honour R. Billings The Lieutenant Governor of the Province of...	Dear Madam Dear Lieutenant Governor	Respectfully yours or Sincerely yours
Premier of Province	The Honourable John Billings, *M.L.A. Premier of the Province of...	Sir	Respectfully yours or Sincerely yours
Minister	The Honourable Mary Billings Minister of...	Madam or Dear Madam	Respectfully yours or Sincerely yours

Judiciary

Chief Justice, Supreme Court of Canada	The Right Honourable Joe Billings, P.C. Chief Justice of Canada	Sir or Dear Sir	Respectfully yours
Chief Justice of Provincial High Court	The Honourable .... Chief Justice of B.C.	Madam or Dear Madam	Sincerely yours or Respectfully yours Very truly yours
Judge (except County and District Court)	The Honourable Mr. Justice John Billings	Sir or Dear Sir	Very truly yours
Judge (County and District Court)	Her Honour Judge Mary Billings	Madam or Dear Madam	Respectfully yours

Religion

Archbishop (Anglican)	The Most Reverend John Dawes, D.D. Archbishop of...	Most Reverend Sir or Your Grace	Respectfully yours

Position	Address	Salutation	Complimentary Closing
Archbishop (Greek Orthodox)	His Eminence the Archbishop of the Greek Orthodox Church	Your Eminence	I am, Your Eminence, Respectfully yours
Archbishop (Roman Catholic)	The Most Reverend John Billings, Archbishop of...	Your Excellency	Respectfully yours
Bishop (Anglican)	The Right Reverend John Billings, D.D., Bishop of...	Right Reverend Sir	Respectfully yours
Bishop (Greek Orthodox)	The Most Reverend Bishop of The Greek Orthodox Church	Right Reverend Bishop	Very respectfully yours
Bishop (Roman Catholic)	The Most Reverend John Billings Bishop of...	Your Excellency	Respectfully yours
Cardinal (Roman Catholic)	His Eminence John Cardinal (surname) Archbishop of...	Your Eminence	Respectfully yours
Moderator	The Right Reverend Carol Dawson, D.D. Moderator of the... Church	Right Reverend Madam Dear Dr. ...	Respectfully yours
Mother Superior (Roman Catholic)	The Reverend Mother Superior, The Congregation of...	Dear Madam Reverend Mother Superior Dear Mother Superior	Respectfully yours

| Pope (Roman Catholic) | His Holiness The Pope | Your Holiness | I have the honour to be, Your Holiness' obedient servant |
| Rabbi (Jewish) | The Reverend Rabbi John Billings | Dear Sir | Respectfully yours |

*Note: (1) The Prime Minister and federal cabinet ministers are members of the Privy Council (P.C.).

(2) The Governor-General is a Privy Councillor (P.C.) as well as a Chancellor of the Order of Canada (C.C.).

(3) All members of the federal parliament have the designation Member of Parliament (M.P.) after their names.

(4) Members of provincial parliaments use the designation Member of Provincial Parliament (M.P.P.) in Ontario; Member of National Assembly (M.N.A.) in Quebec; and Member of Legislative Assembly (M.L.A.) in the other provinces.

Salutations and Complimentary Closings

C51

Consult the following chart to ensure that you use the appropriate salutation and complimentary closing in your business and personal correspondence.

Formal Situation	Salutation	Complimentary Closing
• writing to a person of high political, diplomatic, royal or religious rank	(See Forms of Address Chart, this unit, C50.)	
• writing to a company or organization and addressing no one in particular	Gentlemen or Ladies and Gentlemen	Yours truly
• writing to a person in business whom you have not met but are mentioning specifically in the inside address	Sir, Madam, Dear Sir, Dear Madam	Very truly yours, Yours truly, Yours very truly
• when an attention line is used	Gentlemen, Dear Sirs, Ladies and Gentlemen, Ladies or Mesdames (when the company is totally female)	Very truly yours, Yours truly, Yours very truly

Formal Situation	Salutation	Complimentary Closing
• writing to a person but using only a business title, e.g., Sales Manager	Dear Sir, Dear Madam	Very truly yours, Yours truly, Yours very truly

Less Formal

• writing to a person you know but on a business basis only	Dear Mr. Robinette Dear Miss Jones Dear Ms. Chantrelle Dear Mrs. Kumar	Sincerely, Sincerely yours, Yours sincerely, Cordially yours
• writing to an unknown addressee in a form letter	Dear Friend Dear Customer Dear Homeowner	Very truly yours

Personal

• writing to a friend	Dear Maurice My dear Ginette	Cordially, Cordially yours, Most sincerely, Kindest regards
• writing to a friend in a business situation	Dear Mr. Bird	Yours very sincerely
• writing to a young person	Dear Jonathan	Yours sincerely

Memorandums

C52 The interoffice memorandum is designed for sending messages within an organization and therefore does not need an inside address, salutation, or complimentary closing.

To: T. Pinchon, Sales Rep.   Date: 19–– 04 14
From: Megan Laurence, Sales Manager
Subject: May Sales Meeting
      The next monthly sales meeting is scheduled for Thursday, May 13, at 10 a.m. in my office.
      Will you please give a 15-minute presentation (for the benefit of the new sales people) on the ad campaign which you ran so successfully in January. Let me know if you will need any audio-visual equipment.

Press or News Releases

C53 When a new product is introduced, a senior managerial appointment announced, or other notable event occurs, the occasion is frequently publicized in the media by means of a press or news release. This is a bulletin sent out to newspapers, trade magazines, and other pertinent journals all at the same time in the hope of free publication. The press release follows this standard format:

- Type on standard size typing paper.
- Use wide margins.
- Double space to allow for editing.
- Type the sender's name and title, company name, address, and telephone number in a block at the top left.
- Under the release date, type the story headline in block capitals.
- Type FOR RELEASE (or FOR IMMEDIATE RELEASE) and the date at the top right, and "Mailed (date)" underneath.
- End the release with ### or -30-.

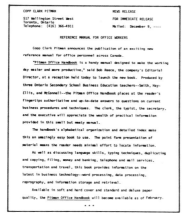 Press release

Contents of the Press Release

Keep the contents to one page if possible and the writing strictly factual. A well-written release enables an editor to do an accurate précis if one is necessary.

The first paragraph should tell a brief story answering the questions of who, what, when, where, why and how. Subsequent paragraphs amplify or expand upon the news. No concluding paragraph is necessary.

Reports and Manuscripts

C54 Reports, surveys, studies, *etc.*, are prepared to present information to an individual or group in answer to a question or before the making of a decision.

Reports come in two broad categories: the *information report*, which provides data; and the *research report*, which outlines a problem, presents facts and findings after research has been carried out, evaluates the data collected, and recommends a solution. The information report is informal and usually brief; the research report is complex and therefore requires a more structured format. (See Unit 18, TT85 for typing style instructions.)

Preparing a Report

Research: Before you start writing the report, gather all the facts to be presented. Go to appropriate and, of course, reliable sources for records, figures, dates, and other pertinent information.

If you need to go beyond your own office to the company or public library, know how to find the information you require. Check card catalogues, encyclopedias, almanacs or fact books, books of quotations, or Who's Who. (See Unit 8, 110, How to Use a Library.) Use an index card for each fact so that it is easy to organize the data in a logical sequence later. Remember to quote your sources in the report.

Headings

"*Headings and sub-headings pinpoint and summarize ideas for easy absorption by the reader.*"

Familoe, Dorothy. Creative Communication for Business Students, Holt, Rinehart & Winston, Toronto, 1977, P.186.

Advocates
1. *Closely written text boring*
2. *Break up text into many sections*
3. *Make reader's task easy*

Report notes

The Outline: Once you have collected all the relevant data, make up an outline for your report.

- First write an introduction stating the purpose of the report.
- Enlarge on the purpose by giving details, comparisons, statistics, *etc.* Write a note or sub-heading for each topic or paragraph to be included.
- End with your conclusions or recommendations.

Rough Draft: Build upon the outline and add the appropriate substance to the report. To be of greatest benefit to the reader, a report should:

- be complete (any questions should be anticipated and answered)
- be concise (this enables the reader to quickly understand what is being presented)
- be clearly written and easy to read (no confusion should be raised in the reader's mind)
- be more objective than subjective
- be developed in logical sequence
- be accurate and contain only verified information
- be supported by specific and accurate evidence that reinforces your arguments

Final Report: Polish the rough draft (several times if necessary) until you are satisfied that your words tell an honest, understandable story. Read the draft aloud to hear how it flows; ask yourself if every point has been clearly expressed; try to see your work from the reader's perspective.

If you plan to mail the report, enclose it with a letter of transmittal which should explain the purpose of the report and your recommendations.

Parts of the Formal or Research Report

This report is usually composed of many of the following parts. (See Unit 18, TT85 for illustrations.)

Title Page or Cover Sheet: The title of the report, name and department or company of the originator, name of the recipient, and the date are attractively typed on this first page.

Table of Contents: Each heading and its page number are set up for easy reference on the second page. The contents page tells the reader what topics are to be covered in the report and where to find them quickly. Illustrations may be listed in the table of contents.

Summary (or Synopsis): In long reports, a summary enables the reader who has not enough time to read the whole report to quickly pick up the main points.

The Body:
• The *introduction* gives the purpose of the report, research methods, background information, conclusions, and recommendations.
• The *report* itself is organized by sections and has many sub-headings.
• The *conclusion* provides results of the research and recommendations. The findings are presented, interpreted, and then conclusions drawn or recommendations made, with supporting reasons.

Footnotes or Endnotes: These are references to specific sources used in the report and are related by numbers to words, phrases, or sentences in the text. A note contains the source's author, page number, line number. Footnotes appear at the bottom of each page; end notes appear on a separate page at the end of the body.

Bibliography: The names of books, periodicals, *etc.,* their authors, date, place and name of publisher comprise this list of sources. It is always arranged alphabetically by author or editor.

Appendix: When a number of graphs, tables, special vocabulary lists, *etc.,* are included in the report, they are collected in an appendix.

Oral Expression of Language

C55 Most people spend more time in speaking than they do in writing (giving instructions, asking questions, selling, *etc.*). With the spoken word, tone, pitch, volume, rate, enunciation, and pronunciation, as well as language skills, are all important considerations. Skillful use of the voice and clever choice of language will permit you to achieve the desired effect on your audience.

Tone: indication of attitude and feelings; tempo of your speech

Pitch: degree of highness or lowness of the voice (variations in pitch add interest and indicate meanings)

Volume: quality that enables you to be *heard* (volume is influenced by size of room, use or not of microphone, size and acoustics of room)

Rate: tempo of your speech (use a rate that makes each word intelligible)

Enunciation: the precision with which you express each word (let your audience hear your words: "What did you say?" not "Wojasay?")

Pronunciation: correct expression of each word (correct pronunciation is the mark of an educated person: film not filum; maintenance not maint*ai*nance)

Introducing a Speaker

C56 Keep the introduction short and simple. Include:
- a warm, welcoming comment
- a statement of the speaker's topic
- a very brief summary of the speaker's background or special interests
- an introduction of the speaker by *name* (Do this *last.* The speaker knows that at this point he/she takes over.)

Thanking a Speaker

C57 Again, say very little. Comment on the importance of the speech, and then simply thank the speaker, expressing appreciation on behalf of everyone present.

Making a Speech or Oral Report

C58
- **Establish purpose.** Is it your purpose to inform, persuade, or entertain (or a combination of these)?
- **Determine your topic** and decide on the key ideas.
- **Consider your audience** — age, type, and size.

- **Collect and organize your reference materials.**
- **Prepare an outline.** Build a "frame" consisting of an introduction (what your presentation is about); a middle (which includes the details needed to satisfy the listeners' curiosity and keep them interested); and a conclusion (which reaffirms the opening statement).
- **Produce your notes.** Enlarge upon your outline until you have produced a speech (either in point form or in full) that is the right length. From this expanded outline, produce the notes you will use as the basis for your speech. You may use your outline, your entire speech with key points underscored, or cue cards (small index cards) showing major points.

> *Speech on Effective Communication*
>
> 1. Choose words with precision
>   - avoid clichés and jargon
>   - avoid ambiguities and redundancies
>
> 2. Structure sentences properly
>   - avoid wordiness
>   - use complete sentences

Speech notes

- **Practise.** The inexperienced speaker may find it helpful to practise the presentation aloud to a friend or a mirror, or to put it on tape and play it back.

Speaking Before Large Groups

C59   When it is time for you to speak, walk calmly to the appointed spot, look up, smile, and make your presentation, bearing in mind these tips:

- Speak slowly, clearly, and loudly enough to be heard by everyone.
- Be enthusiastic.
- Be well prepared. (Preparation breeds confidence.)
- Don't read. Use an outline or cue cards.
- Use visuals to present difficult concepts or statistical information.
- Keep your head up and look at your audience.
- Use a conversational tone.
- Conceal any nervousness as well as you can. (Use a lectern to hold on to; keep taking deep breaths; don't hold on to papers — they rattle!)
- Avoid irritating mannerisms (too many hand movements; moving about; using "uh," "like," "you know," *etc.*).
- *Feel* your audience's reaction and respond to it.

How to Dictate

C60   The ability to dictate is a necessary business skill. Writing your communication is time consuming, costly, and inefficient — particularly in offices equipped with a word processing facility.

Whether you dictate to a person or into a recording machine, advance preparation is the key to success. For greater efficiency, plan to do all your dictating in one session if possible.

Preparation

- Assemble all the information you need — files, correspondence, calendar, address book.
- Organize your thoughts in advance and make notes of the points you want to include.
- When you want to reply to incoming correspondence, make notes in the margins.

Dictation Instructions

- Identify yourself by name, title, and location.
- Identify the type of message (letter, memo, Telex, *etc.*).
- Indicate priority or rush work.
- Specify the number of copies to be made and to whom they should go.
- Give any special instructions regarding spacing, layout, or stationery to be used.
- If you are dictating into a recorder, make an *indicator slip*, if possible, to give corrections and communication lengths.

Dictation

- Hold the microphone or telephone receiver about 10 cm from your mouth.
- Remain stationary and do not smoke or chew gum.
- Use a natural, conversational voice level and speed.
- Give the name and address of the addressee.
- For memos, indicate the subject.
- Dictate numbers slowly and spell proper names not accessible to the typist.
- Spell out troublesome technical and other difficult words or names.
- Give as many punctuation and paragraphing instructions as possible.
- If your job necessitates dictating while you are travelling, roll up the car windows; wait until the plane is cruising before you switch on your microphone.
- Place correspondence being replied to face down on the desk when dictation is finished so the order is correct for the typist's easy reference.

Grammatical Terms

Adjective: A word which modifies (describes) a noun or pronoun.

long dress; *fast* typist

Compound Adjective: Two or more words which combine to describe a noun.

a *good-looking* man, a *ten-speed* bicycle

Adverb: A word which modifies a verb, adjective, or another adverb.

She types *quickly.* That *rather* old typewriter...

Antecedent: The noun or pronoun to which a pronoun refers.

When *Sue* went shopping *she* forgot to buy cheese.
Every *person* is entitled to express *his/her* opinion.

Appositive (in apposition): Expression which agrees in number and case with the expression to which it refers and is used as an explanation.

Our tour guide, *who wears a black beret*, is very experienced.

Case: The English language has three cases:

Nominative (subjective) (initiates action): I, he, she, we, they, who

He can type.

Objective (receives action): me, him, her, us, them, whom

Give *them* the book.

Possessive (ownership): my (mine), your (yours), *etc.*

We use *his* typewriter.

Clause: A group of words which has both subject and predicate, which is a part of a compound or complex sentence.

While the sun is shining, ...

Restrictive Clause: A group of words which is essential to the meaning of the sentence.

The man *who had a broken leg* limped home.

Non-restrictive Clause: A group of words which does not affect the meaning of the sentence.

The man, *whose leg was broken last week*, is our chief accountant.

Conjunction: A word or words used to connect sentence parts.

and, but, as well as, not only...but also

Gerund: A form of the verb (ending in *ing*) which is used as a noun. Note that a noun or pronoun modifying a gerund is in the possessive case.

He appreciated *their* offering to help.
We approve of *their* coming with us.
They awaited the *Prime Minister's* coming.

Interjection: A word of exclamation registering emotion.

Help! My foot is stuck.

Mood: The mood of a verb shows the type of action of the verb and can be either:

Indicative: a statement of fact

She *can* drive a car.

Imperative: a command

Let him be.

Subjunctive: a wish or conjecture

If I *were* you,....

Noun: The name of a person, place, thing, animal, action, or concept.

Proper noun: person—Pierre Trudeau
place—Canada

Common noun: thing—apple
animal—dog
action—labour

Abstract noun (concept): love

Collective noun (groups of things): committee, team

Number: Singular or plural of nouns, pronouns, or verbs.

apple/apples; him/them; she runs/they run

Object: The part of a sentence that receives the action.

The sun is shining on *us.*

Paragraph: A series of sentences developing *one central purpose or idea.* The *topic* sentence opens the paragraph and the *transitional* one (forming a link with the paragraph that follows) ends it.

Golf is a game that many people play. Most of my friends are golf fanatics, and they particularly enjoy competition. (transitional)
The club in town runs four major tournaments each season to test every golfer's mettle.... (topic)

Parenthetical Expression: A word, phrase, or clause which does not change the meaning of a sentence but adds some expression to it.

Every sales representative—63 to be exact—attended the conference.

Participle: A form of the verb in either present or past tense (freezing, frozen) which is used as an adjective.

Freezing January temperatures are uncomfortable.

Phrase: A group of related words without a subject and predicate which functions as a single part of speech.

on the other hand,

Predicate: The verb and its modifiers.

The sun *is shining brightly today.*

Preposition: Any word which relates a noun or its equivalent to other parts of a sentence (to, at, with, by).

He worked *for* his father.

Note: prepositions always take the objective case.
Between you and me, it's too late.
Not
Between you and I, it's too late.

Pronoun: A word used to avoid the repetition of a noun in a sentence.

	Subject form (giving actions)	**Object form (receiving actions)**
Personal pronoun:	I	me
	we	us
	you	you
	he	him
	she	her
	they	them
Impersonal pronoun:	one	one
Relative pronoun:	who	whom
	which	which
	that	that
	those	those
	these	these

Angelo and I arrived at the same time.
Not
Me and Angelo arrived at the same time.

Please distribute the books to her and Carlos.
Not
Please distribute the books to she and Carlos.

Sentence: A group of words which contains a subject and a verb and expresses a complete thought. Sentences may be simple, compound, or complex.

Simple sentence (one independent main thought):

The sun is shining.

Compound Sentence (two independent main thoughts):

The sun is shining and the golfers are out.

Complex Sentence (one independent main thought and one or more dependent thoughts):

While the sun is shining, the golfers are out.

Compound-Complex (two independent main thoughts and one or more dependent thoughts):

While the sun is shining, the golfers are out and the clubhouse is empty.

Subject: The part of the sentence which names the person, thing, or concept to which the verb refers.

The sun is shining.

Tense: Time of the action—present, past, future.

Present: She listens.

Past: She listened.

Future: She will listen.

Verb: A word intended to tell you what is happening in the sentence.

Action words such as run, swim, walk; or linking words (copula verbs) such as is, seems, appears

Voice: Form of a verb which shows whether the subject performs or receives the action.

Active (subject *performs* the action): He read the book.

Passive (subject *receives* the action): The book was read by him.

Unit 3

Data Processing

Information may be processed in a number of ways—by calculators or accounting machines, for example—but the computer is the single most important business data processing device.

The computer can:
- process large volumes of material at incredibly high speeds
- follow instructions repeatedly without making mistakes
- store vast quantities of information in very little space
- function with little human intervention
- supply up-to-the-minute information about all phases of a company's operations, e.g., sales and inventory
- perform routine office work, e.g., payroll and accounts receivable
- control machinery on assembly lines and in processing plants

As an office worker you may not need to become a data processing expert, but you should be aware of what a computer can do and how it does it. You should understand how the work of the computer relates to the overall activities of the company and you must be aware of the roles played by the computer personnel in the firm.

Computer Components

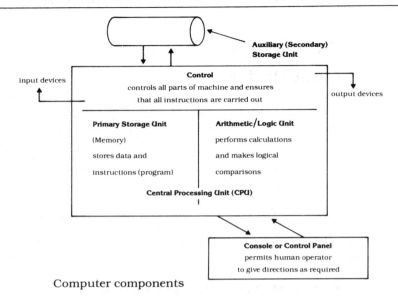

Computer components

D1   **Computer hardware** refers to all the electronic and mechanical parts of the machine (e.g., readers, printers, tape and disk drives).

Computer software refers to all the instructions that tell the computer to perform certain operations.

Computers range in size from room-size to desk-top models; but regardless of size, each features input, storage, processing, and output capability.

The Steps Involved in Processing Data Through the Computer

D2   1. **Input:** From a source document (e.g., employee time card) raw data (hours worked) are transformed into a form acceptable to a computer and fed into the machine via one of the input media discussed later.
    2. **Storing:** The facts, consisting of the information to be processed (hours worked and rate of pay) and the instructions for processing (calculate the wage), are fed into the computer's memory locations.
    3. **Processing:** All required calculating, processing, and other related instructions are carried out [(regular hours × hourly rate) + (overtime hours × overtime rate) − deductions = net pay].

4. **Output:** The processed data (output) is produced and communicated in the required format (payroll cheque).

Input Devices

Before data can be fed into the computer, it must be *recorded* in an acceptable format. The part of a record that contains a specific piece of information (such as an employee number or an account number) is referred to as a *field*. A set of related records is known as a *file* (e.g., all office employees or a set of accounts receivable records).

Information may be recorded from *source documents* (invoices, sales slips, orders, *etc.*) or it can be accepted directly into the computer from either optically read documents or input terminal keyboards. All computers accept one of the following input devices; most can accept a number of them.

Magnetic Ink Character Recognition (MICR)

A special ink containing a trace of iron is used to imprint the MICR code on documents. The iron is magnetized, and sorting machines sense it and interpret the data. This device is used by banks for processing cheques.

Magnetic Tape or Disk

Data can be keyed directly onto magnetic tape or disks without the need for cards. The encoding is done by means of a typewriter-like keyboard.

Optical Character Recognition (OCR)

Certain shapes can be sensed by sophisticated optical reading devices. Data is typed on sheets on a font (shape) acceptable to a computer scanner. The sheets are then placed in the scanner and read.

Optical Mark Reading (OMR)

In this system, pencil marks on cards or sheets are scanned and interpreted by the computer. Market research surveys would be a typical example of the use of OMR.

Paper Tape

Paper tape is a strip of paper on which data can be recorded in the form of punched holes. Such tapes may be made by many different business machines (e.g., cash registers). Paper tape is cheap but fragile, slow to read, and impossible to reuse.

Punched Card

The card has numbered columns and rows which are punched by a keypunch operator with current data. Each batch of cards is verified (checked), sorted, and put onto a *reader* where the holes in the cards are read and converted into electronic impulses.

Punched cards are gradually being made obsolete in favour of the following faster and more accurate input methods.

Video Display Terminal — Also Known as Remote Display or CRT (Cathode Ray Tube)

The device consists of a keyboard and a small TV screen. The terminal can be in the same room as the computer or a considerable distance away. The operator keys the job code and address (location in storage) of the data requested. The contents in the file then flash on the screen. Data can be entered directly into storage, and new records made or existing ones changed immediately. Devices of this type are used in such applications as airline reservations.

Voice Command

This system is based on the uniqueness of each person's voice and permits direct input by means of the spoken word.

Central Processing Unit (CPU)

D4   This unit receives instructions and information from the input device, stores the information until needed, recalls the information and instructions, performs the needed calculations or comparisons, and takes whatever other action may be required. The CPU has three parts, as described below:

Primary Storage (Memory) Unit

D5   This unit provides for the *temporary* storage of data. All data and instructions must be received here before the computer can start its work. The storage area contains a number of *addresses* (storage locations). The size of the computer determines the number of possible storage locations.

Arithmetic/Logic Unit

D6   This unit processes the data. It can do calculations and take logical action (compare possible courses of action and decide between alternatives).

Control Unit

D7 This unit controls the entire system (input and output devices and central processing unit) and sees that everything is working in accordance with the instructions (program) it has received.

Problem Solving (Programming)

D8 The computer can make rapid calculations but it cannot *think*. It is told how to solve a problem by means of a *program*. The program instructs the machine to perform a fixed operation or a group of fixed operations on given data.

The programmer (the person who writes the program) must attempt to foresee every possibility and every alternative that could arise in the solution of a problem. Therefore, the programmer must work in a systematic fashion and take each problem carefully and meticulously through the following stages before feeding the program into the computer.

1. Define the problem.
2. Plan the solution, i.e., develop a visual, step-by-step procedure.
3. Code the solution into a computer language.
4. Test the solution.

From the *statement* of the problem, the programmer develops either a *flowchart*, a *structure diagram*, or some other type of coded diagram to illustrate the steps involved in solving the problem. In flowcharting, *symbols* are used; in structure diagrams, *lines and comments* are used.

Problem: Wage payable = (hours worked × hourly rate) + (overtime hours × overtime hourly rate) − deductions

- From input device (punched card, tape, *etc.*) the computer reads in information needed (wage rate, hours worked, deductions).
- Each time information is read in, the question, "Is this the last piece of information?" is asked. If the answer is "yes," then the process is complete and the machine stops. If the answer is "no," the computer moves on to the next stage.
- The computer is instructed to complete all the necessary calculations to establish the amount payable to the employee.
- As a last stage, the computer is instructed to print out the result of the calculation (this may be in the form of a pay cheque or a report, depending on the instructions).

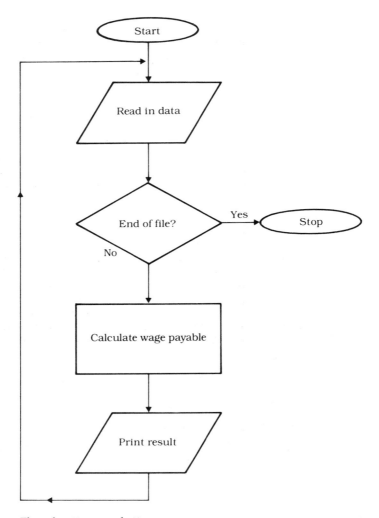

Flowcharting a solution

Computer Languages

D9   Computers work on instructions presented in words and digits. There are several computer languages, but the two most frequently used are:

- COBOL (COmmon Business Oriented Language): this is particularly suited to perform business related tasks.
- FORTRAN (FORmula TRANslation): this is designed primarily to perform mathematical and scientific calculations.

Most manufacturers build computers to accept instructions in either COBOL or FORTRAN, or both.

A set of instructions called a *compiler* is provided by the computer manufacturer. This enables the computer to translate *language* instructions into electronic impulses that activate the circuits through which the machine functions. When the calculations are made, the compiler converts these impulses into *language* again.

After the program is tested and corrected, it can be used repeatedly with different values (data) each time. To switch from one job to another—say from payroll to month-end financial reporting—a new program is loaded into the computer.

Output Devices

There are two basic types of output devices: those that provide permanent (hard copy) records such as statements, reports, and cheques, which are known as print-outs; and those that provide temporary, visual displays (soft copy) which are known as readouts. The type of output is related to the eventual use of the information, e.g., for storage and use in future processing or for immediate use in a visible form.

Key Punch

Holes are punched by this device into blank cards to represent the processed data. The cards may be stored or used for further processing.

Magnetic Tape and Magnetic Disk

Data from these output devices may be retained indefinitely and used as input for new processing.

Microfilm

Because of the vast quantities of paper generated by the computer, devices are available to microfilm reports directly from the computer or from the printed report. (This is known as COM and is described in Unit 5, F49.)

Paper Tape Punch

Processed data can be punched into paper tape and stored for later use.

Plotter

Drawings and graphs can be produced from data fed into the computer.

Printer

Information is printed in alphabetical and/or numerical form on continuous paper in an immediately usable format.

Visual Display (CRT)

Information is displayed on a screen that is positioned away from the computer. Printers can be linked with CRTs if a permanent record of the readout is required.

Voice Response

The processed data is provided in a voice-like response.

Note: Some devices serve as both input and output media, e.g., CRT, magnetic tape, and magnetic disk.

Secondary (Auxiliary) Data Storage

D11 Data fed into a computer must be stored for a while in the primary storage unit to await processing, and data that has been processed may also have to be stored temporarily. However, since there is a limit to how much data may be stored in primary storage, secondary (auxiliary) storage is required when processed data is to be stored for future use. Secondary storage can be achieved in several ways, e.g., processed punched cards, magnetic tapes, magnetic disks, or magnetic drums.

Communicating Facilities (Data Transmission)

D12 Computers and certain of their input and output devices do not need to be in the same room or even in the same building as each other. In fact, many terminals can be attached to one large computer so that computer time can be shared by a number of locations. Terminals can transmit data over a communications network in a process known as *teleprocessing*. The communications link (data transmission service) can be provided by private or public telephone and telegraph companies. (See Unit 16, T44.) The computer receives the data through the link, acts upon it, and sends back the required response.

Word Processing

D13 Word processors can be hooked into the computer so that they can use the computer's storage capacity as well as its data processing and communications facilities. For detailed information on word processing, see Unit 20.

Computer Facilities for the Small Office

D14 If the purchase of a small computer is not economically feasible, these two alternatives are possible.

Service Bureau

D15 You may rent the services of a computer to perform a specific task, e.g., month-end statements.

Time Sharing

D16 The installation of a terminal in your office will give you access to a central computer system and its capabilities.

Data Processing Personnel

D17 Large computer installations require a self-contained department of specially trained people. A list of typical job descriptions of people employed in such a data processing department includes the following:

Computer centre manager: The manager is responsible for the overall running of the department, e.g., for scheduling programs in the computer; managing equipment and supplies; and ensuring that the firm's computing needs are met.

Computer operator: The operator feeds data into the computer for processing and distributes the output. The operator is also responsible for preventive maintenance on the computer and for cleaning its vital parts.

Control clerk: The control clerk is responsible for regulating the flow of documents and information going into the computer for processing.

Data base administration staff: People in this section are responsible for dealing with a firm's computerized information requirements. They co-ordinate data collection and storage needs.

Data entry staff: Data entry staff use machines with keyboards similar to those of typewriters to transfer data to an input medium. Data entry staff may be known as keypunch clerks, keytape clerks, or data entry clerks.

Programmer: This is the person responsible for writing the detailed instructions (programs) on which the computer operates. The programmer solves problems and encodes solutions into a computer language.

Service technician: The service technician is responsible for total maintenance of the equipment.

Systems analyst: The systems analyst studies ways of improving office routines involving the computer, i.e., deciding on the best way of performing the work involved.

Computer Terms

D18

Access: the operation of seeking, reading, or writing data on a storage unit.

Address: an identification for a storage location in the memory of a computer.

ALGOL: Algorithmic Language. It uses algebraic symbols to express problem-solving formulas for machine solution.

Analog: an analog transmission system sends data in a continuous wave form, whereas a digital system breaks data down into separate digital units for transmission.

Analog computer: computer designed to deal with problems of measurement (e.g., the flow of liquid, temperature changes).

BASIC: a simple high-level language which stands for Beginners All-purpose Symbolic Instruction Code.

Batch processing: grouping related information and processing it at one time. Batch processing makes the most efficient use of computer hardware.

Baud: a unit of signalling speed. It is the number of discrete conditions or signal events per second.

Binary number system: a numbering system that uses only two digits (0 and 1) as its base.

Bit: the smallest unit of information recognized by the computer.

Buffer: a storage device used to compensate for a difference in rate of data flow when transmitting from one device to another. It is a temporary location for the transmitted data to occupy.

Bug: an error in a computer program.

Byte: a sequence of eight bits of information.

Chip: thousands of transistors squeezed onto a tiny silicon chip; use of the chip has resulted in the creation of small, powerful computers.

COBOL: programming language particularly suitable for business related tasks.

CPU (Central Processing Unit): the brain of the computer responsible for arithmetical, logical, and control functions.

Crash: refers to a machine's hardware or software failure, which prevents a system from functioning.

Data bank: a collection of data in one place.

Data base: a comprehensive collection of libraries of data in a single location. This electronic filing cabinet contains a series of files which can be stored and updated.

Debugging: a procedure to identify and correct any mistakes found during the testing of a program.

Digital computers: computers designed to make calculations by counting.

Disk: a device for storing data. A flexible disk is known as a floppy disk.

Distributed Data Processing (D.D.P.): decentralized data processing where, for example, branch offices have their own minicomputers that are hooked into a main computer at another location. This speeds up the company's data processing functions because some data processing can be done away from the mainframe (main computer) and then fed into it.

Dump: to copy the contents of all or part of a storage device, usually from a central processing unit, into an external storage unit.

File: a collection of related records.

Floppy disk/diskette: flexible magnetic disk used on mini- or microcomputer systems to store information.

FORTRAN: programming language used primarily for mathematical and scientific procedures.

Hardware: the equipment or devices which make up a computer system.

Intelligent copier (information distributor): a programmable copier capable of simple copying; or of assembling stored information, copying, and distributing it to other compatible equipment. (See Unit 14, R29.)

Intelligent terminal: a terminal with its own built-in microprocessor.

Keypunch: a device which punches the holes in cards.

Microcomputer: a small computer for home use or for small business application.

Minicomputer: a small and relatively inexpensive computer which can be used on its own or hooked into a main (large) computer setup.

On-line data processing: data processing in which transactions are processed through a computer as they actually occur, e.g., in banking transactions where an account is updated as deposits or withdrawals are made.

Peripheral equipment: equipment separate from the CPU, e.g., printers and terminals.

Point of sale terminals (POS): bar code sensors or wand readers capture data from price tags or codes. These terminals automatically record product identification and price, and update inventory records.

Program: as a noun, it denotes the plan or operating instructions needed to produce results from a computer; as a verb, it means planning the method of attack for a defined problem.

Random access: access to particular items in a file (or disk) without the need for searching the whole file.

Real-time data processing: processing of data on transactions as they actually occur, e.g., in airline and hotel reservations.

Software: programs and routines used in operating the computer.

Standalone: a device that is completely self-contained.

Terminal: a device for entering or receiving data from the main computer.

Turnaround time: time between submission of a job to the computer centre and the return of the results.

Turnkey system: a system devised for an untrained user, i.e., where a user wants to *turn the key* and have the computer function for him or her.

Video display: basically a TV screen which displays information going into and coming out of the machine.

Voice recognition unit: an input device that converts spoken words into binary data.

Voice response unit: a terminal that generates output in a voice-like response.

Unit 4

Efficiency: Time and Space Management

Accomplishing all that is required of you in a day, retaining your sanity, and maintaining a high efficiency level is a difficult juggling act. In this unit you will find some ideas on how to become a successful "juggler" and therefore get more out of your *day* without taking too much out of *yourself*.

E1 Time Management

The Starting Point

E2 Find out what you are presently doing with your time by keeping a log of each day's activities for several weeks. Analyze your log and try to determine which time periods were most productive in your typical day and which the least productive. Now start to plan your time for more efficient use.

Planning Your Day

E3 • Make a work schedule for yourself, i.e., list exactly what you must accomplish that day.

THINGS TO DO LIST

Monday Sept. 15

A *Make up weekly sales report.*
A *Give Bob a merit review.*
  See about new typewriter.
B *Call Janis at ad agency re half page ad.*
  Send anniversary card to Muriel.
C *Arrange for lunch with other execs. next Thursday.*

Things to do list

- Assess each task, assign priorities (A, B, C, *etc.*) and establish deadlines.
- Delegate all C jobs (and as many others as you can). For example, if you have a secretary or assistant, delegate:
    the opening and sorting of mail
    the screening of visitors and phone callers
    the annotating of magazine articles
- Do unwelcome jobs first while you are freshest.
- Finish one job before you start another.
- Check each job off the list as you complete it. (This is a positive act and *very* satisfying.)
- Maintain a long-term calendar as well as a daily one, and note on it routine dates (regular meetings, reports due, *etc.*) and other commitments for several months ahead.
- Schedule a specific time of day for dealing with mail, and discourage all interruptions during this time.
- Group related jobs together. For example:

    Save copying jobs until you have several so that you walk to the machine just once.
    Do all the mailing jobs at one time.
    Do *one* batch of filing a day if possible.

- Avoid interruptions. The stop-start approach to a job is time wasted. Resist an "open door" policy, i.e., don't have your desk positioned so that you appear to welcome casual socializers. Sit with your back or side to the door.
- Keep breaks short but take them. A break will keep your energy level up.
- Try to get everything done in the shortest time with the fewest wasted motions. Think out an activity and reduce it to a series of mechanical routines.
- At the end of the day, analyze why each unchecked job was not completed.
- Develop good reminder and follow-up systems. (See Unit 5, F32.)
- Have an easy-to-read phone No. record system that is well cross referenced.
- Pace yourself. Allow sufficient time to complete a job so that you are not under unnecessary pressure.
- Keep a filing system that is easy to use and clean it out frequently. (See Unit 5, F35.) Do not keep records and forms no one needs.
- Keep your desk tidy. Time is wasted in trying to find information on a desk buried under paper.
- If you are faced with a large job which cannot be handled at one time, do it in small "chunks." Work away at the assignment by doing small parts of it in any ten- or fifteen- minute unused time segments which occur during the day.

Procedures Manuals

E4

It is useful to do away with the waste of time involved in having one person explain procedures to another. This is accomplished by creating manuals which can be referred to for all standard procedures.

- Set up an *operations manual for your filing system* which describes all the equipment; explains indexing, coding, cross referencing, and charge-out procedures; and outlines your records retention policy.
- Establish very clear *job descriptions* to aid takeovers when a person leaves or is promoted.
- Make up *job procedures* for reports, *etc.*, which are not done frequently or which are not done by one person all the time. The instructions must be clear enough so that anyone can follow them and produce the job.
- Develop a *company style manual* so that all typists follow the same style and have available an instant reference source.
- Create a manual of *form paragraphs* or *form letters* appropriate for most routine situations.

Become a Better Listener

E5

More effective listening leads to greater understanding and therefore to greater personal efficiency. Since you listen faster than the speaker can speak, you must force yourself to concentrate so that you comprehend what is being said.

- Keep quiet and listen to what is being said. Be an attender not a contender.
- Go over the speaker's statements in your mind.
- Formulate questions as you concentrate.
- Judge the *words*, not the speaker. (Don't concentrate on his tie or the shape of her earrings.)
- Have a notepad handy. Listen and then write down. (Don't trust your memory.)
- Give the speaker your undivided attention. Try not to permit interruptions (e.g., telephone calls) while someone is speaking to you.

Improve Your Reading Skills

E6

Research has shown that the *faster* you read, the more you concentrate and retain. Most people read average material at the rate of 250 wpm; efficient readers read average material at 1000 wpm. Efficient readers do not *word* read, pause, skip back, or silently mouth the words; they skim the page while concentrating on the words. To encourage efficient reading, first determine your present rate and them aim to increase it.

What is Your Reading Speed?

- Start a stopwatch.
- Read a two-page non-fiction article.
- Stop the watch. Calculate the amount of time (in seconds) it took you to read the two pages.
- Count the number of words in the article by adding the number in one line and multiplying this by the total number of lines in the article.
- Divide the words by the number of seconds.
- Now multiply the answer by 60 to get your score in minutes.

To increase your reading speed, follow these steps:

- Decide why you are reading. Before beginning to read a book or article in earnest, it is useful to ask yourself:

    What do I want to find?
    What do I already know?
    Is this new material?
    Should I read all of this?

- Preview the material:

    If it is a book, skim the jacket.
    Review the table of contents.
    Read the first paragraph or first sentence of several chapters or paragraphs to get a feel for the author's style.
    Ascertain what kind of concentration will be needed and whether or not the item or book is worth reading.

- Use an index finger to lead your eyes along the line you are reading.

Avoid Stress

E7   Pace yourself throughout the day so that you eliminate periods of stress and fatigue.

- Plan the toughest jobs or appointments for the start of the day when you are freshest.
- Don't cram too many activities into a short time span. Plan for a breathing space between appointments.
- If you must leave the office or building for any reason, allow yourself sufficient time to arrive at your destination without rushing.
- Resist lunch and evening appointments.
- Allow for rest periods when planning long business trips. Jet lag is a serious stress problem.
- Delegate as many routine tasks as possible.

Dealing With Correspondence

E8

- Don't proscrastinate. Handle each piece of correspondence only once and make decisions *now*. Often you will not know anything more about the subject three days hence.
- Use as many form letters or form paragraphs as possible. (See Unit 2, C39.)
- Become an efficient dictator. (See Unit 2, C60.)
- Use preprinted routing slips.
- *Write* responses on incoming letters or memos, photocopy them for your file, and send the original back to the writer.
- Follow up on unpaid bills by photocopying the invoice or statement and writing or typing a reminder on it.
- Use carbon-interleaved speed memos and handwrite your message.
- Use a dictating machine or a stenographer rather than handwrite material that is to be typed.
- Carry a pocket-size dictating machine for recording correspondence when you are out of the office. (Ensure the recording medium is compatible with the transcribing units in the office, of course.)
- Write short, easy-to-understand letters.
- Don't put everything in writing. Phone. Walk over and talk to people in the office.
- Use rubber stamps. (See Unit 6, FO27.)
- Use stickers for repetitive information.
- Use postcards.

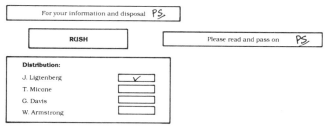

Preprinted stickers

Typing Shortcuts

E9

See Unit 18, TT82 for speedy production hints.
See Unit 18, TT102 for transcription tips.

Meetings

E10

- Don't wait for latecomers. You penalize the people who were punctual and waste their time and your own.
- See Unit 11, MC6 for hints on efficient management of meetings.

Telephone

E11

- Prepare for telephone calls before you dial by having files, calendar, pen, and paper handy. (See Unit 16, T4.)
- Do your telephoning in blocks of time.

Equipment

E12

Having the right working tools and equipment available can save time, energy, and money.

- Where ownership is not possible, consider renting. For example, rent computer time for such large jobs as payroll.
- Consider the advantages of word processing. (See Unit 20.)
- In addition to having available the obvious small items required, check into the advantages of purchasing such specialized items as:

Forms separator: separates both carbon and carbonless continuous forms into stacks.

Burster: will "burst" continuous forms and cheques into individual sheets.

Collator: will automatically gather separate sheets into sets.

Postage meter: will save trips to the post office.

Power stapler: will speed up those big stapling jobs.

E13 # Space Management

Work Area Arrangement

E14

Work areas must be set up with the performance of tasks in mind as well as with consideration for the individual's need for privacy, quiet, and security.

Desk layout: Save time by keeping frequently used supplies and equipment within easy reach.

Telephone: Place this on the same side of your desk as your non-writing hand so that you pick up the receiver with that hand and leave your writing hand free for note taking.

Files and reference sources: Locate these close to the work station. If they are in constant use, position them either directly beside or behind your desk so that you can reach them from your chair.

The Secretary's Desk

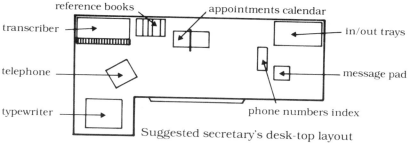

Suggested secretary's desk-top layout

E15 **Centre (shallow) drawer:** Use this for small items such as paper clips, pencils, pens, erasers, elastic bands, rulers, scissors, staples, tape, stamp pads, steno pad, moisteners.

Stationery drawers: Position stationery in the order in which you make up a carbon pack: letterheads first, carbon next, onionskin in the third, continuation next, *etc.*

Office Layout

E16 Office layout has considerable influence on efficiency and productivity levels.

- Consider an open-plan office concept. Its flexibility means that 80 per cent of available space can be used, whereas the conventional plan permits only 40 per cent.
- Provide enough space for people to move around freely.
- Match the positioning of desks and work stations to the paperwork flow. Paperwork must flow smoothly, with a minimum of interruptions and backtracking.
- Choose filing cabinets or shelves to suit the amount of space available and the types of records to be stored. (See Unit 5, F37.)
- Position shared equipment (e.g., copiers) so that the area does not serve as the office socializing spot.
- Group together employees using the same equipment or records.
- Locate service sections (e.g., mailing department) near the departments that use them most.

Office Furnishings

E17 Studies on furniture, furniture arrangement, light, and sound reveal these to be significant factors in office efficiency. Consider these points:

Desks: L-shaped desks provide 80 per cent more work space than conventional ones. Choose light or medium gray for the desk top because this is less tiring on the eyes than dark woods.

"Systems" furniture: This creates the most efficient work station as far as space and employee productivity are concerned. Systems furniture means that the work station consists of pre-wired movable panels of varying heights plus such added components as work surface, files, and individual lighting in whatever configuration is best suited to the task to be accomplished.

Lighting: Desk lighting is better than overhead lighting for productivity.

Noise control: Sounds from office machines bounce off walls, ceilings, and other surfaces and cause noise disturbance. Sound absorbing materials in room-dividing panels and ceilings help alleviate this problem. Carpeting and drapes are also useful in absorbing sounds.

Unit 5

Filing: Records Management

Filing means retaining records in systematic order for future reference. This unit provides an outline of the basic procedures of filing which should be followed whether the business is large or small; whether the filing is centralized or decentralized; or whether the storage medium is paper, punched cards, magnetic tapes or disks, or film. This unit also contains a description of the major filing systems and various storage devices.

The Alphabet

F1   Since the alphabet is the basis of many filing systems, it is obvious that one uniform set of rules for placing names in alphabetic order must be followed by everyone who works with or uses the files. The rules which follow are based on those used in compiling the telephone directory.

Indexing

F2   Before names or other captions (places or subjects) can be placed in alphabetic order, they must be *indexed*. Indexing means determining the most important part of a name or caption and then bringing that word or words to the front, if necessary. The indexed version of the name or caption should be typed on the file folder, index card, or record container.

Normal Order	Indexed Order
Laura L. Fleming	Fleming, Laura L.
The Complete Essays of	Twain, Mark, (The)
Mark Twain	Complete Essays (of)
Jack Bird Plumbing Co.	Bird, Jack, Plumbing Co.

- Commas are used to indicate that the parts of a name or caption have been rearranged.
- Small, unimportant words are ignored for indexing purposes.

Alphabetic Sequencing

F3

Each part of the name or caption is considered as a separate unit, working from left to right until a comparison point is reached.

Unit 1	Unit 2	Unit 3
Bird,	J.	
Bird,	Jack	
Birde,	J.	John

For correct filing order, always follow the rule *nothing before something.*

Names of Individuals

F4

- Surnames are considered first, given names or initials second, middle names or initials third.
- A surname standing alone precedes a surname with initials.
- A surname with initials precedes a surname with a full given name.

> Johnson
> Johnson, N.
> Johnson, Nadia

Note: Names of married women should be alphabetically sequenced by their own names, not their husbands' names.

> Jones, Sara (Mrs. Robert)
> Jones, Sarah (Mrs. Allan)

Names of Companies

F5

Company names are filed as written unless the company is named after a person.

> Spruce Springs Antiques
> Ford Motor Company, The

If the company is named after a person, it is indexed so that the family name is considered first.

Normal Order	Indexed Order
Terence Singh Electronics	Singh, Terence, Electronics

If the *whole* name is the one under which the company is commonly known, it should be filed following the *normal order* and not *indexed*.

John Hancock Mutual Life Insurance Co.	**But**
	Eaton, T., Co. Ltd.
Laura Secord Candy Shops	Heath, D.C. and Co.
Sara Lee Kitchens (Canada) Ltd.	Simpson, Robert, Co. Ltd.

Small Words (an, and, of, by, on, &, the)

F6

These are ignored for sequencing purposes but must be typed in the caption on the file label. They may be placed in parentheses if desired. If *the* begins a name, it is moved to the end; if it occurs elsewhere, it may be typed in parentheses.

Fernando The Butcher	Fernando (The) Butcher
The Valley School of Dance	Valley School (of) Dance, The

Foreign language equivalents of *the* (Le, La, Il, El, *etc.*) and Old English forms (Ye) are considered to be prefixes, i.e., part of the name.

El Matador
La Scala Dining Room
Le Chien Elégant
Ye Olde Cheese Factory

Titles and Degrees

F7

These are disregarded for alphabetic sequencing purposes but are typed after the name on folders, labels, *etc.*

Normal Order	Caption Order
Mrs. Jane Alexander, B.A.	Alexander, Jane (B.A.) (Mrs.)
Dr. Alan H. Draper	Draper, Alan H. (Dr.)

Note: If a title is part of a person's given name or a business name, it is filed as written.

Normal Order	Caption Order
Lord Simcoe Hotel	Lord Simcoe Hotel
Sir Nicholas Restaurant	Sir Nicholas Restaurant
Sister Gabriella	Sister Gabriella

Initials (Single Letters)

F8

Names consisting of initials only are placed before all other names starting with the same letter. Each initial is considered as a separate unit.

	Unit 1	Unit 2	Unit 3
CAC Realty	C	A	C
CIAG Insurance	C	I	A
Cabaret Dance Studio	Cabaret	Dance	Studio

Note: Where the meaning of the initials is known, cross reference to avoid confusion. (See this Unit, F31.)

Abbreviations

F9

These are treated as if they are written out. However, the abbreviated form must appear on the file folder tab or index card.

Caption Order	**Filing Order**
St. John's Bookstore	Saint John's Bookstore
Sanitary Inspectors Inc.	Sanitary Inspectors Incorporated

Bros. (Brothers), Wm. (William), Chas. (Charles), Jas. (James), Inc. (Incorporated).

Prefixes

F10

These are considered as part of the name (i.e., prefix plus name form one word).

P. D'Ambrosia	D'Ambrosia, P. (considered as though spelled Dambrosia)
O. De Kleine	De Kleine, O. (considered as though spelled Dekleine)
D. von der Heidt	von der Heidt, D. (considered as though spelled vonderheidt)

Note: Names beginning with Mc and Mac are filed as written.

Apostrophes

F11

These are ignored in alphabetic sequencing—no matter where they occur. Notice, for example, how the name Lela's is fitted into the following list.

LeLarge Inc.
Lela's Hair Stylist
Lelas, T.
L'Elégant Beauty Salon
L'Elégante Ltd.

Note: Some offices ignore the *s* if it comes after the apostrophe, but current practice is to ignore the apostrophe and include the *s*.

Hyphenated Names

F12

Each word in a hyphenated name is treated as a separate filing unit, i.e., the hyphen is disregarded while filing order is being established but is typed on the file folder label.

	Units 1	2	3	4
Canadian-American Pen Co.	Canadian	American	Pen	Co.
Ellen Curtis-Brown	Curtis	Brown	Ellen	
James William Curtis	Curtis	James	William	
Winston Curtis-Jones	Curtis	Jones	Winston	
Nu-Style Beauty Salon	Nu	Style	Beauty	Salon

Note: Some offices treat the hyphenated name of an individual as one word, but current practice favours the procedure shown above.

Geographic Names (Place Names and Names Including Compass Terms)

F13   These are treated as though each word is a separate unit (i.e., they are filed as written).

> *North* American Press Ltd.
> *North* West Sportswear Ltd.
> *North* Western Auto Service
> *Northwest* Airlines Inc.

Numbers

F14   Numbers are filed as though they are *spelled* in full but are typed as written (i.e., in numerals) on the file folder or other label.

Filing Order
6th (Sixth) Street Boutique
Super Value Market

Caption Order
6th Street Boutique
Super Value Market

Associations, Societies, Organizations, Banks, Churches, Colleges, Schools, Universities

F15   These remain unchanged for filing purposes.

Normal Order
Bank of Montreal
University of Manitoba
L'Amoreaux Collegiate

Indexed Order
Bank (of) Montreal
University (of) Manitoba
L'Amoreaux Collegiate

Note: Cross reference, if necessary, to avoid confusion. (See this unit, F31.)

Boards, Committees, Estates, Trustees

F16   Boards, *etc.*, are rearranged to bring the most important word to the front.

Normal Order
Board of Governors
Estate of D. Chung

Indexed Order
Governors, Board (of)
Chung, D., Estate (of)

Note: Cross reference if necessary to avoid confusion. (See this unit, F31.)

Governments and Their Divisions

F17 These are filed under the name of the particular government (federal, provincial, municipal) with further subdivisions where necessary.

Normal Order	**Indexed Order**
Government of Canada	*Canada*, Government (of)
Ministry of Agriculture	Agriculture, Ministry (of)
Saskatchewan Ministry of	*Saskatchewan*, (Province of)
Health	Health, Ministry (of)
Windsor Board of Education	*Windsor*, (City of) Education, Board (of)

Identical Names

F18 Identical names are filed alphabetically by *location* (i.e., the province or country is compared first, then street name, then street number (numerically)).

General Manufacturing Co., Main Street, Edmonton, *Alberta*

General Manufacturing Co., 73 *Fifth* Street, Vancouver, *British Columbia*

General Manufacturing Co., *49 Third* Avenue, Vancouver, British Columbia

General Manufacturing Co., *150* Third Avenue, Vancouver, British Columbia

F19 Parts of a Typical Correspondence File

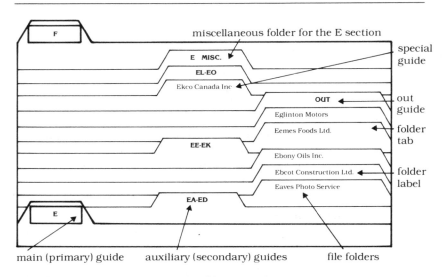

Parts of a typical correspondence file

Guides

F20   *Main* (primary) and *auxiliary* (secondary) guides (folder-size cardboard with metal tabs) are used to separate file folders into divisions and subdivisions to facilitate filing and retrieval. *Special guides* are used when particular subjects or correspondents are frequently referred to and must be speedily located.

Folders (Legal or Letter-Size)

F21
- Individual. An *individual folder* is placed alphabetically in the file behind the proper subdivision for each person, organization, or subject.
- Miscellaneous. Correspondence concerning a new correspondent or subject is placed in a *miscellaneous* folder in the proper subdivision until at least *five* papers have accumulated. An individual folder is then prepared and moved to the appropriate position.

Folder Tabs

Folders are available in a variety of *cuts* which leave a tab visible in the file drawer or on the file shelf.

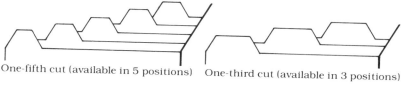

One-fifth cut (available in 5 positions)   One-third cut (available in 3 positions)

One-half cut (available in 2 positions)   Full cut

Folder tabs

The same cut may be used for all folders in a system, or cuts may be varied to stagger folders so that one folder tab is not obscured behind another. For shelf filing, folders, guide cards, and *out* guides are available with tabs at the side for easy visibility.

Folder Labels

Folder captions are usually typed on labels available in roll or sheet form and in various colours. Captions should be typed neatly in a consistent style, and the labels should be positioned carefully so that the captions can be easily seen. Colour may be used to indicate particular years, particular departments, *etc.*

Filing Systems

F22   Records may be arranged alphabetically, by geographic location, by subject, by number, or by a combination of letters and numbers.

Alphabetic Filing

F23
- Names and subjects are filed in simple alphabetic order.
- Main guides indicate each letter of the alphabet.
- Auxiliary guides break down each letter of the alphabet into sections. Folders are arranged alphabetically by name behind these guides. The user merely looks for the first two or three letters on the auxiliary guide and then looks behind for the folder being sought.
- This system is simple, easy to operate, but difficult to expand.
- This system is used in small organizations where specialized breakdown by subject or location is not needed.

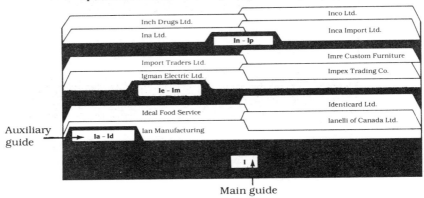

Simple alphabetic file

Geographic Filing

F24
- Files are grouped by geographic location from the largest geographic division to the smallest (e.g., from province to town).
- The largest divisions (provinces) appear on the main guides, and the cities or towns on the auxiliary guides. File folders for correspondents in each city or town are placed alphabetically behind these guides.
- This system is useful to firms or departments whose main interest is territorial data (e.g., sales records); however, it should be noted that successful operation of a geographic system demands sound geographic knowledge.

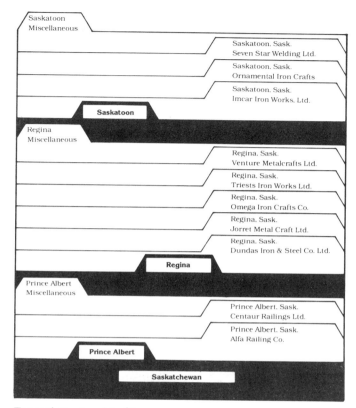

Typical geographic file

Subject Filing

F25

- Subject filing means organizing records by topic (i.e., the content of the material) and then arranging the files alphabetically by those topics.
- The main guide indicates the main topic breakdown in the filing system. Auxiliary guides indicate any necessary subdivisions of the topic. Folders are placed alphabetically by topic behind the appropriate guide.
- Establishing subject classifications demands care and considerable knowledge of the organization's activities.
- An alphabetic master list or card index is needed to show all the main subject divisions, auxiliary (secondary) divisions, and individual folder categories to facilitate retrieval.
- Many cross references are likely to be required.
- This system is used where subject matter is more important than correspondents' names.

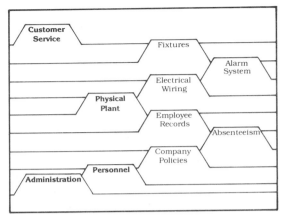

Administration	
Personnel	
Company Policies	
Absenteeism	
Employee Records	
Physical Plant	
Electrical Wiring	
Alarm System	
Fixtures	
Customer Service	

Subject file master list

Simple subject file

Letters and Numbers Used in Subject Filing

F26   Subject filing may also be set up by means of letters and numbers used in combination or by numbers used alone. Such systems are particularly useful in large, centralized filing systems because they can overcome the difficulties generally associated with simple alphabetic subject systems. These variations offer flexibility, diminish misfiling possibilities, eliminate uneven workload problems, and ease expansion difficulties.

Alpha-Numeric

A combination of letters and numbers is used. Main topics are given letters and related subtopics assigned numbers.

A	Administration
A1	Personnel
A1-1	Company Policies
A1-1-1	Absenteeism
A1-2	Employee Records
A2	Physical Plant
A2-1	Electrical Wiring
A2-1-1	Alarm System
A2-2	Fixtures
B	Customer Service

Decimal

This system is based on the notion that all material can be grouped into ten or fewer main categories. Each of the ten major subjects may be subdivided into ten more parts and so on indefinitely.

```
100        Administration
110          Personnel
111            Company Policies
111.1            Absenteeism
112            Employee Records
120          Physical Plant
121            Electrical Wiring
121.1            Alarm System
122            Fixtures

200        Customer Service
```

Duplex-Numeric

A combination of numbers is used. Each primary topic is given a consecutive number, and secondary and tertiary (third subdivision) topics are subdivided down from that number.

```
1-1          Personnel
1-1-1          Company Policies
1-1-1-1          Absenteeism
1-1-2          Employee Records
1-2          Physical Plant
1-2-1          Electrical Wiring
1-2-1-1          Alarm System
1-2-2          Fixtures
```

Subject-Numeric

Subject groups are assigned alphabetic codes (usually of three letters) and secondary and other categories are represented by numerals.

```
ADM.01        Personnel
ADM.01-0        Company Policies
ADM.01-0-1        Absenteeism
ADM.01-1        Employee Records
ADM.02        Physical Plant
ADM.02-0        Electrical Wiring
ADM.02-0-1        Alarm System
ADM.02-1        Fixtures
```

Numeric Filing

F27 **Sequential Numeric System**

In numeric systems, one number is used to cover all the records of a client, case, or account.

- As new folders are required, new numbers are added in sequence.
- Main guides are used to indicate round numbers.
- Auxiliary guides are used to break down the round numbers into smaller categories.

- When a file is opened, a number is allocated and an alphabetic index card is made up.
- The number to be used for a new file is determined by consulting the *Access Register*, a record of file numbers already allocated. The next unused number is allocated to the new file.
- The system *must* have a complementary card system arranged alphabetically which shows the client's name, address, assigned number, and any other pertinent information. If the file number is unknown, the alphabetic card index is consulted and the file number is easily located.
- Numeric filing offers accuracy, confidentiality, and unrestricted possibilities for expansion.
- This system is used by lawyers, doctors, insurance companies or in any situation where records are classified by a number and where records must be continually added to.

Card system for numeric filing

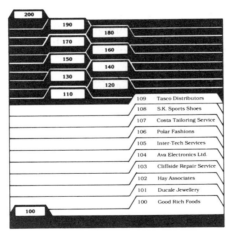

Typical numeric file

Note: Some companies use both name and number on the file folder, but where confidentiality is required, number only is used.

Terminal Digit Filing

- In this type of numeric filing system, numbers are read from right to left in equal groups of numbers (i.e., the first two numbers at the right hand are *primary*; the next two are *secondary*; and the rest are *tertiary*).

File Number 271832 is read as 32 18 27

- To file or retrieve, users first look under section 32 of the file, then under section 18, and finally under section 27.
- Users of this system include insurance companies and hospitals, where the primary and secondary digits could identify the type of claim or service and the tertiary numbers identify the individual's name.

Systems Management and Control

F28

In some organizations records are kept in a centralized storage area under the direction of a records manager; in others, records are retained in individual departments, i.e., they are decentralized. Regardless of the size or sophistication of the filing system, a consistent and careful routine is necessary if it is to be managed successfully. All documents must be routinely checked to ensure proper releasing for filing; then they should be coded and, if necessary, marked for cross reference and follow-up. In addition, efficient charge-out and transfer procedures must be used.

Releasing

F29

- No document should be filed until somebody has released it, i.e., indicated that *all necessary action has been taken.*
- Initials, a rubber stamp, or a carbon copy of a reply attached to the original document are generally used as filing releases.

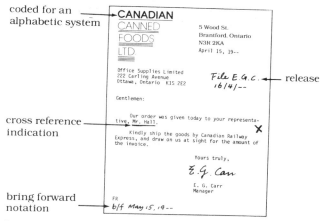

Letter coded for alphabetic filing, showing typical release, cross reference, and bring-forward (follow-up) notations

Coding

F30   Coding means identifying on the record where it is to be filed.
- The word(s) under which the document is to be filed is (are) underscored or circled, or the appropriate caption is inserted.
- The filing units may be indicated by the use of one or more underscores, if required.

Unit 1	Unit 2	Unit 3
Liontos	James	Antiques
Canadian	Canned	Foods

- In the case of a numeric system, the appropriate number or code is written on the document.

Note: Coding makes refiling easier if papers taken from the system must be replaced.

Cross Referencing

F31   Cross referencing means indicating in one or more places where a record may be located. Records are filed under the most important classification and cross referenced under the other(s).

Cross references are advisable when a document refers to more than one subject or where a file might be looked for under more than one heading. For example:
- where names contain several important words

    Vancouver Board of Education
- for names with similar sounds but different spellings

    Noel — Nowell
- for companies referred to by initials but where the meaning of the initials is known

    CBC — Canadian Broadcasting Corporation

Three cross-referencing devices are:

Cross-referencing sheets. Specially designed letter-size sheets which may be filed inside the cross-referenced folder as though they were correspondence so that they direct the searcher to the correct folder.

Cross-referencing folders. These are tabbed half folders placed in the file drawer or shelf in the cross-referenced position as though they were actual folders. These half folders are labelled to indicate the position of the actual correspondence folder.

Cross-referencing index cards. These are small cards kept in a separate file drawer. They are used in a large system where many cross references occur.

```
              C R O S S   R E F E R E N C E

NAME OR
SUBJECT    Dixon Pencil Co Ltd.           Folder No. _____

   Address  531  Davis Drive
            Newmarket , Ont.
            L3Y 2P1


REFER TO  Eberhard Faber (Canada) Ltd. Folder No. _____
            531 Davis Drive
            Newmarket, Ont  L3Y 2P1
            (Division of Dixon Pencil Co )
          Date of letter or paper:  November 8        19--
          Remarks:  Enquiry about automated
                    storage systems

SEE ALSO  _____    Folder No. _____
          _____
          _____
          _____
          _____

   File this cross reference under the name or subject written at the
   top of this page.
```

Cross reference sheet

```
Dixon Pencil Co. Ltd.

See: Eberhard Faber
     Canada Ltd.
```

Cross reference shown on the tab of a half folder

```
DIXON PENCIL CO. LTD.
531 Davis Drive
Newmarket, Ontario  L3Y 2P1

See:  Eberhard Faber (Canada) Ltd.
      531 Davis Drive
      Newmarket, Ontario  L3Y 2P1

Note:  Eberhard Faber is a division
       of Dixon Pencil Co.
```

Cross reference card

Follow-Up or Reminder (Tickler) Systems

F32   A good follow-up system ensures that documents which will require attention in the future are brought forward at the proper time. Any document which has a "bring forward" notation on it should have the request recorded in one of the following devices before the document is placed in the files.

Desk Calendar

On the appropriate day, a note is made of the reminder request and the location of the material.

Follow-Up File (Sometimes Referred to as the Chronological File)

- Thirty-one folders (one for each day of the month) and 12 folders (one for each month) are labelled.
- The folders are placed in a file drawer.
- A follow-up request for the current month is filed in the appropriate *day* folder. If the follow-up is for a future month, it is placed in the appropriate *month* folder.
- Material in each day's folder is dealt with on the appropriate day, and the empty folder is then moved to the back of the *day* folders.
- At the beginning of each month the previous month's empty folder is moved to the back, and papers from the current month's folders are transferred into the daily folders.
- Dates of weekends or holidays are not used for bringing forward correspondence.
- For a very large system, daily folders for a *year* might be set up.

Note: The material in the folder may be the original, a copy, or simply a note to serve as the follow-up.

Tickler File

This system is identical to the follow-up file except that it is in card form and is housed in a small card index container. Reminder notes are made on separate cards and these are inserted behind the appropriate day or month guides.

Charge-Out Procedures (Borrowing Filed Materials)

F33   - Every filing system should have an efficient charge-out procedure for establishing the whereabouts of a record or a file while it is out on loan.
- When materials are to be borrowed, a dated requisition describing the record or file should be completed.

- While the record is out on loan an *out* guide or an *out* folder should be used to replace it. (*Out* guides are satisfactory for single documents. *Out* folders are best for replacing complete folders because new records can be safely stored in them while the folders are out on loan.)
- A careful record must be kept of all documents and files out on loan in case they are needed by someone else. Simple ways of achieving this are by means of the completed requisition form or by means of small index cards which show the name of the borrower, date of borrowing, description of the record, or title of the file.
- Strict follow-up of overdue material is advisable to ensure that borrowed material is returned. A bring forward tickler system (see this unit, F32) or a desk diary might be used for this purpose.
- Should the record be given by the borrower to another person (rerouted), the borrower should inform the file department, and the *out* guide and follow-up record should be changed to show the new borrower's name.

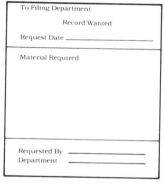

Charge out requisition

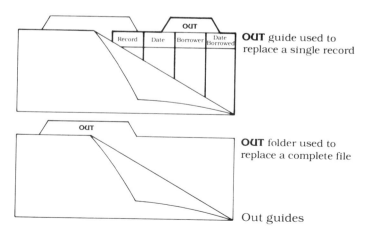

OUT guide used to replace a single record

OUT folder used to replace a complete file

Out guides

Filing Tips

F34 • For faster filing, sort papers into large groupings which follow the arrangement used in the cabinets or shelves, e.g., A-G, H-L, M-S, T-Z. Sorters are available in desk top types or large portable tub types.

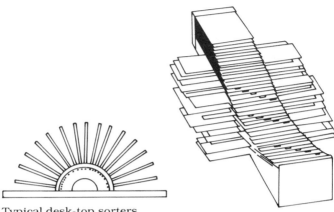

Typical desk-top sorters

• Place documents in folders with the left edge against the crease in the folder.
• Place documents in chronological order with the most recent date on the top.
• Keep a *miscellaneous* folder at the back of each alphabetic or numeric division to hold correspondence that is not designated to a specific file. When five documents have accumulated for a client or subject, make up an individual folder.
• A folder should hold a maximum of 100 sheets. Do not exceed the space provided by the creases. Open an expansion folder for heavy correspondence.
• Suspension folders in cabinets keep materials neater and make files easier to handle.
• Do not overcrowd file drawers or shelves. Allow 10 cm of unused space.
• Use coloured labels. Colour can assist in speeding retrieval and can prevent misfiling because misfiles are automatically indicated by the interruption they would make in the bands of colour used.
• Colour can also be used effectively to indicate time periods and therefore can make the job of transferring old files easier.
• File every day.

Records Retention

F35   A periodic cleanout of files to dispose of outdated or unnecessary material is customary. Routine correspondence may be destroyed, but legal considerations control the retention of some materials. The advice of legal counsel or a C.A. should be sought as to which documents must legally be retained in each particular type of business.

The paper pollution problem can be eased by looking very carefully at which records must be kept and which should be discarded, which can be kept on film or tape, and which — because of legal requirements — must be retained in the original form.

A *records retention schedule* (a timetable for the life of a record) is a useful device. The schedule should show the types of records and the time periods for which they should be kept; it should contain instructions for their eventual disposal or destruction (e.g., transfer from active to inactive storage, microfilmed, or authorized destruction). The records retention schedule is usually drawn up by management, the file supervisor, and the company's legal counsel.

Transfer Methods

F36   Inactive files containing documents and correspondence which are old and not in use, but which should be kept for some reason, should be removed (transferred) from the active files and stored elsewhere so that there is no unnecessary crowding of the active files. The transfer method to be used will be determined by the nature of the business.

Perpetual

When a particular piece of work (e.g., a legal case) is finished, the file is transferred into storage.

Periodic

After a certain period of time (e.g., on a particular date each year) all the files are transferred. (Colour coding file labels by time is helpful in this method.)

F37   Records Storage Equipment

Front (or Vertical) Cabinets

F38
- These cabinets have up to five pull-out drawers that extend 75 cm.
- Available in letter and legal size, front cabinets are best suited to the filing of correspondence.

- The drawers may be fitted with a cradle over which hanging folders may be hooked either to serve as file folders or to house other, smaller folders.

Side (or Lateral) Cabinets

F39　These cabinets have the length of the file against the wall and offer a considerable saving in space requirements over front cabinets.

Shelves

F40
- Shelves, which may be open or closed, are advantageous where large quantities of files are maintained. Shelves save space and offer a plentiful storage area.
- Shelves offer great adaptability and can, for example, be adapted to house computer print-outs, tape reels, and other non-standard size records.
- Most systems use boxes which attach to the shelves to house materials.
- Where maximum filing capacity in limited floor space is needed, shelves are ideal.

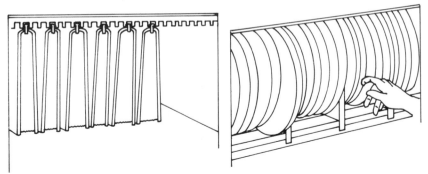

Shelves adapted to house tape reels and print-outs

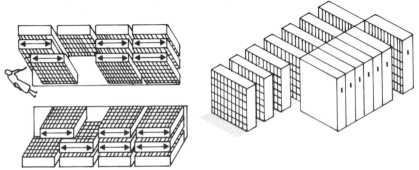

Types of mobile carriage systems

Mobile Carriage Systems (Laterally Rolling Modular Filing Systems)

F41 Such space-saving systems may have movable rows or may have stationary back rows and laterally rolling middle and front rows. (The rows may be moved electronically or manually.) This system allows easy access to whichever row a file is stored on. Built-in safety features ensure that staff members cannot be caught between moving shelves.

Rotary (Circular) Files

F42 These are available in electronically driven versions. They reduce waste motion because by push-button controls they *bring* files to the operator.

Special Files

F43 Special equipment to suit particular needs — plan files, card record systems, binding cases, magnetic media storage devices, *etc.* — is available from office supply companies. Alternatively, manufacturers will build special equipment and provide expert consultation services if necessary.

Automated Storage Equipment (Electronic Retrieval Systems)

F44 Automated storage means that the location and replacement of a particular record (file, tape, reel, card, cheque, *etc.*) is handled by push-button command.

- The system is controlled by an operator who sits at a simple keyboard console work-station.
- The operator keys in the record identification and the *start* command is given.
- A mechanism then moves to the appropriate location, couples itself to the requested file container, and transports the container to the work station.
- After the file has been dealt with, the operator gives a *re-store* command and the mechanism automatically returns the file container to its proper position.

Automated storage equipment offers great speed, space efficiency, security, and ease of operation. The system can also be interfaced, if required, with a computer by means of specially coded label systems.

Micrographic Storage (Microfilm)

F45   Micrographic storage involves microfilming (microminiature recording on film) which permits records storage in 2 per cent or 3 per cent of the space needed for storage of original documents. Micrographic storage provides better protection for the record, fast access to information, greater durability, simplicity of copying, and improved ease of transmittal.

Equipment needed in micrographic storage is:
- a *camera* to film (record) documents
- a *processor* for processing and duplicating exposed film (exposed film may be sent to a specialist for processing or may be processed on the company's own premises)
- a *microfilm reader* to magnify the microfilm back to readable size (microfilm can be enlarged to its original size without loss of detail)
- A *printer* to produce hard copy print-outs of the microfilmed documents of the same size as the original documents.

Note: The reader and printer are frequently one combined unit rather than two separate units.

Microfilm Types

F46   The most commonly used film is 16 mm. However, for drawings or other records which would suffer if too small a reduction were made, 35 mm is used. Film may be negative or positive. Negative provides a white image on black background; positive provides a black image on light background. Negative is the more commonly used film.

Microfilm Storage Devices (Microforms)

F47   Storage may be handled in the following ways. The choice will depend on the nature and the amount of the material to be stored.

Reels (or Cartridges)

These are rolls of uncut film which are used when all the microfilmed documents are related to each other (e.g., when libraries store old newspapers). Reels and cartridges offer low cost and high density (i.e., they can hold up to 6000 images), but they are difficult to search and update.

Film Jackets

These are covers used for storing strips (up to 75 per jacket) of microfilm. This device is particularly suited to *active* systems where frequent consultation and update are involved.

Aperture Cards

These are computer input cards which house a microfilm frame. This storage medium combines the microfilm with electronic data processing because the input card can be coded with related data.

Microfiche

This is the term for 150 mm $\times$ 100 mm flat sheets which contain rows of microfilm frames. Each microfiche can hold from 30 to 420 images. This method is suited to situations where, for example, film versions of entire reports or print-outs are to be kept. Microfiche is easier to update than the other film storage devices.

Microfilm Storage Systems

F48

Equipment designed specifically for housing the various types of microfilm storage devices (binders, cabinets, small tubs) is available from office equipment suppliers. An indexing system for locating microfilmed material could take the form of a card index, a punched card index, or any record identification method used in numeric systems, alphabetic systems, or combination alpha-numeric systems. (See this unit, F26.)

Computer Output Microfilm (COM)

F49

Microfilming and computers have been linked in a system known as Computer Output Microfilm (COM). In this system, computer output is transferred directly onto film instead of onto paper. An operator can call up a specific document within seconds for viewing on a cathode ray tube and for hard copy printing if needed.

The system is advantageous because it is space saving, speedy, and permits very rapid retrieval. The high cost of COM makes it best suited to large, sophisticated records management situations. For smaller companies, the Yellow Pages lists service companies which specialize in COM work.

Computer Assisted Retrieval (CAR)

F50

In CAR the capability of the computer is linked to the searching of microform files. Microfilmed records are located within seconds and the microform can be read on a separate viewer or on the screen of the terminal from which the request was initiated.

Computer Input Microfilm (CIM)

F51

This is a process which permits microforms to be transmitted to remote locations where they may be processed.

Points to Note

F52

- Despite the advantages of saving floor space and reducing operating costs achieved by using microfilm as a storage device, original documents are required to satisfy certain legal requirements. Advice of legal counsel should be sought as to which documents are admissible in court as legal evidence.
- Although special training is not essential, it might be wise to take a course in all facets of microfilming and micrographics. Such courses are available at some community colleges in major centres.
- If it is not feasible for an organization to purchase microfilming equipment, micrographic service companies will undertake the work. Consult the telephone directory.

Filing Terms

F53

In addition to those terms already defined, the following may be useful.

Access register: used in a numeric filing system to record the file numbers allocated.

Active record: a record referred to frequently (e.g., more than once a month), regardless of age.

Archival records: the permanent record of an organization.

Block numeric: a numeric filing system in which blocks of numbers are assigned to particular subject groupings.

Caption: the heading (or description) used on a file folder label.

Case file: a file containing only material relating to a specific action, event, person, place or thing, usually filed by name or number.

Chronological filing: filing by date order.

Indexing: the selection of the caption under which a record is to be filed.

Middle digit: a numeric filing system in which the middle digits in a series of numbers are used as the primary caption under which records are to be filed.

Reading file: a chronological file of extra copies of correspondence.

Rerouting: the process of lending a record out on loan to another borrower without returning it to the records centre first.

Soundex: a filing system based on the phonetic spelling of a name.

Variadex: an alphabetic filing system in which the second letter of the family name is colour coded.

Unit 6

Forms

Regardless of size, nature of business, or type of ownership, firms tend to be organized along very similar lines because they must all deal efficiently with certain fundamental activities. These activities are purchasing, receiving and stockkeeping, producing, selling, shipping, billing, and keeping records of money received and money paid out. These separate activities are linked by means of *forms*, each designed for a particular purpose and each prepared in sufficient quantities to satisfy the firm's needs.

The illustrations which follow describe the flow of activity around *purchasing* and *sales*, the two systems which are the life-blood of any business organization. The illustrations indicate the interdependence of the various departments involved and identify the forms used at each stage of activity.

Following these illustrations are descriptions and illustrations of most typical business forms plus an indication of the minimum number of copies needed to permit interdependent departments to fulfill their functions.

The concluding section of this unit contains information on how to obtain preprinted forms and how to design forms. Additional information is provided about forms that can act as short cuts and time savers within a department.

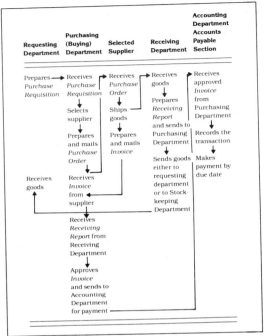

Flow of activities in a typical purchasing system

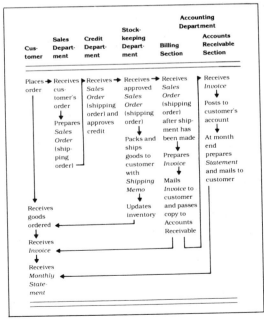

Flow of activities in a typical sales system

Forms Used in Basic Business Activities

FO1 *Note* 1: When a computer is used in a firm's system, the forms will look a little different from those illustrated but their effect will be the same.

Note 2: In each case, only the *minimum* number of copies of each form is indicated.

Purchasing (Buying)

FO2 Purchasing means obtaining everything an organization needs in its operation — from paper clips to delivery trucks. In a small company, buying may be done quite informally (a telephone call or a letter, for example), but a large company needs forms to control and record purchasing functions. In most organizations buying is handled by a purchasing department, which acts only on receipt of an approved purchase requisition.

Purchase Requisition

FO3
- an approved purchase request from within the organization
- 2 copies: 1 to Purchasing Department
         1 for issuing department file

		REQUISITION (NOT A PURCHASE ORDER)			007266
TO	Purchasing Dept.			DATE Aug. 20 19 - -	
ADDRESS			FOR		
SHIP TO	Production Dept.		DATE REQ'D. Sept 17		
QUANTITY		PLEASE SUPPLY		PRICE	AMOUNT
1	50	oak frames, 50 cm x 35 cm			
2	25	mahogany frames, 70 cm x 60 cm			
3	50	panes non-glare glass, 50 cm x 35 cm			
4	25	panes non-glare glass, 70 cm x 60 cm			
5	3	rolls canvas, 80 cm wide			
6					
7					
8					
9					
JOB NO	SALES TAX CHARGEABLE NOT CHARGEABLE	ORDERED BY W. Stanley		APPROVED BY Fche	

Purchase requisition

Purchase Order

FO4
- prepared from the purchase requisition and sent to the vendor (supplier) who offers the best price and delivery terms
- 3 copies: 1 to supplier
  1 to Receiving Department
  1 for Purchasing Department file

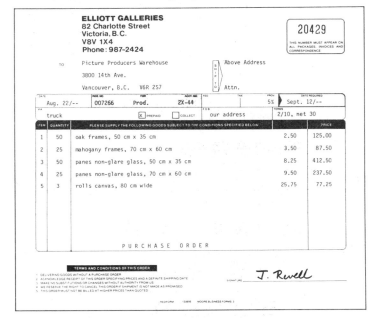

Purchase order

Receiving

FO5
Goods received must be matched against the original purchase order for accuracy in quantity and condition. It is the responsibility of the Receiving Department to make the check and complete a Receiving Report on the incoming goods.

Receiving Report

FO6
- prepared after incoming goods have been checked against the purchase order
- 4 copies: 1 to Accounts Payable Section
  1 to Purchasing Department
  1 to Stockkeeping Department
  1 for Receiving Department file

Receiving report

RECEIVED FROM: Picture Producers Warehouse
3800 14th Ave. Vancouver, B.C. V6R 2S7
DATE: Sept. 11/--
VIA: Truck
FOR: Production Dept.
PRO BILL NO. BY 4720
NO. OF PKGS. 9
PURCHASE ORDER NO. 20429

ITEM NO.	QUANTITY	✓	WEIGHT	ACCEPTED	REJECTED	DESCRIPTION
1	25			✓		oak frames, 50 cm x 35 cm
2	25			✓		oak frames, 50 cm x 35 cm
3	25			✓		mahogany frames, 70 cm x 60 cm
4	25			✓		panes non-glare glass, 50cm x 35cm
5	10			✓		panes non-glare glass, 50cm x 35cm
6	25			✓		panes non-glare glass, 70 cm x 60cm
7	1			✓		roll canvas, 80 cm wide
8	1			✓		roll canvas, 80 cm wide
9	1			✓		roll canvas, 80 cm wide

PARTIAL: ✓ COMPLETE: POSTED BY: RECEIVED BY: am INSPECTED BY: am STORES LOCATION:

15354

Stockkeeping

FO7 This department is responsible for the storage, care, and distribution of finished goods and raw materials.

Inventory (Stock) Record

FO8
- kept for each product and shows quantity received and issued, and the balance presently on hand
- only 1 copy is essential

ELLIOTT GALLERIES
82 Charlotte Street
Victoria, B.C.
V8V 1X4
Phone: 987-2424

PERPETUAL INVENTORY CARD

ITEM: Oak frames, 50 cm x 35 cm Maximum: 200
CODE: S342   STOCK NO: PR89 Minimum: 20

Date 19--	Mdse. on order P.R.#	Amt.	STOCK Received P.O.#	In	Issued S.R.#	Out	Balance
June 6							130
July 7					347	10	120
July 13					703	35	85
July 27					912	50	35
Sept.11	7266	50	20 429	50			85

Inventory record

Stock Requisition

FO9
- sent to the Purchasing Department by the Stockkeeper when it is necessary to replenish supplies which have reached minimum quantity levels
- dealt with by the Purchasing Department as though it were a purchase requisition
- 2 copies: 1 to Purchasing Department
  1 for Stockkeeping Department file

Producing

FO10
In manufacturing firms or in service businesses (such as garages or equipment repairers) an authorization form is required before the actual production of goods or servicing of equipment can begin.

Production Order (Work Order)

FO11
- given to the person or section doing the job
- 2 copies: 1 to the worker or section
  1 for Production Department file

ELLIOTT GALLERIES
82 Charlotte Street
Victoria, B.C.
V8V 1X4
Phone: 987-2424

PRODUCTION CONTROL NO: 100-4981

JOB. NO: F.276   DATE OF ORDER: Aug. 19   CUST. P.O: AE49

CUSTOMER: Scott's Art Stores   SHIP TO: Same address
739 Appian Way
Coquitlam, B.C.
V9T 9P6

DATE REQUIRED: Sept. 30/--   VIA: Express

QUANTITY: 60 framed prints   UNIT PRICE: $50

JOB DESCRIPTION: B.C. scene prints No. 101-160 to be framed in oak frames with non-glare glass, 50 cm x 35 cm

FINISH: UNIT PRICE: BY:

PACKING INSTRUCTIONS: CARTON FROM:

SHIPPING MEMO	QUANTITY	INVOICE #	QUANTITY	AMOUNT

Production order

Selling

FO12
A customer who wishes to buy merchandise or services places an order with a firm.

Sales Order (Also Known as Shipping Order in Some Organizations)

FO13
- made up by a sales representative or sales department clerk after taking an order in person, by telephone, or through the mail
- 6 copies: 1 to Credit Department
  1 to customer
  1 to Stockkeeping Department
  1 to Shipping Department
  1 to Accounts Receivable Section
  1 for Sales Department file

Picture Producers Warehouse
3800 14th Avenue
Vancouver, B.C.
V6R 2S7

SOLD TO *Elliott Galleries*
82 Charlotte St.
Victoria, B.C. V8V 1X4

SHIP TO *same*

DATE	SHIP VIA	CUSTOMER ORDER NO	SALESMAN	
Sept. 8/--	truck	P35-5901	Kenneth Ramsey	

QUANTITY ORDERED	DESCRIPTION	UNIT PRICE
50	oak frames, 50 cm x 35 cm	2.50
25	mahogany frames, 70 cm x 60 cm	3.50
50	panes non-glare glass, 50 cm x 35 cm	8.25
25	panes non-glare glass, 70 cm x 60 cm	9.50
3	rolls canvas, 80 cm wide	25.75

Sales order

FO14
Note: In retail sales situations, a *Sales Slip* is issued at the time of sale and given to the customer with the goods purchased.
- 3 copies: 1 to customer
  1 to Accounts Receivable Section—when sale is a credit one
  1 for Sales Department file

Shipping

FO15
When goods are shipped, acknowledgement of their receipt is frequently necessary. The form used to obtain the acknowledgement may be a copy of the invoice or it may be a shipping memo.

Shipping Memo (Delivery Receipt)

FO16
- signed by the customer and given back to the carrier on receipt of merchandise
- 2 copies: 1 (signed) to customer
  1 (signed) for shipper

```
                                                    040573
FROM  Picture Producers Warehouse      DATE  Sept 11/--
TO    Elliott Galleries                 YOUR ORDER
ADDRESS  82 Charlotte St.       CITY  Victoria
PACKAGES    RECEIVED IN APPARENT GOOD ORDER          WEIGHT
   9      Contents - frames
                   - glass
                   - canvas rolls




RECEIVED BY  A. McLaughlin      TOTAL PACKAGES  9    TOTAL WEIGHT
                                C.O.D. CHARGE       DELIVERY CHARGE
                                                    REDIFORM 6M51
```

Delivery receipt

Bill of Lading

FO17
- the standard shipping document which serves as a contract between consignor (the supplier) and the carrier of goods
- used for rail, water, air, or road transportation of goods
- signed by the customer or carrier

(See Unit 7, G3.)

Billing

FO18
After the supplier has shipped the articles ordered, or after delivery of the merchandise, the customer is billed (sent an invoice).

Invoice

FO19
- sent by the Billing Section of the Accounting Department to the customer
- shows details of merchandise ordered, cost, shipping charges, terms of payment, discounts applicable, tax, and total amount due
- 3 copies: 1 to customer
  1 to Accounts Receivable Section
  1 for Billing Section file

- additional copies of invoice can be used by:
  credit department
  accounting department
  sales department (to acknowledge order or to
     indicate that shipment was made)
  stockkeeping department (for inventory control)
  shipping department (as a packing slip)

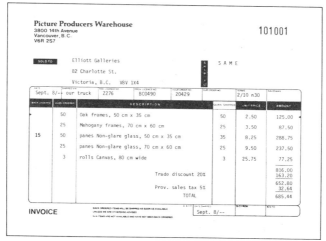

Invoice

    If the total order cannot be shipped, the invoice shows that fact. For example, if a quantity of 100 were ordered and only 40 were available for shipment, 60 would be entered in the *back order* column and 40 in the *quantity* column. The outstanding 60 would be shipped and invoiced at a later date.

Credit Invoice

FO20
- issued by the Billing Section of the Accounting Department to a customer in case of returned or damaged merchandise or an overcharge
- tells the customer that his/her account is reduced (credited) by the amount shown
- 3 copies, as for the invoice

Collecting

FO21   If a customer does not pay for each order as it is invoiced, he/she is sent a monthly statement.

Statement

FO22
- sent by Accounts Receivable Section to customer
- itemizes purchases, returns, and payments made during the month and shows total balance due
- 3 copies: 1 to customer
  - 1 for collection follow-up
  - 1 for Accounts Receivable Section file

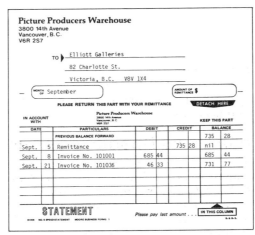

Statement

Disbursing

FO23
Disbursing, the paying out of funds by a company, is carried out either by the Accounts Payable Section or by the Payroll Section. The *Accounts Payable Section* makes all the company's payments other than payroll. The *Payroll Section* handles salaries and wages for employees. (See Unit 1, B38.)

Preprinted Basic Business Forms

FO24
Where the size of the business does not justify specially printed forms, preprinted forms may be purchased. These forms may be rubber stamped with the company name and a number if necessary. Preprinted forms which may be purchased include:

Billing forms (duplicate and
  triplicate)
Carbon-set memos
Delivery receipts
Expense accounts
Invoices

Ledger sheets and
  accounting paper
Petty cash vouchers
Purchase orders (duplicate and
  triplicate)
Receipts

Requisition forms
Sales representatives' order
books (duplicate and
triplicate)

Statements
Time and payroll forms

Preprinted Specialized Forms

FO25

Legal forms: mortgages, leases, wills, *etc.*, are obtainable from several sources, e.g., Dye & Durham, Newsome & Gilbert.

Tax forms: available through the local Revenue Canada Taxation office.

Banking forms: can be obtained from branches of chartered banks or other financial institutions.

Telegram and Teletype forms: available from CNCP Telecommunications.

Miscellaneous Business Forms

FO26

Some business forms exist which cannot be identified with one of the key activities but are still important to the smooth running of a business. For typical forms used in the filing, personnel, transportation, and communications functions, see the relevant units of this handbook.

Rubber Stamps

FO27

In some situations, rubber stamps can be used in place of forms to provide necessary information. Information can be stamped on documents to indicate *date of receipt, date of shipment, priority in handling, department routing of documents, filing information, etc.*

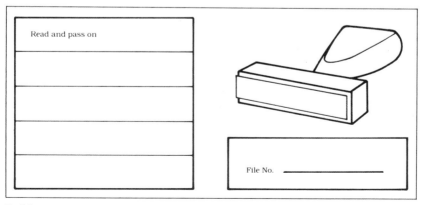

Read and pass on

File No.

Rubber stamps

Design of Business Forms

FO28 Business forms should be drawn up with the goal of speeding up the flow of information. These are the basic characteristics of a well-designed form:

Data should be easy to enter. The captions must be clear and the lines far enough apart to make writing or typing on them easy.

Data entered should be easy to read and use. The instructions should be adequate, titles correct, the type face a simple one, and the colours of ink and paper appropriate.

Data obtained must accommodate the firm's needs. The information requested must be full enough.

Size requirements of a computer must be considered. A computer form can be designed for any purpose—payroll, statement, invoice, purchase order, *etc.*,—but it must be of a size the computer can handle, be preprinted on continuous forms, and have side-punched holes.

Copy requirements must be met. A *masterset* (an original, carbons, and copies all attached to one form) might be considered. The masterset saves the typist's time by eliminating the need to assemble a carbon pack.

Unit 7

Goods Transportation

This unit provides information on the transportation services available for shipping goods within Canada and internationally, a description of the procedures to be followed in shipping goods out of the country and into the country, and guides to obtaining expert assistance.

Chart of Transportation Services

G1   Unless otherwise stated,

1. Charges are based on destination and mass or volume, whichever is greater.
2. Services may be prepaid or collected.

135

Chart of Transportation Services

Type	Shipping Area	Pick-Up and Delivery	Insurance
Rail Express	Canada and major U.S. cities	available in all but remote areas	not included
Rapidex	Canada	included	free up to S50 value: additional protection available at 50¢/S1000 value
Rail Freight	Canada and major U.S. cities	customer must arrange to get boxcar to siding	usually included
Air Express	Canada and major U.S. cities	usually included	free up to S50 value: additional protection available at 35¢/S100 value
Air Parcel/Courier Services 1) Fastest (Expedair)	Canada and major U.S. cities	not included. airport to airport service only	not included. but S500 max. declarable value may be purchased
2) 2nd priority (small packets) (Airvelop)	Canada and major U.S. cities	included	not included, but S500 max. declarable value may be purchased
3) 2nd priority (larger packets) (Couriair)	Canada and major U.S. cities	included	not included, but S500 max. declarable value may be purchased
Air Cargo/Freight	Canada and major U.S. cities and international	not included. airport to airport service only	free up to S50 value: additional protection available at 30¢/S100 value
Truck	Canada and major U.S. cities	included, except for out-of-way locations	usually included
Bus	Canada and major U.S. cities	not included. parcel *taken* to terminal 2 hours before departure	not included, max. S500 in Canada. S250 in U.S. may be purchased
Boat (Steamship)	Canada, U.S., international	not included	not included
Courier Services U.P.S. (United Parcel Service)	Southern Ontario and U.S.	included in weekly service charge	free up to S100 value

Restrictions	Special Services	Points to Note
	C.O.D. service	• best suited to out-of-town packages up to 60 kg where post office service is not possible
• max. 34 kg • total length and girth 3 m	heated service at extra cost	• suitable for fast (road or road and rail) delivery of parcels • maximum value of parcel $1000 • prepaid parcels only
full boxcars only	• refrigerator cars • animal care • containerization • piggyback • fishyback	• best suited to large out-of-town shipments • full boxcars only are accepted (but see Freight Forwarders) • charges based on contents, perishability, mass and destination
maximum 60 kg	C.O.D. service	• best suited for small packages in need of high priority treatment where cost is not important
• max. 23 kg • max. dimensions 225 cm (max. 122 cm 1 side)		• service available from 06:00 to 00:30 • highest priority (max. delivery time 8 hours) • most expensive • prepaid service only
• max. 1 kg • 30 × 41 cm		• picked up before 17:00, guaranteed next-day delivery
• max. 40 kg • 122 × 229 cm		• picked up before 17:00, guaranteed next-day delivery
over 50 kg	• animal care • perishables • refrigerator	• cheaper than air express, but expensive • full container rate is cheaper than partial
	• heater • refrigerator • flatbed cars • C.O.D.	• delivery possible to places not served by a railroad • charge based on classification tariff, type of licence, quantity and distance • full truckload rate is cheaper than partial load
• max. 48 kg • 61 × 61 × 122 cm		• for U.S. packages, export documents must accompany parcel • packages must be prepaid
containers only	• refrigerator • tank containers	• best suited to heavy, bulky goods and machinery where speed is not a consideration • personal effects must be prepaid
• max. 35 kg • 22 kg to U.S. • max. girth and length 2.75 m	• C.O.D. • acknowledgement of delivery for additional charge	• a good alternative to the postal service (see Unit 13, PO44) • next-day delivery available in an extensive area.

Shipping Goods Within Canada

Documentation

G3   The *bill of lading* (sometimes known as the straight bill of lading) is the standard contractual document used for all but express shipments between the shipper and carrier. (For express shipments, this document is referred to as the express shipping contract.) The bill of lading serves as a receipt for goods, as documentary evidence of ownership of goods, and is not negotiable.

Bill of lading

The form is completed in triplicate:

- Copy 1 is mailed by the shipper to the consignee.
- Copy 2 is retained by the carrier.
- Copy 3 is retained by the shipper.

When ownership of the goods may change during shipment (as, for example, when perishable goods are shipped before a buyer has been found), an *order bill of lading* (a negotiable bill of lading) is used.

Obtaining Transportation Services

G4

When an organization is not large enough to have its own shipping department, it frequently uses freight forwarders or international freight forwarders. These are agencies which specialize in gathering small shipments (usually within a city) and combining them into boxcarloads, containers, *etc.* They make up documents for shipments; take care of legal fees; arrange charges for freight; organize pickup and delivery; arrange for agents at the consignee's end; distribute documents; and provide any other required transportation services. Forwarders charge fees according to the value of the goods handled on each shipment. Freight forwarders often act as customs brokers as well.

Exporting Goods

G5

Shipping goods to foreign nations is more complex than shipping within Canada because of customs regulations, documentation, and foreign exchange problems.

Documents Used

G6

A considerable number of documents are required to satisfy the demands of Canada Customs and customs authorities in the importing country. The shipper may be required to provide all or most of the following documents.

Confirmation of Sales

• an acknowledgement that the order has been received and will be shipped

Invoices

• Commercial Invoice (Form B13): the standard invoice issued for all regular sales.
• Consular Invoice or Special Customs Invoice: needed by authorities in the importing country (depending on the rules of that country).
• Pro-Forma Invoice: a mock invoice used by the prospective buyer to request permission from his government to buy the necessary Canadian currency.

Special Certificates

These are required by the importing country to assist in clearing goods through customs and establishing tariff rates.

• Certificate of Origin or Combined Certificate of Value and Origin: a declaration of the country of origin of the goods which must be notarized by the Board of Trade.

- Certificate of Mass (Weight List): needed when duties are calculated according to mass. This depends on the importing country's regulations and is usually required when payment is made by letter of credit.
- Certificate of Health (Sanitary Certificate): required when animals or plants are being shipped.

Export Permits

- obtainable from the Export Permit Branch of the Department of Industry, Trade and Commerce
- may be required depending upon the commodity being exported and Canada's relations with the relevant country

Import Permits

- required by some countries
- issued by importing country to Canadian exporter

Bill of Lading

- the basic document required in any shipment (see this unit, G3)

Export Entry Form

- required before any goods above $500 in value are allowed to leave Canada
- used by Canada Customs for statistical information

Shipping Notice (Advice of Shipment)

- informs the importer that the shipment has been made

Packing List

- an itemized list of the contents of each package in the shipment.

Obtaining Export Services

G7 Because of the complexity of exporting, most large organizations employ their own experts, and smaller firms use a customs house broker (international freight forwarder) (see this unit, G13) to prepare the documents and arrange for transportation of the goods.

Importing Goods

G8 Usually included in the duties of the traffic manager or shipping clerk is the responsibility for goods being imported.

Customs

G9 Every article entering Canada must pass through Canada Customs at official ports of entry. Canada Customs controls both the entry of goods into the country and the collection of the required duties (tariffs) and taxes. Canada Customs maintains offices in all major cities.

Duty Rates

The rate of duty payable on goods entering Canada is determined by the classification of the goods and the tariff to be applied. Duty rates are calculated in three ways: *ad valorem* (a percentage of value), specific (according to mass, number, or size), or a combination of the two.

Clearing the Goods

G10

Goods are held in bond at a port of entry until they have been cleared; i.e., until the importer has presented the required clearance documents and paid the necessary customs duties and taxes.

Clearance Documents

G11

Customs Entry Form

- shows the items shipped, the method of transportation, duty and taxes payable, country of export, country of origin, names of the exporter and importer, and quantity of goods shipped.

Customs Invoice

- required for all shipments valued at $500 and over (the form of the invoice to be used is determined by the tariff rate which applies to the goods and whether they were shipped on consignment or sold before shipment)

Packing List, Bill of Lading, Shipping Advice Note, and Import Permit

(See this unit, G6.)

Drawbacks (Refund of Duties Paid)

G12

Duties and sales taxes are recoverable in the following three situations:

- when goods are imported, duty and sales tax paid, and the goods are used in the manufacture of products to stay in Canada (manufacturer's drawback)
- when goods are imported, the duty and sales tax paid, and the articles are then exported to a third country (export drawback)
- when such errors as overpayment of duty or short shipment of goods have occurred

Drawbacks may be obtained by applying to the Drawback Department of Canada Customs.

Obtaining Import Services

G13   Some organizations use a customs house broker/international freight forwarder to clear shipments on their behalf. Customs house brokers clear shipments through customs, providing whatever assistance may be needed in the process (obtaining permits, finding out duty rates, making up documents, *etc.*). The payment they receive is based on the value of the goods cleared.

Transportation Terms

G14   **Ad valorem duty** (Ad val., A/V): customs tax levied on value of imported goods.

Bill of lading (b.l, B/L): document issued by a carrier to a shipper which acknowledges receipt of goods and promises to make delivery under the conditions stated.

c.i.f. (carriage, insurance, freight): these charges have been or will be prepaid by the shipper.

CL (Carload): a shipment large enough to fill a rail boxcar.

C.O.D. (cash on delivery): collection of the invoice value of the goods is made before the goods are given to the buyer.

Common carrier: the transporter of the goods between the consignor and the consignee.

Consignee: the recipient of the goods shipped.

Consignor: the sender of the shipment.

Container service: shipments made in a metal container which may be carried by either road, rail, or sea (or all three) without the need for unloading and reloading.

Demurrage: charge for storage payable to a carrier for goods not collected within the time limit permitted.

F.O.B. (free on board): delivery of goods free of charge to the destination named, e.g., F.O.B. Toronto.

Fishyback: a trailer placed on a ship or barge.

LCL (less than carload): a quantity that is less than a full rail boxcar.

Manifest: list of cargo, which shows the masses, dimensions, values, destinations, and consignees.

Piggyback: one method of transportation carried on the back of another (e.g., a trailer on a flat railroad car).

Tariff: a fee schedule of transporting companies; or a government tax schedule on imports.

Waybill (W.B.): dispatcher's written description of goods shipped.

Unit 8

Information Sources

The efficient office worker must know where to find business-related information quickly. Some sources of this information you will use frequently and will therefore want to own; others you may need infrequently but should be aware of.

This unit is organized around the topics the business person is most likely to need information on and shows the reference sources generally considered to be the most authoritative. For those situations where more specialized information is required, the local reference library is invaluable. Included also, therefore, is a section on how to find information in a library.

The reference books available in your particular office will, of course, depend on the type of business you are involved in. But remember that *no* desk is complete without a good dictionary.

Almanacs and Year Books

I1   These annual publications provide statistics and short, factual statements on various current topics such as exports, imports, mining, population, political personalities, and government structure, as well as holidays and memorable dates.

Canada Year Book
Hull, Quebec: Canadian Government Publishing Centre, Supply and Services Canada

Canadian Almanac and Directory
Toronto: Copp Clark Pitman

Canadian Annual Review
Toronto: University of Toronto Press

The Corpus Almanac of Canada
Toronto: Corpus Publishers Services Ltd.

Whitaker's Almanack
London: J. Whitaker & Sons

World Almanac and Book of Facts
Garden City, N.Y.: Doubleday & Co., Inc.

Atlases

I2   Atlases contain statistical and descriptive data about various regions and countries of the world, as well as detailed maps and indexes of Canada and foreign countries.

The Canadian Oxford Desk Atlas
Don Mills, Ont.: Oxford University Press

The Canadian Oxford School Atlas
Don Mills, Ont.: Oxford University Press

Rand McNally Commercial Atlas and Marketing Guide
Chicago: Rand McNally & Co.

Webster's New Geographical Dictionary
Springfield, Mass.: G. & C. Merriam Co.

Biographical Dictionaries (Who's Who)

I3   These supply factual data about famous living persons. Each entry includes background, date of birth, education, marital status, positions held, achievements, and honours.

The Canadian Who's Who
Toronto: University of Toronto Press

International Who's Who
London: Europa Publications

Who's Who in America
Chicago: Marquis Who's Who, Inc.

Who's Who in Canada
Toronto: International Press Ltd.

Note: For information about notable people no longer alive, refer to encyclopedias or the *Dictionary of National Biography* of relevant countries.

Business Information

The following books will help you locate data relating to business and trade, people and products, finance and commerce.

City Directories provide information on residents and companies in a community. They contain the following sections:

> *Buyer's Guide*: similar to the yellow pages of the telephone directory with companies and services listed alphabetically.
>
> *Alphabetic List* shows adult residents, their addresses, occupations, and marital status. Also included are business and professional organizations with the address, type of business, and official personnel of each one.
>
> *Street Directory* lists each street alphabetically, and indicates where intersections occur. The numbers of the residences and business organizations are arranged numerically under each street, and the names of householders and companies and their telephone numbers are placed opposite them.
>
> *Telephone Number Directory* contains a numerical listing of numbers with names and addresses of the subscribers appended to them.
>
> *Miscellaneous Section* provides information about population statistics and municipal governments.
>
> Toronto: Might Directories

Classified Telephone Directory (Yellow Pages) lists businesses, classified by type, in a particular area.

Directory of Associations in Canada/Répetoire des associations au Canada is a listing of clubs, federations, and societies.
Toronto: University of Toronto Press

Directory of Directors lists Canadian executives and the companies they represent.
Toronto: Financial Post

Dun and Bradstreet Reference Book supplies credit information. Upon request, Dun & Bradstreet will also provide updated individual credit reports to subscribers.
Toronto: Dun & Bradstreet Canada Ltd.

Trade Directories provide names of manufacturing and commercial companies, their products and brand names, their branch offices, and their chief executives.

Canadian Trade Index
Toronto: Canadian Manufacturers' Association

Fraser's Canadian Trade Directory
Toronto: Maclean-Hunter Ltd.

Guide to Canadian Manufacturers (classified by industry)
Toronto: Dun & Bradstreet Canada Ltd.

Standard & Poor's Register of Corporations, Directors and Executives
New York: Standard & Poor's Corporation

15 Dictionaries

Dictionaries contain words which are listed alphabetically, usually with the following information:

- *meanings* and definitions
- *preferred form of spelling* if more than one is acceptable
- *syllabic division* shown by a heavy accent, light accent, centred period, or hyphen
- *correct pronunciation* indicated by accent marks—a heavy one ē shows special emphasis; a lighter mark ĕ denotes less stress
- *part of speech*: if more than one is indicated, any change in pronunciation will also be shown
- *derivation of words* (their origins) in square brackets at the end of an entry
- *synonyms and antonyms* indicated by *syn* and *ant* at the end of an entry
- *usage examples* in phrases and clauses to complement the common definition and clarify usage
- *prefixes and suffixes* with their definitions

Consult the front of the dictionary for greater details on etymology (word origins), pronunciation, and abbreviations used in the dictionary. The alphabetic list of words is usually followed by an appendix of words with special uses, a section on abbreviations, and foreign words and phrases. Some dictionaries also supply information on international currencies, scientific and technical terms, titles of address, and weights and measures.

The Concise Oxford English Dictionary
London: Oxford University Press

The Senior Dictionary
Agincourt, Ont: Gage Educational Publishing

Webster's New Collegiate Dictionary
Springfield, Mass: G. & C. Merriam Co.

Specialized dictionaries are available for most professions, as well as for scientific, technical, and trade specializations. Examples include:

Black's Law Dictionary
St. Paul's: West Publishing Co.

Black's Medical Dictionary
Toronto: A. & C. Black

Blakiston's Pocket Medical Dictionary
Toronto: McGraw-Hill Ryerson Limited

Terminology for Accountants
Toronto: Canadian Institute of Chartered Accountants

English Usage Books

16

These indicate the fundamental rules of grammar, punctuation, usage, and style.

A Dictionary of Modern English Usage, H.W. Fowler,
London: Oxford University Press

McGraw-Hill Handbook of English, 3rd Canadian Edition,
Shaw,
Toronto: McGraw-Hill Ryerson Limited

A **thesaurus** (directory of synonyms and antonyms) is useful when you have an idea of what you want to say but need a particular word to convey the exact meaning; or when you need a variation for a frequently repeated word. A thesaurus comes in two forms: the words are arranged alphabetically as in a dictionary, or they are listed according to the ideas they express.

Roget's Thesaurus of the English Language in Dictionary Form
Garden City, N.Y.: Garden City Books

Roget's Thesaurus of English Words and Phrases
Toronto: Longmans Canada Ltd.

The Synonym Finder
Emmaus, Pa: Rodale Books, Inc.

Webster's Collegiate Thesaurus
Springfield, Mass: G. & C. Merriam Co.

Government References

I7   Government publications on many topics are obtainable
       through government book stores all across Canada. Ottawa's
       publishing agent is the Department of Supply and Services,
       which handles material from all Canadian Government
       Departments. Examples of these publications are:

       Canada Year Book (annually)
       Statistics Canada

       Canadian Civil Aircraft Register (every three months)
       Transport Canada

       Exports by Commodities (annually)
       Statistics Canada

       Parliamentary Debates
       Canadian Publishing Centre, Supply & Services Canada

       *Travel, Tourism and Outdoor Recreation—A Statistical
       Digest* (every two years)
       Statistics Canada

             Also available at government book stores are provincial
       government publications on a variety of subjects. Each
       government department produces its own publication.

Postal Information

I8   *Postal Code Directories* give a postal code for every location
       in Canada. Use the appropriate provincial directory to ensure
       correct addressing of envelopes and faster mail delivery. For
       information on how to obtain copies of Postal Code
       Directories see Unit 13, PO1.

       Post Office Guide
       For complex or unusual mailing situations, consult this
       guide at your nearest post office.

Secretarial and Office Procedures

I9   For guidance on typing techniques, business practices, and
       English language conventions, refer to this handbook or one
       of the others available, such as:

       Reference Manual for Secretaries and Typists
       Second Canadian Edition, SI Metric, Sabin
       Toronto: McGraw-Hill Ryerson Limited

How to Use a Library

I 10 All libraries, regardless of size or specialization, provide *card catalogues* to indicate which books the library owns. There are usually three card index files—author, title, and subject, each alphabetically arranged. If you know the title or author, check one of these files; if not, look in the subject file. From the card, note down the reference number and then locate the book on the shelves.

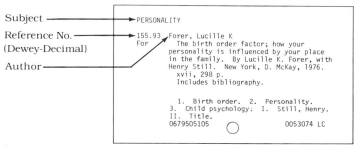

Subject

Reference No.
(Dewey-Decimal)

Author

```
PERSONALITY

155.93  Forer, Lucille K
For       The birth order factor; how your
          personality is influenced by your place
          in the family.  By Lucille K. Forer, with
          Henry Still.  New York, D. McKay, 1976.
          xvii, 298 p.
          Includes bibliography.

          1.  Birth order.  2.  Personality.
          3.  Child psychology:  I.  Still, Henry.
          II.  Title.
          0679505105                       0053074 LC
```

Library reference card

Most libraries use a numerical classification system known as the Dewey-Decimal system to catalogue their books. Here are the ten major categories under which all books are listed:

000-099	General
100-199	Philosophy
200-299	Religion
*300-399	Social Sciences
400-499	Language
500-599	Science and Mathematics
*600-699	Applied Sciences and Industries
700-799	Fine Arts and Recreation
800-899	Literature
900-999	History, Travel, and Biography

*Most business information is contained in these sections.

The first three digits (155) in the card illustrated tell you that the book falls under the Philosophy classification.

Libraries also have a *Periodicals Index* which lists articles published in a particular field. The index is a computer list of material available from a central source. The librarian can obtain listed items for you.

Data Bases

I 11 Data bases are computer encyclopedia which provide access to information on a broad variety of topics. Such information may be bibliographic (i.e., a list of publications on a given topic) or full text. The information may be available by means of a telephone call or on-line (i.e., through a telephone compatible computer terminal or word processor).

Data bases are provided by such sources as university libraries, so that a worldwide bibliographic service is available; by departments of government; and by organizations such as newspaper publishers.

The use of such services is highly specialized and the assistance of a professional librarian is recommended because of the problem of indexing — i.e., determining the words or expressions which will lead to retrieval of the fullest possible bibliography.

Videotex

I12

Videotex is the transmission of words, pictures, and graphics to specially adapted television receivers via airwaves, cables, or telephone lines. Videotex can supply information to businesses or homes from a central data base or can allow messages to move from individual to individual on the network.

Telidon is the name of the Canadian government-sponsored two-way videotex system.

Unit 9

Job Search and Application

Finding the right job entails careful thought and considerable effort. In this chapter are some ideas on how to search for the job you want, how to present yourself to best advantage in a written application, how to promote yourself effectively at the interview, and how to follow up afterwards to ensure you are chosen for the position.

J1 The Search

The Newspaper

J2 Advertisers do not always word their advertisements as you might expect. Do not read only the *headings* or *titles*; they may be misleading. Read *all* the advertisement. You may find you have the qualifications and that the job would interest you. On the other hand, you may not be interested in or qualified for a job to which you are attracted by the heading or title only.

Try not to be discouraged if you do not have precisely the qualifications listed. Advertisers seeking "minimum grade 12 education" may well consider someone with grade 11, experience, and enthusiasm. Go ahead and apply. At this point, your goal is to obtain an interview.

The Employment Agency

J3 Many companies use the services of employment agencies in filling their vacancies. The service these agencies offer has certain advantages for prospective employees:

- No fee is charged to prospective employees.

- The agency conducts tests and, ideally, only sends applicants after jobs for which they are suited.
- Time is saved because mail service is not involved.

Other Sources

J4
- The local Canada Employment Centre (formerly Manpower) maintains a listing of jobs in your particular area.
- Friends or relatives already employed by companies you would like to join may be able to tell you of vacancies.
- You may consider writing directly to the personnel manager of a firm which interests you. There may be an opening now or in the near future.

The Application

J5 Once you have located an appealing advertisement, you must next convince someone to interview you. This is done by sending an application letter and a résumé which "sells" you.

The Letter

J6 Your letter of application must be carefully worded so that it
- sells you in relation to the job for which you are applying
- summarizes why you are applying for this job and which of your qualifications are most directly applicable to the job
- provides all the facts asked of you in the advertisement
- is concise, specific, and to the point

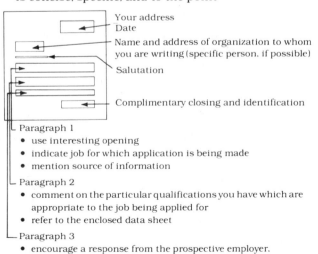

Your address
Date
Name and address of organization to whom you are writing (specific person, if possible)
Salutation
Complimentary closing and identification

Paragraph 1
- use interesting opening
- indicate job for which application is being made
- mention source of information

Paragraph 2
- comment on the particular qualifications you have which are appropriate to the job being applied for
- refer to the enclosed data sheet

Paragraph 3
- encourage a response from the prospective employer, i.e., request an interview or say you are looking forward to a reply

Outline of application letter

In producing your letter of application:

- Use businesslike stationery (plain white, unlined).
- Type your letter if possible.
- Include some reference to the source of your information about the job.
- Ask for some action (e.g., a phone call or written reply).
- Keep to one page (if you can).
- Carefully check any doubtful spelling or grammatical points.
- Type or neatly print your name beneath the signature, if your signature is less than perfect.
- Address your envelope correctly.

Never submit a duplicated letter of application.

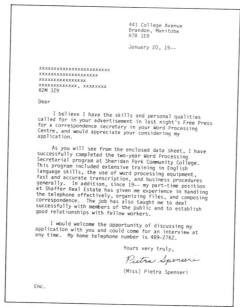

Application letter

The Résumé

The résumé (also known as the data sheet or *curriculum vitae*) is rarely read thoroughly. It must, therefore, be short, easy to read, and organized so that it will draw attention to your most significant achievements and skills. Ideally, every résumé should be tailored to the job being applied for; however, many people find a well-thought-out résumé can be used for *many* situations and that the covering letter can be used to zero in on the specific job being applied for.

Information in a résumé is usually presented in this sequence: personal information, education, work experience, interests or hobbies, and references (optional). A unit entitled "Career Goals" may be valuable but is not essential. Keep the résumé short and start with the most recent dates.

Personal Information

Provide your name, address, and telephone number. Any other personal information you provide is *voluntary*. The law prohibits discrimination against anyone on grounds of sex, race, religion, marital status, age, or nationality. This information is not relevant to any job.

Education

- Include the name of the institution(s) you attended; your major concentration; certificates or degrees earned; dates; and any honours, scholarships, or special awards.
- Note any work-related training—evening courses, professional workshops, special training courses.
- Do not include elementary school information.

Work Experience

- List your previous jobs, starting with the most recent one.
- Provide approximate starting and ending dates.
- Indicate what areas you were responsible for in your previous jobs. Do *not* simply list the titles of those jobs.
- Do not mention salaries.

Interests or Hobbies

Information contained here can provide useful insights for prospective employers, e.g., valuable administrative experience is indicated by volunteer work; leadership potential is indicated by work with youth groups.

References

- Ask permission from people you quote as references *before* you use their names.
- Do not use relatives as references.

It is possible to organize your résumé by function rather than by time spent in various endeavours. Sometimes this kind of organization can help an employer see your qualifications more easily. For example, if an advertiser demands someone with proven writing, speaking, organizational, and clerical skills, you might use these headings in the "work experience" section and match your experience to the headings.

It *is* acceptable to mail a duplicate of your résumé, but it is *not* acceptable to submit a duplicated letter of application.

Résumé

The Application Form

J8

Although you have provided an extensive résumé, you will still be required by most organizations to complete an application form. In doing do:

- Complete the form neatly and accurately. (This might be the only handwritten document the interviewer has on which to judge your writing skills.)
- Have a copy of your résumé available to remind you of dates of previous jobs, education, *etc.*
- Be truthful but not unnecessarily modest.

The Interview

J9

The interview is designed to provide information for both the employer and the applicant. Most interviews follow a pattern. Being aware of this pattern will make you a more confident interviewee.

You can expect a few minutes of introductory small talk, followed by a short introduction to the firm, its activities, and products. Next, the interviewer will ask you questions about your education and experience. Details of the vacancy will then be provided, and you will be invited to ask questions. Finally, you will be asked if, after hearing about the job first hand, you are still interested.

Here are some important points to note in successfully presenting yourself at an interview.

- Be prepared. If you feel comfortable, you will probably appear confident.
- Have a positive attitude.
- Find out in advance what you can about the firm or organization.
- Coordinate your wardrobe so that you will look your best but will also be comfortable.
- Take along a pen and paper.
- Be prepared to be tested.
- Take a copy of your application with you (letter and résumé).
- Go alone. Leave family and friends at home.
- Arrive in plenty of time. (Make the trip a day or two before to get the travelling time worked out. Also, the cost and convenience of travel are factors to be considered in deciding whether or not you *really* want this job.)
- Let the interviewer guide the interview. Wait for an offer to shake hands and an indication of where you should sit.
- Remember your interviewer's name.
- Avoid "yes" or "no" responses. Expand on your answers.
- Look at the interviewer. Direct eye contact signifies confidence.
- Smile!
- Keep the discussion to the job only. Home or social concerns have no place here.
- Do not smoke, even if you are invited to. (You may find yourself needing both hands at some point.)
- Be honest about your capabilities but do not be too modest.
- Raise the question of salary late in the interview.

Answering and Asking Questions

You will be asked questions, of course, and these will vary from job to job. Here are some typical ones which you would be well advised to review and prepare answers to before you go for your interview:

- Why are you interested in this particular job?
- What experience do you have that makes you feel you would be useful in this job?
- What do you think are your best personal qualities?
- What are your limitations?
- What did you like most/least about your last job?
- What do you know about our organization?
- What are your ambitions?

In addition, you will be invited to ask questions. Again, go prepared. Even if your interviewer seems to have dealt with all the information you require, try to ask at least one sensible question when invited to do so. Ones you might consider are:

- Why is the present employee leaving?
- What is the prospect of advancement/development with the company?
- What fringe benefits are provided by the company?

Not all interviews are the same, of course. You may find it informative to refer to Unit 12, P9 of this book on the subject of "How to Conduct an Interview" so that you are aware of what an employer is trying to find out about you.

Follow Up

J10

- At the end of the interview ask for a date by which you could expect to have an answer. If you have not heard anything within ten days, write or call.
- Go home and review the interview. Carefully analyze what took place and then decide whether to accept the job should it be offered to you.
- You may like to consider a thank-you letter to the interviewer. It should express your thanks for the interview and indicate that you are looking forward to a reply.

441 College Avenue
Brandon, Manitoba
R7A 1E8

January 28, 19--

XXXXXXXXXXXXXXXXXXXXXXX
XXXXXXXXXXXXXXXXXXXX
XXXXXXXXXXXXXX
XXXXXXXXXXXX, XXXXXXX
R2M 3Z9

Dear

    Thank you for the time you spent with me at the interview today.

    I appreciated the opportunity to talk with you and hope to hear from you very soon.

Sincerely,

Pietra Spenseri

(Miss) Pietra Spenseri

Thank you letter

Final Thoughts

J11   If you are offered the job, congratulations! If you are
unsuccessful, try not to be discouraged. Most firms do not
provide a reason for rejecting candidates. You may even have
been passed over because you were too good for the job and
you may not have stayed very long—who knows?

Remember that the three key qualities of a prospective
employee are:

- genuine interest
- the ability to perform the job well
- willingness to learn

If you have demonstrated these, and follow the job search
hints given here, it will not be long before you secure the job
that is just right for you.

Unit 10

Mathematics in Business

Dealing with business problems involving commissions, taxes, billing, etc., demands a certain level of mathematical skill. To solve such problems the office worker must be able to work with fractions, decimals, and percentages. While calculators are available to perform the routine computations involved, the operator of the calculator must know how to instruct the machine properly.

Fractions

M1

Note: Calculators cannot work with fractions unless these are *decimal* fractions. However, an understanding of common fractions, their functions and uses, is helpful in working with decimal fractions. Having a knowledge of fractions is also useful in dealing with algebraic expressions.

Terms: $\dfrac{1}{15}$ *numerator*
denominator

Improper fraction (numerator larger than denominator): $\dfrac{4}{3}$

Proper fraction (numerator smaller than denominator): $\dfrac{1}{2}$

Mixed number (combination of whole number and fraction): $7\dfrac{2}{5}$

Equivalent fractions (fractions of the same value but different numerators and denominators): $\dfrac{1}{4}$ and $\dfrac{2}{8}$

Product (result of two numbers multiplied by each other): $2 \times 3 = 6$

159

To Add and Subtract Fractions

1. Find the lowest common denominator (i.e., the smallest amount into which each denominator can be evenly divided).

   $\frac{1}{3} + \frac{3}{5}$ —lowest common denominator is 15

2. Rewrite each fraction as an equivalent fraction using the lowest common denominator.

   $\frac{1}{3} + \frac{3}{5} = \frac{5}{15} + \frac{9}{15}$

3. Add or subtract the numerators.

   $\frac{1}{3} + \frac{3}{5} = \frac{5}{15} + \frac{9}{15} = \frac{14}{15}$

To Add and Subtract Mixed Numbers

1. Add or subtract the whole numbers.
2. Add or subtract the fractions.
3. Add or subtract the results.

   $$6\frac{1}{2} + 3\frac{5}{8} + 3\frac{3}{4} - 2\frac{1}{16}$$

   Step 1: $6 + 3 + 3 - 2 = 10$

   Step 2: $\frac{1}{2} + \frac{5}{8} + \frac{3}{4} - \frac{1}{16} = \frac{8 + 10 + 12 - 1}{16}$

   $$= \frac{29}{16} = 1\frac{13}{16}$$

   (To express an improper fraction as a mixed number, divide the numerator by the denominator.)

   Step 3: $10 + 1\frac{13}{16} = 11\frac{13}{16}$

To Multiply Fractions

Multiply the numerators and divide by the product of the denominators.

$$\frac{1}{3} \times \frac{3}{5} = \frac{1 \times 3}{3 \times 5} = \frac{3}{15}$$

To Multiply Mixed Numbers

Express the mixed numbers as improper fractions and multiply as you would proper fractions. (To express a *mixed* number as an improper fraction, rewrite the *whole* number as a fraction with the same denominator as the other fraction and add the two $1\frac{1}{2} = \frac{2}{2} + \frac{1}{2} = \frac{3}{2}$.)

$$1\frac{1}{2} \times 3\frac{4}{5} = \frac{3}{2} \times \frac{19}{5} = \frac{15}{10} \times \frac{38}{10} =$$
$$\frac{570}{100} = 5\frac{70}{100} = 5\frac{7}{10}$$

To Multiply a Fraction by a Whole Number

Rewrite the whole number as a fraction with denominator 1 and multiply as you would proper fractions. Reduce your answer to its lowest value.

$$\frac{5}{8} \times 2 = \frac{5}{8} \times \frac{2}{1} = \frac{10}{8} = 1\frac{2}{8} = 1\frac{1}{4}$$

To Divide by a Fraction

Multiply by its reciprocal (the inverse of the fraction).

$$\frac{5}{6} \div \frac{2}{5} = \frac{5}{6} \times \frac{5}{2} = \frac{25}{12} = 2\frac{1}{12}$$

Decimals

Note: always precede a decimal value less than 1 with a zero. 0.43 not .43

To Change Fractions to Decimals

To express a fraction as a decimal, divide the numerator by the denominator.

$$\frac{3}{5} = 3 \div 5 = 0.6$$

$$\frac{2}{3} = 2 \div 3 = 0.6667 \text{ to 4 places}$$
$$= 0.667 \text{ to 3 places}$$

To Change Decimals to Fractions

To change a decimal to a fraction, write the decimal figure as the numerator and the denominator as a power of ten (the number of digits to the right of the decimal point is the number of zeros after the 1 in the denominator).

$$0.1 = \frac{1}{10}; \quad 0.01 = \frac{1}{100}; \quad 0.001 = \frac{1}{1000}$$

$$0.6 = \frac{6}{10} = \frac{3}{5} \text{ (reduced to its lowest value)}$$

$$0.06 = \frac{6}{100} = \frac{3}{50}$$

$$0.43 = \frac{43}{100}$$

To Add or Subtract Decimals

Write the numbers so that the decimal marker is in line and add or subtract in the normal way.

$$\begin{array}{r} 0.07 \\ 21.314 \\ \underline{2.6183} \\ 24.0023 \end{array}$$

To Multiply With Decimals

Multiply the numbers as though the decimals did not exist. To arrive at the number of decimal places in the product (total), *add* the number of decimal places being multiplied and insert the decimal that number of places to the left of the final digit.

$$4.\underset{2}{\underbrace{54}} \times 2.\underset{1}{\underbrace{2}} = 9.\underset{3}{\underbrace{988}}$$
$$2 \quad + \quad 1 = \quad 3 \text{ decimal places}$$

To Divide With Decimals

Divide as though the decimals did not exist. To arrive at the number of decimal places in the quotient (final result), *subtract* the number of decimal places in the divisor from the number of decimal places in the number to be divided and insert the decimal point that number of places to the left of the final digit.

divide 15.625 by 2.5

$$15.625 \div 2.5 = 6.25$$
$$3 \quad - \quad 1 = \quad 2 \text{ decimal places}$$

Percentages

M3

A per cent of a number is a hundredth of that number. Therefore, 5% of a number is 5 hundredths of a number and may be expressed as $\frac{5}{100}$, or 0.05, or 5%.

To Change a Per Cent to a Fraction

Divide by 100 and remove the percentage sign.

$$30\% = \frac{30}{100} = \frac{3}{10}$$

To Change a Fraction to a Per Cent

Multiply by 100%.

$\frac{4}{5}$ as a percentage is $\frac{4}{5} \times 100\% = 80\%$

To Change a Per Cent to a Decimal

Divide the rate per cent by 100, i.e., move the decimal marker two places to the *left*.

$$35\% = \frac{35}{100} = 0.35$$

Note: When a calculator is used, a per cent must be expressed as a decimal.

To Change a Decimal to a Per Cent

Multiply the decimal by 100%, i.e., move the decimal marker two places to the *right*.

1.34 as a per cent is $1.34 \times 100\% = 134\%$

To Find What Per Cent One Number is of Another

Divide the number that has *of* in front of it into the other number and multiply by 100.

What percentage is 15 of 75?

$$= \frac{15}{75} \times 100 = \frac{1500}{75}$$
$$= 20\%$$

To Find the Full Number of Which a Percentage Is Already Known

Divide the number known by the percentage known and multiply by 100.

35% of a number is 56. Find the number.

$$\frac{56}{35} \times 100 = \frac{5600}{35} = 160$$

To Find the Percentage Increase of One Number Over Another

Subtract the base number from the increased number to find the *amount* of the increase. Divide the *base* number into the amount of the increase and multiply by 100.

Sales rose from $4000 (base number) to $5000 (increased number). What is the percentage increase? Sales increased by $1000.

$$\frac{1000}{4000} \times 100 = 25\%$$

To Find the Amount of Increase or Decrease When the Base Number and Percentage Increase or Decrease are Known

Add the percentage rate of increase to 100, divide the result by 100, and multiply by the base figure.

$4000 increased by 25% of itself equals what?

$$\frac{125}{100} \times 4000 = 5000$$

i.e., $4000 increased by 25% of itself equals $5000

To find a decreased rate, subtract the percentage rate decrease from 100.

$4000 decreased by 25% of itself equals what?

$$\frac{75}{100} \times 4000 = \$3000$$

Common Equivalents

M4 Certain percentages and their decimal and fractional equivalents are used so frequently that knowing them can save a great deal of unnecessary calculation time.

Per Cent	Decimal Fraction	Common Fraction	Per Cent	Decimal Fraction	Common Fraction
1%	0.01	1/100	37½%	0.375	3/8
5%	0.05	1/20	40%	0.40	2/5
6¼%	0.625	1/16	50%	0.50	1/2
8 1/3%	0.083	1/12	60%	0.60	3/5
10%	0.10	1/10	62½%	0.625	5/8
12½%	0.125	1/8	66 2/3%	0.666	2/3
16 2/3%	0.1666	1/6	70%	0.70	7/10
20%	0.20	1/5	75%	0.75	3/4
25%	0.25	1/4	80%	0.80	4/5
30%	0.30	3/10	87½%	0.875	7/8
33 1/3%	0.333	1/3	90%	0.90	9/10
			100%	1.00	

Table of common equivalents

Algebraic Equations

M5   Business formulas are frequently expressed as algebraic equations. Algebra means working with one or more unknown variables; an equation is a *sentence* of two expressions connected by an equal sign.

$I = Prt$ [Interest (I) equals principal (P) multiplied by rate (r) multiplied by time (t).]

As you work with an equation, it must be kept constantly in balance, i.e., if you add, subtract, divide, or multiply something to one side then you must do the same thing to the other side.

Rearranging Formula Terms

Where one numerical value in a formula is not known, it is necessary to isolate the unknown quantity. To do this, keep the equation in balance, i.e., what you do to one side you must do to the other.

The simple interest formula is $I = Prt$
Find P when $I = \$18$, $r = 9\%$, $t = 2$ years.
Since P is the unknown, it must be isolated, i.e., both sides must be divided by rt.

$$P = \frac{I}{rt}$$

$$P = \frac{18}{0.09 \times 2}$$

$$P = \$100$$

Rules to Observe in Reducing Algebraic Expressions to Their Simplest Form

- To multiply powers having the same base, add the indices:
  $a \times a \times a$ is a^3
  The base is a and always has an index of 1; the sum of the indices in this case is 3.
  $a^3 \times a^2 = a^5$
- To divide a power by a power having the same base, subtract the indices:
  $a^3 \div a^2 = a$
- Only like terms may be added or subtracted:
  $3a + 3a = 6a$ but $3a + 3b = 3a + 3b$
- The order of operations used to reduce an algebraic expression to its simplest form is:

  1. Simplify any expressions inside brackets.
  2. Remove brackets.
  3. If the word *of* is used, replace it with a multiplication sign.
  4. Divide and multiply next. Do these operations in the order given, working from left to right.

5. Add and subtract last. Do these operations in the order given, working from left to right.

The true interest rate formula is $r = \dfrac{2Nc}{A(n+1)}$

r = annual interest rate
c = cost of borrowing
n = number of payments needed to pay the loan in full
N = number of payments in one year
A = amount borrowed

What is the *true* interest rate on a loan of $2500 to be repaid in monthly instalments in 18 months at 13½%? The cost of borrowing is quoted as $275.60.

$$r = \frac{2 \times 12 \times 275.60}{2500\,(18 + 1)}$$

$$r = \frac{2 \times 12 \times 275.60}{2500 \times 19}$$

$$r = \frac{6614.4}{47\,500}$$

$$r = 0.1392$$

Expressed as a percentage, the true interest rate is 13.92%.

Calculators

M6

When you work with mathematical expressions on a calculator, be careful about the sequence of completing the operations.

Evaluate $x = 2a + 4c$ when $a = 7$ and $c = 5$
1. Multiply 2 by 7, note down this partial answer (14), and clear.
2. Multiply 4×5, note down this partial answer (20), and clear.
3. Add 14 and 20 = 34.

M7

Business Formulas

Accounting Equation

M8

$A = L + OE$

A = assets, L = liabilities, OE = Owner's Equity

Amortization Formula

M9

$$p = \frac{Pi\,(1 + i)^n}{(1 + i)^n - 1}$$

p = amount to be paid per payment period
i = interest rate per time period
n = total number of payment periods
p = principal

Interest

M10   There are two types of interest:

- **Simple**: where interest is calculated only on the original principal.

  $I = Prt$
  I = interest, t = time in years, r = annual rate, and
     P = principal

- **Compound**: where interest is calculated periodically and added to the principal so that for succeeding periods both the original principal and the accumulated interest earn interest.

  $A = P(1 + i)^n$
  A = amount that the principal (P) will accumulate to at i rate of interest per interest period for n interest periods. (If time is expressed in days, show as, for example, $\frac{30}{365}$; if time is one year show as 1.)

Selling Price

M11 $S = C + M$
S = selling price, C = cost, M = markup

Taxes (Property)

M12 $T = Ar$
T = taxes, A = assessment, r = rate (mills)
($\$1$ = 1000 mills)

True Interest Rate

M13 $r = \dfrac{2\,Nc}{A\,(n + 1)}$

r = annual interest rate
c = cost of borrowing
n = number of payments to pay the loan in full
N = number of payments in one year
A = amount borrowed

Pricing Goods For Sale

M14   Pricing means establishing the price at which goods can be sold. Pricing takes into consideration discounts and allowances to be given, transportation costs, pricing legislation, demand, the type of business, competition, and the level of profit sought, e.g., a certain *percentage return* on sales or on investment.

Retail and Wholesale Prices

Markup and Margin

Most retail and wholesale prices are established by using markups, i.e., adding a set percentage to the price at which the goods were purchased which the seller feels will cover operating expenses and provide a reasonable net profit.

If the owner of a business seeks a net profit of, for example, 12% of sales and the operating expenses of the business are expected to be 27% of sales, he must establish his selling price to produce a gross profit (or margin) of 39%. The cost price of each article should, therefore, be 61% of its selling price.

Sales (100%) − Cost Price (61%) = Gross Profit or Margin (39%)
Gross Profit (39%) − Expenses (27%) = Net Profit (12%)

> If cost price = \$56
> then 61% of the selling price is \$56
> then selling price = $56 \times \dfrac{100}{61} = \$91.80$

Therefore markup = \$91.80 − \$56.00 = \$35.80

Note: Margin and markup are the same in amount but different in percentage because margin is related to selling price and markup is related to cost price.

If selling price is known to be \$91.80, then margin is \$35.80, or 39% of the selling price; if cost price is known to be \$56, then markup is \$35.80, or 64%.

Markdown

A markdown is often called a discount. It means a reduction in the regular marked price and is usually offered by the seller to attract customers and increase sales.

Discounts

Discounts in the form of percentages off list prices are offered as inducements to buy.

Trade discounts: These are given by manufacturers to wholesalers or retailers and by wholesalers to retailers. When a series of discounts is quoted, this is known as a *chain discount*. The first discount is always taken off the list price. The second discount is taken off the remainder and so on. Successive discounts cannot be added together.

List price \$1000	
− 200	1st trade discount 20%
800	
− 80	2nd trade discount 10%
720	
− 36	3rd trade discount 5%
\$ 684	

Cash discounts: Sometimes these are offered as an inducement to pay a bill quickly. For example, if the expression 2/10, n/30 is shown on an invoice, it means that if the invoice is paid within 10 days a 2% discount may be deducted from the net (total) amount. If the invoice is not paid within 10 days, the 2% may not be deducted and the net amount is due in 30 days. The 2% discount may not, of course, be deducted from any shipping charges shown.

Break Even Point

M17   For a business to be worthwhile, income must exceed expenses. The point at which income and expenses intersect is known as the *break even point* (BEP). (Above the *BEP*, profit; below the *BEP*, loss!) The break even point is calculated to determine the minimum output or sales necessary for income to cover costs. The break even point analysis is particularly useful for comparing pricing alternatives.

Break even point

$$= \frac{\text{Total fixed costs (costs that cannot be changed)}}{\text{Suggested selling price per unit } - \text{ variable costs per unit (costs that can be changed)}}$$

Total fixed costs for a small book are $32 000, variable costs per unit $0.75, and suggested selling price is $1.25.

$$BEP = \frac{32\ 000}{1.25 - 0.75} = \frac{32\ 000}{0.50} = 64\ 000 \text{ units}$$

Therefore, 64 000 copies of the book must be sold before a profit is achieved. To improve this position, the selling price might be raised or some way of cutting variable costs (e.g., using less expensive paper) might be sought.

Statistical Data

M18   Frequently, business information is presented in the form of averages and ratios to indicate comparisons and trends.

Averages

M19   **Mean**

An average (or mean) is a single number that represents a central value in a group of numbers. Averages (means) may be simple or weighted.

Simple average. Find a simple average by dividing the sum of a series of numbers by the total number of members of the series.

T-shirts sold for \$4.90 in the spring sale, \$6.25 at regular price, and \$5.44 in the fall sale. Average selling price was $\frac{4.90 + 6.25 + 5.44}{3} = \frac{16.59}{3} = \$5.53$

Weighted average. The *simple* average is based on only one unit of each number being added and then being divided by the sum of the units. However, in some situations this may not provide a true average. Find a *weighted* average by multiplying each quantity by its unit value, add the products, and then divide by the sum of the quantities.

120 T-shirts were sold at \$4.90 in the spring sale, 230 at \$6.25, and 90 at \$5.44 in the fall sale. Average (weighted) selling price was
$$\frac{(4.90 \times 120) + (6.25 \times 230) + (5.44 \times 90)}{120 + 230 + 90}$$

$$= \frac{588 + 1437.50 + 489.60}{440} = \frac{2515.10}{440} = \$5.72.$$

Compare with \$5.53 as the simple average.

Mode

Mode is the figure occurring most frequently in a list of numbers.

6, 7, 9, 6, 7, 8, 7, 8. The mode is 7 (occurs 3 times).

This type of statistical information is most interesting to, for example, a shoe retailer who wishes to know the most common selling shoe size.

Median

The median (middle value) in a series of numbers arranged in numerical order is the quantity that appears at the mid point of the list. One half the quantities have a higher value and one half have a lower value. Find the median figure by arranging the series of numbers in order of size or value and then selecting the middle one.

Seven students earned these marks: 24, 76, 10, 73, 74, 70, 66. Arrange in order: 10, 24, 66, 70, 73, 74, 76. The median mark is 70. There are three numbers higher than 70 and three lower. (When the number of items is even, the median is the average of the two middle numbers.)

Ratio

M20

The ratio of two numbers compares the size or value of one number with the size or value of another number.

There are 20 females and 10 males in the office. The ratio of females to males is 20:10 or 2:1 (reduced to the lowest form).

Proportion

M21 The term proportion is used to indicate that two ratios are equal.

> 1:4 is proportional to 2:8.

When two ratios are equal, their cross products are also equal.

$$\frac{1}{4} \times \frac{2}{8}$$

If three terms in a proportion are known, the fourth is easily found.

> x:16 is proportional to 3:12

$$\frac{x}{16} \times \frac{3}{12} \qquad \begin{aligned} 12x &= 48 \\ x &= \frac{48}{12} \\ x &= 4 \end{aligned}$$

> 4:16 is proportional to 3:12

Charts and Graphs

M22 Ideas for presenting statistical data in pictorial form may be found in Unit 18, TT40.

Foreign Currency Exchange

M23 This is the rate at which one country's currency can be exchanged for that of another at a bank. Newspapers frequently publish lists of exchange rates, but the bank rate may vary from these because of the constant fluctuations caused by economic and political factors. Most currencies are now expressed as decimals and conversions are simple.

> Change $25 U.S. to Canadian dollars where $1 U.S. = $1.15 Canadian.
> $25 U.S. = 25 × 1.15 = $28.75 Canadian
> Therefore $25 U.S. = $28.75 Canadian

> Change $25 Canadian to U.S. dollars where $1 Canadian = 85¢ U.S.
> $25 Canadian = 0.85 × 25 = $21.25 U.S.
> Therefore $25 Canadian = $21.25 U.S.

Unit 11

Meetings and Conferences

Meetings and conferences are a regular and important part of business activities. Most meetings are *informal* and held to permit participants to exchange ideas and information about new procedures or products. However, some meetings are *formal* and must be conducted strictly according to procedures laid down in the constitution and bylaws (i.e., the governing rules of conduct of the corporation or organization). Examples of formal meetings are regular meetings of the Board of Directors, Annual Shareholders' Meetings, and Annual General Meetings. These are held to obtain authority to act in a specific way, e.g., to distribute profits, amend the constitution, or receive reports.

Although there are variations of purpose, size, and degrees of formality, the planning, announcing, conducting, and recording of meetings have many similarities. Advance plans must be well laid, the meeting must be conducted efficiently, and the points raised and decisions made must be recorded accurately. This chapter provides the information needed to conduct *any* meeting successfully, regardless of its type or purpose.

MC1   Planning the Meeting

Advance Planning

MC2
If the meeting is to be held *on the company's premises*, book the room needed well in advance. Make a list of things to be dealt with before the required date. Be sure to do each job on this list in sufficient time to guarantee that everything is available for the meeting.

- Reserve the meeting room and *double check* the booking later.

- Check availability of coat hanging space.
- Order refreshments.
- Plan and confirm lunch or dinner needs.
- Make and confirm hotel accommodation for out-of-town participants.
- Ensure availability of pads, pencils, ashtrays, glasses, drinking water.
- Check equipment. Be sure that audio-visual and sound equipment is in working order.

Note: Name tags may be a good idea when participants are coming from several firms or organizations.

When a *hotel* or *convention centre* is to be used, confirm the booking in writing and be absolutely positive that the hotel can cope with everything needed. Send them a checklist such as that illustrated and *insist on confirmation*.

```
Checklist of requirements for meeting on May 19, 19--

*  The meeting room can accommodate _____ people.   _____

*  A particular arrangement of tables and chairs
   can be made.                                     _____

*  Water pitchers, glasses, and ashtrays can be
   provided.                                        _____

*  Lectern or podium available.                     _____

*  Microphones can be placed as directed.           _____

*  Audio-visual equipment--such as overhead
   projectors (and pens), movie or slide
   projectors and screens--are available.           _____

*  ___ telephones are in the room or nearby.        _____

*  Typing and copying equipment is available.       _____

*  Coffee will be served at _____.         _____
   Lunches will be served at _____.        _____

*  Arrangement for receptions, dinners, cocktail
   parties, etc., are as agreed.                    _____

                             (signed) _____

                                     Manager
```

Checklist of meeting requirements

Again, confirm the booking a few days in advance of the meeting.

Announcing (Convening) the Meeting

MC3   When you invite participants to the meeting, note the following:

- Be sure to include the time, date, location, and purpose of the meeting in the notice.

- Send out the notice far enough in advance so that people can fit the meeting into their plans but not so early that it can be forgotten.
- For formal meetings, provide the necessary length of time for advance notices which is specified in the constitution or bylaws.
- A formal notice of meeting may be sent out on letterhead paper or on a postcard.

```
ATLANTIC TRADING COMPANY
437 Atlantic Road, Charlottetown, P.E.I.  C1A 3Z9

19-- 10 01


NOTICE OF MEETING

A meeting of the Board of Directors will be held at 13:30

on Wednesday, October 15, in Board Room A of the

Atlantic Trading Company at 437 Atlantic Road, Charlottetown.



Atlantic Trading Company
S. Dominelli
Executive Secretary
```

Notice of meeting

The Agenda

MC4   The agenda is the *plan* for the meeting. It lists the place, date, and time of the meeting, as well as the items of business and the order in which they are to be dealt with. There is no fixed format that needs to be followed. An interoffice memo indicating the discussion topics serves well for small, informal meetings. A detailed program indicating discussion topics and length of discussion times may be advantageous for large gatherings with much to talk about. It is a good idea to send the agenda out in advance of the meeting so that participants may be properly prepared.

Agendas for formal meetings contain discussion topics that come within the scope of the organization as outlined in the constitution and bylaws. A typical formal agenda might include: call to order, apologies for absence, minutes (reading and approval), business arising from the minutes, new business, reports, nominations and elections, date of next meeting, adjournment.

```
                Meeting of the Board of Directors

                          Board Room A

                          19-- 10 15

                            13:30


                          A G E N D A

    13:30    Reading and approval of minutes of September 18 meeting.

    13:40    Matters arising from the minutes.

    13:45    Reports:

             (a)  Report from Mr. Glover on the progress of the

                  proposed plant move.

             (b)  Report from Miss Wilson on the purchase of a

                  new printing machine, and proposed installation date.

    14:30    New Business.

    15:30    Date and time of next meeting.

    15:40    Adjournment.
```

Agenda

Last-Minute Preparations

MC5

- Conduct a last-minute check of all details.
- Have available:
  extra agendas
  extra copies of the minutes of the last meeting
  the minute book or file
  copies of the constitution and bylaws
  any previously submitted motions
  copies of reports to be presented
- Check that the room temperature is comfortable.

Conducting the Meeting
(The Chairperson's Role)

MC6

The meeting is conducted by the chairperson. With informal meetings, the chairperson's role is simply to maintain order, to ensure that the meeting follows the agenda, and to ensure that the proper communication of ideas and dissemination of information takes place.

In formal meetings, it is customary to employ parliamentary procedures (formal rules of debate) and it is the chairperson's task to see that these rules are adhered to. While the rules might seem cumbersome, they do give everyone an equal right to be heard, have his/her point of view considered, and to vote on an issue.

In particular, the chairperson:

- ensures there is a quorum present (i.e., the legally required number of participants)

- calls the meeting to order (i.e., makes sure that it starts on time)
- maintains order
- explains and decides all questions of procedure
- announces and clarifies all business under consideration
- states motions and resolutions
- conducts the votes
- decides on tie votes

Parliamentary Procedures (Formal Rules of Debate)

MC7 **Presenting a Motion**

When a proposal is made at a formal meeting it is referred to as a *motion* and must have the support of another person, who is referred to as the *seconder*.

The participant making the motion should rise and be recognized (acknowledged) by the presiding officer (usually the chairperson).

A typical motion begins, "I move that ..."

A typical motion support begins, "I second the motion ..." Discussion, and, perhaps, amendment of the motion follows.

Note: While motions to amend a motion may be made, only *one* main motion at a time may be dealt with. Motions to amend must be discussed and voted upon so that the main motion is properly amended before it is finally discussed and voted upon. For example:

Main Motion	I move that the staff receive a bonus this year.
	seconded J. Brown
Amendment	I move that the motion ... that the staff receive a bonus this year only if the company earns a profit in excess of 10%.
	seconded J. Green. Discussion. Vote carried.
Amended Main Motion	That the staff receive a bonus this year provided the company earns a profit in excess of 10%.

The chairperson finally conducts voting (by ballot or show of hands) on the motion and announces the result of the vote. If more than half the voters vote in favour, the motion is adopted (carried). If a motion is not voted upon, the procedure for disposing of it is to "lay it on the table" (or, as it is more commonly expressed, "table" it).

Point of Order

Should a member feel that a debating rule has been broken, that member may interrupt the person speaking and address the chairperson directly, without waiting for recognition. Points of order must be made immediately after the alleged violation. They are not debatable, and the member who was interrupted must yield until the matter is clarified.

Note: Only a brief outline of the commonly used aspects of parliamentary debating procedures has been included here. Full details are contained in *Robert's Rules of Order*, available in paperback or hardbound editions. Anyone who is required to conduct or take notes of an important formal meeting should become familiar with Robert's rules.

Proxies

MC8 The constitution and bylaws of most organizations permit a person who cannot attend important meetings to be represented by proxy. A proxy may be either:

- another person who can attend the meeting with authority to vote and make decisions on behalf of the absent person
- a ballot (voting) card which has been sent out before the meeting and has been completed and returned by the absent person

Minutes (Record) of the Meeting

MC9 Minutes are designed to record that, firstly, a meeting was held and, secondly, the decisions made at the meeting. In addition, some minutes record proposals made and rejected as well as a summary of the discussion, i.e., they provide sufficient information for those not present to have a clear picture of what took place.

Properly prepared minutes

- clearly state the name, purpose, time, and place of the meeting
- note who was present
- are accurate, concise, and unbiased
- provide a summary of the results, not a complete description of the proceedings
- contain exact statements of motions, movers, and seconders
- state the terms of any resolutions adopted
- note appointments made

```
                        ATLANTIC TRADING COMPANY

                          BOARD OF DIRECTORS

                        Minutes of Meeting, 19-- 10 15

        TIME AND        The monthly meeting of the Board of Directors of the Atlantic
        PLACE           Trading Company was held at 13:30, 19-- 10 15, in the Company
                        Board Room.

        ATTENDANCE      Present:  Mr. P. Reynolds, Mr. N. McCune, Ms. J. Ackroyd, Mr. S.
                        Dominelli, Miss R. Wilson, Mr. D. D'Aoust, Mrs. B. VanLaarhove,
                        Mr. W. Glover, Ms. G. Kotzell.
                        Absent:  Mr. I. Brinkmann.
                        Mr. Reynolds, the President, chaired the meeting and requested
                        the Secretary, Mr. Dominelli, to read the minutes.

        APPROVAL OF     Mr. N. McCune moved that the minutes of the meeting held 19--
        MINUTES         09 18 be approved as read and Mr. D. D'Aoust seconded the motion.
                        CARRIED.

        MATTERS         Since there were no matters arising from the previous minutes,
        ARISING         the Chairman proceeded with the business at hand.

        REPORTS         Mr. Glover, the Production Manager, reported that construction
                        of the new plant site was progressing slightly ahead of schedule.
                        Decreased profits mentioned in the Treasurer's report pointed
                        up the desirability of a new location, and Mr. Glover was
                        confident that the company could move before the end of the year.

                        Miss Wilson, Purchasing Agent, informed the meeting that tenders
                        were still coming in from printing machine manufacturers and
                        that her committee would make their decision next week.

        NEW BUSINESS    The advantages of a Suggestion Plan were outlined by the
                        Chairman, who then asked Ms. Kotzell if she would head a group of
                        four members to investigate a Plan. Ms. Kotzell agreed to
                        proceed as requested.

        NEXT MEETING    The next meeting of the Board will be held on 19-- 11 14.

        ADJOURNMENT     The meeting adjourned at 15:10.

                                            CHAIRMAN _____
        DATE _____
                                            SECRETARY _____
```

Minutes

Taking Notes for the Minutes

MC10

- Sit close enough to the chairperson so that you can get his or her attention if you miss a detail.
- Study the agenda in advance and read over any specified papers prior to the meeting so that you are familiar with names and terms.
- Go over the minutes of the previous meeting to familiarize yourself with previous discussion topics.
- Prepare in advance a list of people who *should* be in attendance so that only a check mark is needed to designate their absence or attendance.
- Make a seating plan and assign a number to each person present. Try to identify each person by some feature which will help recall names.
- Plan your pad so that you have room for names and discussion topics. Organize notes so that all discussion on any one subject is kept together. Note the name of each person introducing a topic.
- Take more notes than necessary; they can be cut down later.
- For formal meetings, a preprinted notemaking sheet would be useful. It is especially helpful for motions because they must be recorded *verbatim* (word for word). Record whether a motion was adopted, lost, referred to a committee, or tabled.
- Note anything that demands action after the meeting.
- Do not hesitate to interrupt discreetly to ask for restatement of a motion, clarification of a point, or identification of a speaker.

Tape Recording the Minutes

MC11   Before planning to use a tape recorder, remember these disadvantages:

- objections by some people
- technically difficult to set up so voices of all members are audible
- time consuming in playing back and transcribing
- difficulty of identifying speakers

If you *do* use a tape recorder:

- Change tapes during pauses in meetings, or use two recorders and start the recording on the next tape while the previous one is ending.
- Number and identify each tape.

Producing the Minutes

MC12
- Produce a rough draft while the information is still fresh in your mind.
- Follow the pattern of topics established in the agenda.
- Refer to previously prepared minutes and use the same style.
- Make resolutions stand out in some way, e.g., use capitals.
- Be objective, i.e., do not include personal opinions.
- Record whether a motion was adopted, lost, referred to a committee, or tabled.
- Reports, depending on their importance, may be:
    summarized and attached
    attached in their entirety
    referred to in the body of the minutes
- Submit the final draft to the chairperson of the meeting for approval.
- Produce sufficient copies for participants, others on the distribution list, for the file (or official minute book), as well as extras for use at the next meeting.

Follow-Up After the Meeting

MC13
- Distribute the minutes.
- Deal with any requests that may have arisen at the meeting, e.g., for additional information.
- Send reminders, if necessary, about action to be taken.
- If possible, circulate minutes with notice and agenda of *next* meeting so that participants can check items in advance for accuracy, and absentees can be kept informed.
- Send out appropriate thank-you notes.

Unit 12

Personnel Planning: Staffing the Office

Since the operation of any business organization, large or small, is strongly influenced by its office employees, it is important that a firm have a fair and consistent personnel policy (recruiting, training, motivating, paying, and generally caring for its employees).

Administration of the personnel policy in a large organization is the responsibility of the *Personnel Manager*; in a small organization it is the responsibility of anyone who has the welfare of another employee as part of his or her day-to-day responsibilities. The comments that follow describe personnel policies appropriate to most firms.

Personnel Planning

P1   What are the firm's needs for office staff and how are these needs to be met? Most organizations favour the type of systematic procedure which follows.

1. Study existing use of staff to see if greater efficiency can be obtained.
2. Forecast future volume of work, based on the firm's long-range plans.
3. Forecast future numbers and types of employees needed to deal with the anticipated work volume.
4. Consider the present employee inventory so that the anticipated contribution of the present staff to future needs is known.
5. Plan the recruitment of the right numbers of appropriately qualified personnel.

Job Analysis

P2   People involved in the hiring process must be properly prepared; therefore, an analysis of any vacancy must be undertaken and a job description drawn up. A typical job description shows: title, location, duties and responsibilities, hours of work, machines and equipment used, skills needed, working conditions, salary, opportunities for promotion, and qualifications needed (including education, experience, skills).

Recruitment

P3   Anyone involved in any aspect of hiring must be aware that legislation exists which prohibits discrimination as to race, colour, nationality, or religion. Some provinces prohibit discrimination on the grounds of age, sex, and marital status. Advertisements, application forms, or questions pertaining to hiring may not express or imply discrimination on any of the forbidden grounds.

Sources of Personnel

P4
- local Canada Employment Centres (formerly Manpower)
- advertisements placed in local or national newspapers
- student services departments of schools, colleges or universities
- employment agencies
- local union offices
- professional associations
- applications already on file
- recommendations of other employees
- personnel already employed (i.e., promotion from within)

Advertisements

P5   The job description (see this unit, P2) will serve as the only advertisement needed for most of the sources shown above. Advertisements placed in local or national newspapers will, of course, require special treatment. The well-written advertisement provides a full, clear description of the job and a suitable balance between overselling and underselling the position.

Hints on Effective Advertising

P6
- Be specific. Avoid vague expressions such as "good wages," "good conditions," "good personality needed," "large," "progressive," "expanding," or "leading company."

- Confine each advertisement to one job only.
- Aim to attract the most suitable people for the job, not just to obtain a large response.
  - Choose your newspaper with care. Some papers are best for management positions and others for clerical positions.
  - Advertise towards the end of the week as there is a larger readership then.
  - Remember that mention of salary can be a natural screening device.
  - Choose the right size advertisement for your purpose.
- Follow the provisions of your provincial Human Rights Code.
- Provide factual information. Do not hide the truth if the job has many routine aspects. (Applicants do not want to waste their time and the employer does not want to screen many unsuitable applicants.)

Word Processing Co-ordinator

We need an experienced (3 years) word processing operator with supervisory ability to co-ordinate work flow and user communication for our 10-operator centre. The person hired will have a typing speed of 60 wpm, excellent dicta-typing skills, and be required to operate Xerox 800 and AES equipment.

Three weeks' annual holiday; \$15 000 to \$20 000 salary; dental scheme. CALL TODAY to find out more about this career opportunity.

745-1892

Concisely worded advertisement

The Application Form

P7

The application form must provide a full yet pertinent description of the candidate. Care must be paid to its design so that the form:

- obtains sufficient relevant information
- provides enough writing space for full responses
- adheres to the law on what may or may not be asked
- is worded so that the purpose of each question is clearly understood

The information asked for in the typical application form is divided into five sections: *personal, education, work experience, recreational pursuits,* and space for any *additional information* the candidate may wish to provide.

Since the form may be the *only* source of information on some applicants, it should provide room for starting and finishing dates with other employers so that gaps which may require explanation are revealed.

The Interview

P8

The interview is designed to:

- *obtain* for the prospective employer relevant facts not provided by the completed application form and/or letter and data sheet (e.g., appearance, attitudes, ambitions, skills) so that an objective assessment can be made
- *provide* for the prospective employee information such as salary, working conditions, promotion possibilities, and fringe benefits not contained in the advertisement

How to Conduct an Interview

P9

Be Properly Prepared

- Prepare in advance a list of the essential characteristics of the person being sought, e.g., qualifications and experience, personality and attitudes, general intelligence, special aptitudes, interests, and career goals.
- Be familiar with the details of the *job* and the special skills needed.
- Review the information already provided by the applicant (letter, résumé, application form).

Make the Applicant Comfortable

- Do not keep the applicant waiting.
- Be the first to offer a handshake.
- Indicate clearly where he or she is to sit.
- Provide a comfortable chair and be sure not to put the candidate at a disadvantage, e.g., ensure that the chair height is not lower than the interviewer's or that the sun is not shining in the applicant's eyes.
- Use a language level appropriate to the candidate.
- Be warm and friendly and give your full attention so that a good rapport is established.
- Lead the discussion at first.
- Avoid interruptions, e.g., telephone calls.
- Do not take notes.

Give the Applicant a Turn

- Be a good listener.
- Word questions so that they require more than a "yes" or "no" answer.
- Provide sufficient talking time so that you can find out about each applicant's confidence level, oral communication skills, and attitudes.

- Invite questions.
- Ask applicants to tell you their specific interests and goals and why they feel suited to the position.
- Gently probe any vague answers, gaps, tendencies to change jobs, or personality conflicts.

Provide All the Details of the Job

- Offer a full description of the position.
- Go over company policy, fringe benefits, promotion possibilities, *etc.*

Try to Establish Your Short List

- If the person is obviously unsuitable, try to impart this gently at the interview.
- If the person is a likely candidate, try to provide some definite date by which you will be in touch again. He or she may be considering other jobs.
- Find out when the applicant could start if the job were offered.

Record Your Reaction

- Before you go on to the next interview, write up a full impression of the applicant who has just left.

Tests

P10
- Don't test for the sake of it. A folder of job samples (typed reports, complex tabulations) might serve just as well.
- Test only skills relevant to the job being applied for.
- Make allowance for nervousness.
- Provide a comfortable setting and adequate equipment and supplies.
- Make reasonable demands, e.g., five minutes of typing and three minutes of dictation are sufficient.
- Make your testing realistic, e.g., ask a secretary to produce a *letter* rather than type a five-minute speed test.
- Use testing material that is free of language and terms peculiar to your particular firm or organization.

Follow Up to the Interview

P11
The interview may be followed up, depending on the firm's policy, by:

- checking a candidate's references
- a medical examination
- a second interview with the candidate's prospective superior

Regular Review (Evaluation)

P12   Reviews are designed to reveal dissatisfied employees; unsuitable employees; employees in need of assistance, transfer, or another job elsewhere; particularly able employees who are ready for promotion; or employees eligible for salary increases or bonuses.

To keep the evaluation as unbiased as possible, a carefully designed rating sheet might be used.

EMPLOYEE RATING SHEET

Name: _____

Job: _____

Department:_____Supervisor: _____

Date of last review: _____Present salary: _____

Supervisor's comments:	Excellent	Good	Fair	Poor	Unacceptable
Performance	5	4	3	2	1
Attitude	5	4	3	2	1
Punctuality	5	4	3	2	1
Attendance	5	4	3	2	1

Supervisor's comments and recommendations: _____

_____

_____

_____
SIGNATURE

Employee's comments: _____

_____

_____
SIGNATURE

Date of review: _____

Employee Rating (Evaluation) Form

The evaluation might be made on quality of work, quantity of work, initiative shown, relationship with others, attitude and cooperativeness, punctuality, and attendance.

Several approaches might be used in the evaluation process:

- The superior might complete the application, then discuss it with the employee and invite reaction.
- The employee might be invited to fill out the evaluation form for discussion with his/her superior.
- The evaluation might be kept entirely confidential. (This is not recommended, however, because there is no learning experience involved for the employee and the objectivity of the evaluator might be questionable.)

The firm's personnel policy should provide for a review with a new employee after the first few days and then for a regular review either at yearly or six-monthly intervals, depending on the job. (The more routine the task, the greater the need for shorter review intervals.)

Promotion Policy

P13 A firm's promotion policy should be to strive to promote someone already on staff (promotion from within). To encourage the fairest arrangement, a firm's policy might encompass: *equality of opportunity* (any suitably qualified employee is invited to apply); *merit* (the ability to do a job well); and *seniority* (length of service).

Merit or seniority used separately as the basis for promotion decisions has definite disadvantages:

- Merit alone may cause poor morale in very experienced senior, but less able, employees.
- Seniority alone may prevent the best candidate from getting the job and can be discouraging to newer, ambitious, and able staff members.

A fair promotion policy, therefore, is one that uses a mix of merit and seniority.

P14 Leaving

Dismissal

P15 The dismissal of an employee may be unavoidable because of loss of business, automation, take over, or closure. It may arise because of problems of incompetence, personality conflicts, dishonesty, or failure to comply with company policy. Whatever the cause, dismissal is a very serious matter and should be the subject of a clearly defined policy.

- All dismissals should be based on careful documentation. Employees should first be warned and given an opportunity to change.
- Care should be taken not to influence badly a person's chances for employment elsewhere.

Except in rare circumstances, e.g., discovery in a criminal act, notice of dismissal must be given in writing. The length of notice will depend on the nature of the job, the length of employment, and the contractual arrangement with the company. A check with your provincial department of labour will clarify the legal requirements in your province.

Resignation

P16   Resignations should be treated with the greatest seriousness. A reason for every resignation should be obtained so that:

- a valued employee might be encouraged to stay
- the underlying problem might be resolved

Records

P17   A file on each employee should be kept in a system in which confidentiality is assured. The file might contain:

- application form and correspondence (including references from previous employers, if appropriate)
- periodic evaluation reports
- attendance records
- salary record
- courses and additional training taken
- job description of the position presently held

     This file will be consulted in the event of promotion opportunities. Therefore, in the employee's best interest, it must be complete and up to date.

Payment Policy

P18   A firm's payment policy will be based on these considerations:

- legally prescribed minimum rates
- the need to attract and keep the right kind of employee
- the need to keep employees properly motivated and content

     A payment policy must be competitive with that of other firms in the area and in similar businesses, and provide for regular pay increases to cover:

- increases in cost of living
- rewards for length of service
- particular merit

     When a labour union is involved, payments will also be influenced by the union contract.

Job Evaluation

P19 The decision as to how much one employee should be paid in relation to another is best determined by an accurate and fair evaluation of each job. This might be achieved by ranking or classifying jobs in order of importance or difficulty and then placing each job in a category for which a pay scale is established.

Fringe Benefits

P20 Fringe benefits are supplements to salary or wage payments. They are designed to encourage more and better work and to keep employees contented. The benefits will vary with the size and success of the business. Paid annual vacations, paid sick leave, and some insurance payments are mandatory. (See Unit 1, B42.) Other benefits that might be offered are: profit-sharing plans, bonuses, flexible working hours, supplementary pension plans, supplementary health insurance schemes, dental plans, group life insurance, staff discounts, payment of education fees, subsidized recreational facilities, Christmas gifts.

P21 Temporary Help

Finding Temporary Help

P22 If the need arises for additional help for short periods of time (to cover vacations, inventory time, *etc.*), temporary workers may be obtained from a number of sources.

- Agencies that specialize in providing skilled help of all kinds. The employer pays the agency and the agency pays the "temporary employee."
  Be sure to:
  > Investigate more than one agency (check the Yellow Pages for a list of local agencies).

  Find out how each agency operates:
  > Are employees bonded (insured as to their honesty)?
  > Have employees been tested?
  > Does the agency handle *all* payment details?
  > Is satisfaction and a fast replacement guaranteed?
  > Can the agency handle requests at short notice?
- Advertisements
- Canada Employment Centres (formerly Manpower)

Making the Best Use of Temporary Help

P23   To get the best value for your temporary help dollar, organize the temporary helper's work in advance.
- Have a properly equipped work place ready.
- Have all necessary supplies available.
- Provide as many written instructions as possible, e.g., the style manual or job models.
- Keep your expectations reasonable.
- Be available to answer questions.

Unit 13

Postal Services

Advances in office technology permit information to be exchanged between organizations by many means, e.g., communicating word processors, facsimile transmission, and a considerable range of telephone and telecommunications services. However, the sending and receiving of *original* documents and other items is still a vital part of a company's operation. Provided in this unit are suggestions for dealing with outgoing mail, a presentation of the key services of Canada Post, and a discussion of alternative delivery methods to those offered by Canada Post.

Mail Technique

PO1   The following tips will help to ensure prompt delivery of your mail by Canada Post.

- **Address envelopes carefully.** Follow Canada Post guidelines (see Unit 18, TT46) and be sure to include a postal code on mail for Canadian destinations. If the code is unknown, look it up in the appropriate Postal Code directory. To find the code in the directory, locate the town (arranged in alphabetical order), the street (again, alphabetically arranged), and then the street number. The set of four Postal Code directories (Atlantic, Quebec, Ontario, and Western) is issued free by Canada Post upon completion of a request card at any post office.

NEW BRUNSWICK

Street Number from	to	Postal CODE	Street Number from	to	Postal CODE
N° de la maison de	à	CODE Postal	N° de la maison de	à	CODE Postal
LEGION DR			Even/Pair 98	104	E3A 1V4
Odd/Impair 101	105	E3A 2K9	200	228	E3A 1V6
107	-	E3A 2L1	**MACKENZIE RD**		
Even/Pair 100	122	E3A 2K8	Odd/Impair 15	-	E3B 6B5
LEICESTER ST			55	65	E3B 6B6
Odd/Impair 7	23	E3B 4N3	Even/Pair 30	-	E3B 6B7
63	75	E3B 4N5	**MACLAREN AVE**		
Even/Pair 4	-	E3B 4N2	Odd/Impair 537	603	E3A 3K9
22	70	E3B 4N4	623	639	E3A 3L1
LESLIE ST			713	767	E3A 3L4
Even/Pair 52	-	E3A 5B2	771	777	E3A 3L6
LEVERMAN ST			781	807	E3A 3L8
Odd/Impair 9	-	E3A 4H7	Even/Pair 528	-	E3A 3K7
LILAC CRES			542	614	E3A 3K8
Odd/Impair 3	27	E3A 2G7	626	668	E3A 3L2
29	65	E3A 2G8	672	686	E3A 3L3
Even/Pair 2	24	E3A 2G6	732	758	E3A 3L5

Excerpt from Postal Code Directory

- **Use a return address.** In case of non-delivery, this information will assist in speedy return. Non-delivery of mail is usually caused by lack of a proper address or the absence of a return address. Such undelivered mail is kept by Canada Post for a reasonable time, then opened and the contents sold at an annual public auction.
- **Use the correct Canada Post service and affix sufficient postage.** If there is a deficiency in the amount of postage paid, the delivery is slowed down and on mail to Canadian destinations, the addressee must pay double the amount due. On mail to the United States or overseas destinations, the sender must pay double the deficiency.
- **Mail early and pre-sort.** Avoid the end-of-the-day rush by mailing early, and sort your mail into in-town and out-of-town batches.
- **Wrap parcels carefully.** Packages must be carefully wrapped to avoid damage, breakage, leakage of contents, or injury to postal handlers. See this unit, PO7 for information on prohibited articles.
- **Use the right equipment.**
  Postage Meter/Mailing Machines. The manual type accepts hand-fed mail, seals it, and stamps it. Automatic models can feed in the mail, seal it, postmark it, meter-stamp it, and count the number of pieces and stack them. These machines may be rented from a postage meter manufacturing company. An amount of postage is purchased from the post office and entered into the meter. When that

amount of postage has been used up, a further amount may be purchased.

Postage Scales. These are used to ensure that correct postage is affixed in accordance with Canada Post mass regulations.

Canada Post Service

PO2   The amount of postage payable depends on the class of service used, the mass of the package, the destination, and any additional services required. Because postal rates change from time to time, it is wise to keep current postal information in your office. The Canada Postal Guide may be purchased from the Publishing Centre, Supply and Services Canada, Ottawa, Ontario, K1A 0S9; and Canada Post rate leaflets are available free at any post office.

Canada Post Service Within Canada (Domestic)

PO3   (See this unit, PO25 for Canada Post Service to the United States and this unit, PO32 for Canada Post Service to overseas destinations.)

First Class

PO4   Mail in this category consists of written or typed matter— letters, printed business forms, receipts, documents, and post cards up to 500 g. In Canada all first class mail is sent by air where airmail service is available.

Parcels from 500 g to 30 kg (not exceeding 1 m in length, width, or depth and 2 m combined length and girth) may also be sent first class. A surcharge is added for parcels which exceed the specified limit but fall within a size of 2 m in any dimension and 3 m combined length and girth. First class parcels receive priority air service and are costlier than fourth class parcels.

Second Class

PO5   This service is available to printers and publishers only for shipment of printed matter which they publish, e.g., periodicals, magazines. The general public does not have access to second class mail.

Third Class

PO6 Third class mail consists of printed matter mailed by individuals or companies other than publishers. This material must be of a non-personal nature, e.g., newspapers, magazines, and advertising circulars. Also included in this category are greeting cards with up to five written words. Third class mail has lower priority and is cheaper than first class mail. Maximum mass is 500 g.

Householder mail is unaddressed third class mail. This is the most economical postal service for distributing catalogues, samples, promotional leaflets, *etc.* The company sending out the samples specifies to the post office the district to be covered; the letter carrier then distributes one mailing piece to every householder or occupant within that district. The charge is a fee per item, plus a sum per kilogram.

Fourth Class (Parcel Post)

PO7 Use parcel post for packages between 500 g and 16 kg. The same size restrictions (1 m X 2 m) apply as to first class parcels. All fourth class parcels receive surface transmission and are cheaper than first class parcels.

Prohibited articles include perishables, plants, liquor, drug samples, and explosives. For fuller information, consult the Canada Postal Guide.

PO8 Additional Canada Post Services

Business Reply Cards and Envelopes (Canada Only)

PO9 These are used by companies who wish to encourage enquiries in response to advertisements, *etc.* The post office levies a charge per card or envelope plus the postage on each one returned to the sender.

C.O.D. (Canada Only)

PO10 This service is available to organizations that mail items requiring payment on delivery.

The amount to be collected (maximum amount $200) is collected upon delivery by the letter carrier and a receipt is given as proof of payment. The sender pays a small fee (depending on the amount to be collected) for the service, and receives payment for the goods mailed by means of a money order. If the goods are lost or damaged, the post office will reimburse the sender for their value.

Certified Mail (Canada Only)

PO11 This is a low-cost proof-of-delivery service for important but not valuable items. The sender purchases from the post office a kit consisting of a special envelope with a receipt card. The addressee signs the receipt for the item when it is delivered, and the post office sends this card to the sender as proof of delivery. The charge is based on regular postage plus the certification fee.

Change of Address Cards (Canada and United States Only)

PO12 These cards are available free of charge from the post office. *Note:* For a small fee the post office will readdress mail to your next address for three months.

Franked Mail

PO13 First, second, or third class mail to or from the Governor-General, senators, and members of the Federal Government either in Ottawa or in their constituencies may be sent free of charge.

Insurance

PO14 Compensation for damage or loss is provided up to a maximum of $1000 in Canada and $200 in the United States and other specified countries. The insurance fee (plus regular postage) is based on the value of the article. Check the Canada Postal Guide for a list of insurable articles.

Intelpost

PO15 This is a facsimile transmission service which permits rapid transmission of documents via satellite. You can send (or receive) a high-quality black and white facsimile of any written material, document, or graphic. The sender must take the document to the Intelpost centre at the main post office in any of the cities mentioned below. Within minutes, the copy will be available for pickup by your correspondent. The service is available between Vancouver, Edmonton, Calgary, Winnipeg, Toronto, Ottawa, Montreal, Halifax, Amsterdam, Berne, London, New York, and Washington, D.C. Future plans call for an expansion of Intelpost.

International Reply Coupons

PO16 These are purchased in the sending country and may be exchanged by the recipient at a post office in the foreign country for stamps to be used in the reply.

Money Orders

PO17   Money orders permit the safe sending of money almost anywhere in the world. They can be cashed at the recipient's post office at no cost. They can be replaced if lost.

Money Packets (Canada and United States)

PO18   This service is for sending valuables of over $100 (such as coins, jewellery, stocks and bonds, and lottery tickets). The post office charges postage, which includes a registration fee, but only accepts an indemnity of up to $100, because the sender is expected to carry adequate insurance.

Post Office Boxes

PO19   These are rented by businesses and individuals not wishing to use a full address or when letter carrier service is not available. The renter pays an annual fee, is allocated a box number and given a key. He or she has sole access to the contents.

Postpak (Canada Only)

PO20   This service is for bulk shipments of second, third, and fourth class mail which are sent to one address on one day. Quantity discounts are available.

Priority Post

PO21   This service exists to provide next-day delivery of packages to certain designated areas in Canada and overseas. A contract arrangement is possible when packages are mailed frequently from one address to another, e.g., head office to branch office communications. Pickup and delivery service is available. Consult your postmaster for details of designated areas and contract terms.

Registered Mail

PO22   This service is useful when a document or article of value is to be mailed.
     The item to be registered must be taken to the post office. On payment of postage plus a registration fee (based on the value of the article), the sender is given a numbered receipt. The receipt (registration) number is stamped on the registered package and is recorded by the postal clerk. When the package is delivered, the addressee must sign for it.
     If a registered item does not arrive at its destination, the registration number enables the package to be traced. In

case of loss or damage, the post office liability is up to $1000 on Canadian mail, up to $200 on mail to the United States, and up to $15.76 on mail going overseas.

Acknowledgement of Receipt Card

For a small fee, the sender of a registered package may request an acknowledgement of receipt card. Upon receipt of the package, the recipient signs the card, which is then returned to the sender as proof of delivery.

Special Delivery

PO23 This service is used when high-speed delivery is required. The sender must take the item to the post office. The amount paid is postage plus an additional fee.

Telepost

PO24 (See Unit 16, T41.)

Note: Canada Post provides many other services, e.g., lock box and bag service, pre-cancelled stamps, and special rates for literature for the blind. Refer to the Canada Postal Guide or your local post office for complete information on these and other services.

PO25 # Canada Post Service to the United States

First Class to the U.S.

PO26 Mail in this category costs the same as mail to be delivered in Canada for the first 30 g but is more expensive after that. It includes written or typed matter of a personal nature, business forms, *etc.*, up to 500g.

Small Packets and Printed Papers to the U.S.

PO27 This service is for unsealed packages up to 500 g. Postage rates are the same as third class rates for delivery in Canada. Packets may be registered but not insured.

Airmail Packages and Letters to the U.S.

PO28 For urgent mail between 500 g and 30 kg, airmail service is available. There is a size restriction of 1 m in any dimension × 2 m combined length and girth.

Surface Packages (Parcel Post) to the U.S.

PO29   Mail from 500 g to 16 kg with the same size restrictions as the airmail packages above but of a less urgent nature may be sent for a much lower price by parcel post.

Additional Canada Post Services to the U.S.

PO30   The following special services are available for mail to the United States. See this unit, PO8, for details: Insurance, Intelpost, Money Orders, Money Packets, Priority Post, Registered Mail, Special Delivery.

Customs Declaration

PO31   Customs regulations demand that the contents, their value, and the name and address of sender be declared on every package leaving Canada. The proper forms are available at the post office.

PO32
Canada Post Service to Overseas Destinations

Letter Mail and Post Cards (Overseas)

PO33   Letters of a business or personal nature and post cards to a maximum of 500 g travel by air only.

Aerogrammes (Air Letters)

PO34   A self-contained stamped letter/envelope form can be purchased from the post office for the same price as an airmail stamp. Writing space is limited and no enclosures are permitted.

Small Packets, Printed Papers, Books (Overseas)

PO35   Articles which fall into this category and have a mass of up to 500 g may be sent unsealed by airmail or by surface mail, depending on the urgency. Airmail is costlier than surface mail. Packets may be registered but not insured.

Direct bags go by surface mail only and are for the use of publishers and other mailers sending a quantity (up to 30 kg) of mail to one address.

Parcels (Overseas)

PO36   Parcels weighing more than 500 g and less than 10 kg may be sent by air or surface mail.

Additional Canada Post Services to Overseas Destinations

PO37 The following special services are available for mail to many countries. See this unit, PO8 for descriptions: Insurance, Intelpost, International Reply Coupons, Money Orders, Priority Post, Registration, Special Delivery. Consult the Canada Postal Guide or your postmaster for a list of those countries to which these services apply.

Customs Declaration

PO38 Customs regulations demand that the contents, their value, and the name and address of sender be declared on every package leaving Canada. The forms are available at the post office.

PO39 # Alternatives to the Postal Delivery Service

Airline (Air Express)

PO40 (See Unit 7, G1, Chart of Transportation Services.) Several airline companies offer fast, economical air delivery of letters and packages in North America. Refer to the Yellow Pages under "Courier Service" or contact an airline company.

Bus

PO41 Bus companies will transport letters or packages. The sender must take the items to the bus depot two hours before departure time. The addressee must pick them up at the destination terminal.

Courier Services

PO42 (See Unit 7, G1, Chart of Transportation Services.) Couriers deliver mail on the same day within a city, and on the next day within the driveable area, e.g., Toronto to London; Kenora to Winnipeg. Companies offer pickup and delivery on weekdays. The charge per article (maximum 2 kg) is based on mass and destination. Check the Yellow Pages under "Courier Service" or "Delivery Service."

Taxi

PO43 If a courier is unavailable for same-day delivery, a taxi might be considered if the mail is urgent.

United Parcel Service (UPS)

PO44   This organization provides a rapid package delivery service between points in Ontario and between points in Ontario and the United States. The charge is based on mass and destination. Maximum size restrictions are 35 kg within Ontario and 22 kg to the United States; maximum dimensions are 2.75 m combined length and girth. If pickup service is required, it is available on payment of a weekly fee.

Unit 14

Reprographics: Copying and Duplicating

Although computer memories and micrographics (microfilm, microfiche, etc.) have reduced the need for paper copies, the demand for written records of correspondence and documents remains. This unit describes copying processes which are used to produce paper copy. The term *copying* means that the original document is used to make copies; the term *duplicating* means that a master is prepared (by writing or typing, or by a heat process) from which copies are then produced. The term *reprographics* is used to describe both processes.

The responsibility of the office worker is to use the best and cheapest method of copying or duplicating to meet each job's intended purpose. This unit contains the information needed to permit you to select the best process, produce top quality masters, use copying and duplicating machines properly, and choose the most appropriate equipment for your office.

Comparison of Reprographic Processes

Process	Quality of Reproduction	Number of Copies	Advantages
Photocopier (electrostatic)	Excellent (will produce an exact black and white copy of the original)	unlimited	• speed • quality • accepts single sheets or 3-dimensional objects (e.g., books) • machines available with many features (see this unit, R28 for full listing) • ease of operation
Thermal Copier	Good (if original is clear and high in carbon content)	unlimited	• speed • ease of use • copier can produce thermal dittos and stencils, overheads, and single copies
Carbon copies	Low	• up to 5 on a manual typewriter • up to 8 on an electric	• low cost
Spirit Duplicator	Fair	• up to 100 normal master • up to 200 long-run master	• low cost • variety of colours • masters can be stored and reused • masters may be typed or handwritten • masters can be made on thermal machines
Stencil	Good	• up to 5000 standard stencil • up to 1000 direct master	• low cost • colours possible • stencils can be stored and reused • electronic or thermal stencils of originals can be made
Offset	Excellent	• up to 20 000	• high quality • colours possible

Limitations	Relative Cost	Most Appropriate Uses i.e. Choose This System
• high cost	expensive	...where quality is more important than cost. Copies are good enough for most needs in or out of the company.
• copies fade • will not pick up colours • accepts only single sheets	expensive	...where reasonably good-quality copies for internal distribution are needed and the original is clear enough to be copied.
• low numbers • low quality	cheapest	...where very few copies of communications are needed; generally for internal use only.
• low quality • master must be prepared	extremely cheap	...where copies are needed for internal distribution and high quality is not a consideration.
• master must be prepared	very cheap	...where good-quality copies of a typed document for in-house or external use are needed.
• trained operator needed • equipment is expensive	expensive	...where long runs of high-quality copies are needed for any situation in or out of the office.

Machine Copying

R2
The easiest way to obtain reproductions is to use a copying machine. While there are many copying machines available, there are basically only two processes involved: photocopying (electrofax and xerography) and thermal (heat transfer) copying.

Photocopying

R3
- This technique uses positive and negative electric charges which attract each other to print the required image.
- Copiers can produce extremely high-quality permanent copies from black and other colour originals taken from single sheets, books, reports, *etc.*
- This process can produce single or multiple copies.

To operate this type of copier, lift the protective cover, place the original face down on the glass, replace the cover and press the print button. For several copies, turn the print dial to the number required and then press the print button.

Note: Both electrofax and xerography have the same capabilities but electrofax needs specially treated paper and xerography does not.

Thermal Copying

R4
- This method uses an infra-red heat lamp to transfer images onto special, heat-sensitive paper.
- Documents to be copied must have high carbon content (as from a pencil or carbon typewriter ribbon).
- Copies will fade with time and exposure to light.
- Copies must be produced one at a time.

To operate this copier, place a sheet of specially treated paper on top of the original and pass the two sheets into the machine with the original face up.

Economical Use of Your Copier

R5
Copying machines are simple to operate and require no special instruction. However, while the convenience factor is high, so is the cost. Be sure to avoid such wasteful jobs as:

- producing copies for distribution to staff members when circulation of the original document would do
- producing copies when carbon copies might be typed
- using a copier when a cheaper process would serve

When the copier is the best choice, use it as economically as possible:

- Save your copying until you have several items. This way you avoid walking to and from the machine several times.
- Put the counter back to "1" when you are through so that the next user does not risk making unnecessary copies.
- Use the right size of paper for the job.
- Make only the *exact* number of copies needed.

Carbon Copying

R6

The cheapest method of producing up to eight good quality copies of a communication to be typed is with carbon paper and carbon copy paper (known as flimsy paper or onion skin).

To Assemble the Carbon Pack

R7

1. Place a piece of flimsy copy paper on the desk.
2. Place a piece of carbon paper (shiny, carbon-coated side down) on the copy paper with the precut corner of the carbon at the left top corner. Repeat steps 1 and 2 as many times as the number of copies you require.
3. Place the top sheet (letterhead or other bond stationery) on top of the final carbon sheet, printed side up.
4. Pick up the pack, tap it at the top end to line up all the edges, and insert it into the typewriter. Be sure to keep the shiny (coated) side of the carbon away from you. *Do not permit the carbon paper to crease.*

Note: An envelope or folded sheet placed over the top edge of the pack makes it easier to insert the pack into the typewriter and keep all the sheets straight. Roll the pack into the machine and then remove the envelope or folded sheet.

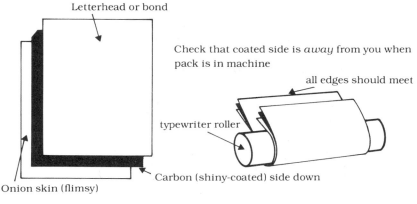

Letterhead or bond

Check that coated side is *away* from you when pack is in machine

all edges should meet

typewriter roller

Carbon (shiny-coated) side down

Onion skin (flimsy)

Carbon pack

Correcting Errors on Carbons

R8
1. Place a piece of card or paper in front of the first sheet of carbon behind the error.
2. Erase the error or use liquid paper or correction tape.
3. Move the card or paper in front of the next sheet of carbon.
4. Remove the error using a pencil eraser or correction aids designed for correcting carbon copies.
5. Continue erasing or correcting until all the copies have been fixed.
6. Type the correct character on the top copy.

Note: This process works equally well if you start from the back of the pack and work forward.

Spirit Duplicating

R9
This is an inexpensive method of making copies suitable for interoffice use. In this system, a master must be prepared from which the copies are produced.

- Spirit masters are available in both letter and legal sizes and in various colours.
- Short-run quality masters produce up to 100 good copies; long-run qualities produce up to 200 copies.
- Masters may be prepared by typing, writing, or drawing on them, or via thermal copying machines.
- Masters may be stored for reuse.

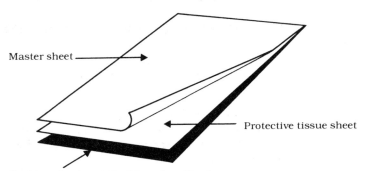

Master sheet

Protective tissue sheet

Backing sheet coated with carbon-like dye

Spirit master set

As the typewriter keys or your ballpoint pen make contact with the master sheet, a carbon-like dye is picked up from the backing sheet and deposited on the back of the master sheet. When the master sheet is attached to the cylinder of the spirit duplicator, fluid moistens the master sheet and gradually releases the dye onto sheets of paper.

Typing the Spirit Master

R10
- Clean the typewriter keys.
- Plan your typing layout as you would with any other typing job.
- Slide the rubber paper bail rollers to the side.
- Remove the protective tissue sheet.
- Insert the *open* end of the master into the typewriter. (This makes correcting easier.)
- When the job is completed, replace the protective tissue sheet.

Note: If any part of the work is to be produced in colour, simply change the backing (carbon) sheet for a backing sheet of the required colour.

Making Corrections on the Spirit Master

R11
1. Roll up the master and pull the white sheet forward.
2. Scrape off the error from the back of the master sheet with a correction knife or razor blade.
3. Insert a small piece of unused spirit master carbon behind the error and type the correction. (Since this is a one-time carbon only, snip a fresh piece from an unused corner.) Remove the piece of spirit master carbon before you continue typing.

Note: If the error does not have to be typed over, cut it out, cover it with cellulose tape or special correcting tape, or block it out with a special crayon or correcting fluid.

Points to Note in Operating the Spirit Duplicator

R12
- Check that the container holds sufficient fluid.
- Use the right type of stationery (shiny, non-porous).
- Fan the paper to prevent sheets from sticking to each other.
- Check that the holes are on the correct side if you are using punched paper.
- Run one or two copies only and check that the image is correctly balanced on the page. Make any necessary adjustments.
- Adjust the back stop on the receiving tray to the length of paper being used so that the printed sheets stack properly.
- Adjust the impression control if the colour strength weakens on the printed copies.

Storing the Master for Future Use

R13
1. Reassemble the master set to its original shape, i.e., carbon, protective sheet, master.
2. Staple and file as you would any other document.

Stencil Duplicating

R14

The stencil duplicator produces better quality copies than the spirit duplicator. A typewriter or special stylus is used to cut images into the stencil (a fine, wax-coated fibre sheet) and the duplicating process is achieved through ink (in various colours) being pressed through the cut stencil to produce printed copy.

- This process is suitable for both interoffice and external correspondence, reports, and forms.
- A small number or thousands of permanent, good-quality copies can be produced economically from one stencil.
- Stencils may be produced by typing, writing, or drawing on them or may be produced by electronic or thermal copying machines.

Types of Stencils

R15

Two kinds of stencils are available: the *standard* type and the *direct master* type.

- The *standard* stencil consists of a waxed sheet and a backing sheet which are joined at the top edge, plus a carbon sheet, inserted coated side up, between the two. This type of stencil is capable of producing up to 5000 copies.
- The *direct master* is a single sheet stencil (i.e., without interleaved carbon) which has the appearance of the standard stencil master but is easier to use. The direct master provides excellent copy quality for up to 1000 copies. Stencils of this type are particularly suited to word processing equipment or electronic typewriters because of their ease of use.

Typing the Standard Stencil

R16

1. Clean the typewriter keys thoroughly.
2. Move the ribbon indicator to "stencil" position.
3. Use the guidelines printed on the stencil to assist in planning the layout of the job.
4. Make whatever pressure adjustments may be needed to ensure that keys do not cut right through the stencil and leave holes. (Experiment with the "o" key on a part of the stencil outside the duplicating limit.)
5. Avoid wrinkling the stencil.

Note: A plastic typing sheet may be placed between the backing sheet and the carbon to provide a firm surface for clearer type. In addition, a clear plastic (pliofilm) sheet may be placed on top of the stencil to prevent damage from sharp keys and to prevent wax buildup on the typewriter keys.

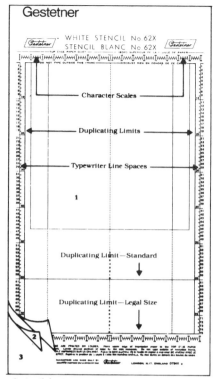

1. stencil sheet
2. carbon paper
3. backing sheet
The stencil guide marks are also shown.

Gestetner stencil

Making Corrections on the Standard Stencil

R17

1. Roll up the stencil and pull forward the plastic sheet if you are using one.

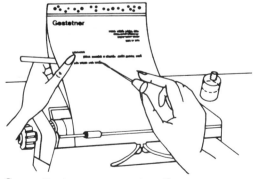

Correcting errors on a stencil

2. Insert a pencil between the carbon sheet and the stencil close to the error.
3. Lightly rub over the error with the end of a paper clip. Coat the error with a thin layer of correcting fluid.
4. Let the fluid dry for about 30 seconds.
5. Remove the pencil and type the correction.

Typing the Direct Master Stencil

R18 This type of stencil requires the use of a carbon (film) ribbon.

1. Clean the typewriter keys thoroughly.
2. Use a carbon (film) ribbon and type directly onto the stencil—i.e., *do not* move the ribbon indicator to the stencil position.
3. Use the guidelines printed on the stencil to assist in planning the layout of the job.

Making Corrections on the Direct Master Stencil

R19
1. Lightly coat the error with correction fluid.
2. Allow the fluid to dry (about 30 seconds) and type the correction.

Points to Note in Operating the Stencil Duplicator

R20
- Do not overload the machine with ink. Depress the ink switch and simultaneously turn the handle until the ink screen has a slight silky sheen.
- Print one or two copies and check for placement of the image on the page. Make any necessary adjustments.
- Use the correct paper for the process (thick, porous duplicating paper).
- Ensure the holes are on the proper side if you are using punched paper.
- Allow sufficient drying time if other than thick, porous duplicating paper is used.

Storing the Stencil for Future Use

R21
1. Place the stencil in an absorbent folder produced especially for the purpose or place it in sheets of newspaper and then in a file folder.
2. Attach a printed version of the original to the folder *or* print a copy onto the folder before taking the stencil off the machine.

Special Equipment

Styli and Signature Plates

Signatures may be written on stencils with ball point pens, but a rolling ball stylus gives better results.

Rolling ball stylus

The rolling ball stylus is best for handwriting on stencils.
Use it along with a signature mask and a signature sheet, for signatures.

Illuminated Drawing Board

Hand-written or drawn stencils can be more easily produced by tracing, using an illuminated drawing board and special styli, lettering guides, and shading plates.

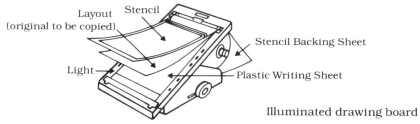

Illuminated drawing board

Note: Stencil manufacturers sell styli, signature masks, and other items of special equipment.

Offset Duplicating

R23 This lithographic process can produce thousands of high-quality copies close in appearance to that of commercial printing. Specially trained operators must run the duplicating machine, but preparation of the offset master requires only typing skills.

Typing the Offset Master

R24
- Clean the typewriter keys, the cylinder, and the paper bail rollers.
- Place a special offset grease ribbon in the typewriter.
- Type directly onto the master.
- Avoid putting fingerprints on the main part of the master.

Making Corrections on the Offset Master

R25
- Erase the error with a special, grit-free offset eraser or a regular firm one using light strokes so the surface of the master is not damaged.
- Type in the correction.

Special Equipment

R26
Aluminum plate masters can be prepared by a photographic process, but special equipment and training are required.

Choosing Reprographic Equipment

R27
For the greatest efficiency at the lowest cost, obtain the right equipment for the job. There are several basic considerations to keep in mind:

- Cost: Which is best — buying, leasing, or renting?
- Speed: How important is speed? Is the extra cost involved in faster copying or duplicating justified for your needs?
- Space: How large a space do you have available in an area that is accessible yet removed enough that noise is not a problem?
- Monthly needs: How much copying or duplicating do you need? The system should be the right size: not so powerful that its capability is wasted; not so small that overuse poses a problem of frequent breakdown.
- Quality of copy produced: Will the copy quality meet all the firm's requirements?
- Type of material to be copied: Is the system capable of handling all your needs for both in-house and outside use?
- Needs for the future: Will the system fit in with future expansion possibilities?

Copier Selection

R28
Considerable care must go into the selection of the office copier because many types and makes are available. Compare copiers on at least the following basic points:

- warranty details
- noise level
- speed
- trade-in value of present machine
- service response time
- amount of storage space required for supplies
- ease of restocking the machine with paper and toner (ink)

- movability
- special wiring or power supply needed
- size
- instant on or warm-up period
- control devices available so that the machine use can be measured
- type of stationery needed
- additional features available

Additional Copier Features to Consider

The basic copier reproduces sheets in standard and legal size from written, typed, or printed copy. Copiers are also available with a variety of features but these usually add to the cost. Before you select a copier, identify the additional features you *need* from the list below and resist obtaining a more sophisticated machine than necessary.

- collating, stapling, and stacking
- copying colours
- copying large documents
- producing projection transparencies
- handling unusual widths and/or lengths
- duplexing (copying on two sides)
- reducing originals to various sizes
- using regular stationery
- using stationery in rolls or sheets of legal or letter size
- copying from bound materials, brochures, magazines
- producing cardweight copies
- printing on coloured paper
- automatically feeding in originals
- reproducing from three-dimensional objects
- making offset plate masters
- copying photographs (half tones)
- offering hookup to communications lines so that copies may be sent to other locations
- a self-diagnostic device to indicate problems with the machine

Intelligent Copiers (Information Distributors)

R29

The intelligent copier is a sophisticated, computer-based piece of equipment which can be instructed to assemble prefabricated (form) paragraphs; locate information from a computer memory; print it; and copy it at high speed. The machine is also capable of distributing the information to other compatible equipment.

The intelligent copier has the added advantage that it can also be used simply as a convenience copier.

Duplicator Selection

R30 Duplicating processes are much cheaper than copying processes, and a duplicator may be useful in your office either as your only system or as a complement to your copier. Consider the following points:

- cost (much cheaper than copying)
- ease of operation
- quality of reproduction (see this unit, R1, chart)
- quantity of copies needed at one time (see this unit, R1, chart)
- flexibility: will this system meet the future needs of the business?
- compatibility: how well will this system fit with copying or duplicating facilities already in the office, e.g., can masters for the duplicator be made on the existing copier?

Unit 15

Social Skills In Business

The social skills demanded of people in their business lives are essentially no different from those demanded of them in their private lives. Tact and good manners in dealing with other people are the keys to successful relationships. However, there are a few specific business-related situations in which some guidance as to acceptable behaviour may be useful.

- For guidance in situations requiring written communications, see Unit 2, C30.
- For guidance in situations requiring oral communications, see Unit 2, C55.

Dining Out

S1   Should you be called upon to represent your employer at a club, restaurant, or social event, do not let inexperience deter you from enjoying the occasion.

Dress

S2   If you are doubtful as to what is appropriate, check with your host or consult a more experienced colleague or another member of the party.

At the Table

S3   If you are faced with many pieces of silverware, work from the outside in.

water   red wine   white wine

2. fish   3. meat   4. salad   1. soup

Table setting

When you have finished eating, place the knife and fork together diagonally across the plate.

Knife and fork in finished position

Cocktails: Garnishes (except citrus fruit) may be eaten.

Soup: If soup is served in a cup with two handles, use both to pick up the cup. If soup is served in a bowl on a serving plate, leave the spoon in the bowl when you have finished.

Wine-tasting: The wine waiter, after uncorking the wine, pours some into the glass of the person who placed the order. After the approval of the wine, the waiter fills all the glasses. If you are the person who placed the order and you are not satisfied with the temperature of the wine, say so.

Bread: Break (do not cut) the bread or roll; butter enough for only one or two mouthfuls at a time.

Vegetables: If they are served in individual dishes, you may eat them from the dish or transfer them from the dish onto your dinner plate.

Bones: These belong on the plate at all times.

Seafood: It is quite acceptable to use your fingers when peeling shrimp or cracking lobster or crab shells. If lemon is to be added, use a fork to hold the lemon wedge and your other hand to squeeze the lemon.

Fresh Fruit: Use a knife to cut and a knife and fork to eat fresh fruit such as oranges, apples, pears, plums. With oranges, cut the outer skin in quarters and peel it off. Then cut the fruit itself into quarters and smaller sections for eating. With apples, *etc.*, cut the fruit into quarters, remove the core, and then cut into bite-size pieces.

Tipping

S4   The customary tip for good service is 15 per cent of the cost of the meal. If you are dissatisfied with the meal or the service, the amount of the tip (if any at all) is your choice. If a group dinner has been arranged, it would be wise to check about tipping. On these occasions, service is often included in the total charge per person.

Introductions

S5   When you are called upon to introduce a caller, a prospective employee, a friend or relative, or any one person to another, there are three general guidelines which you may follow:

1. **Introduce the person holding the less important position to the person holding the more important one.** For example, the president of a company (Mr. Hobhouse) is to be introduced to a new accounts receivable clerk. "Mr. Hobhouse, I'd like you to meet Sandy Ross who joined us on Monday." In reply to Mr. Hobhouse's greeting, the new clerk would say, "How do you do?"
2. **Introduce the younger person to the older one.** For example, a person is about to introduce his or her mother to a colleague. "Mother, may I introduce Miss Savage (Ann)?" "Ann, this is my mother, Mrs. Duncan."
3. **Introduce the man to the woman.** For example, when two people of equally important positions are introduced: "Mrs. Fleming, may I introduce Mr. Weir?" However, if the male president of a company is meeting a female employee for the first time, the woman would be introduced to the man. "Mr. Stanley, I'd like you to meet our new staff member, Carol Robertson."

Note: If you develop the habit of saying the name of the person holding the more important position or older person first, the rest follows automatically.

Invitations

S6   For such special occasions as weddings and formal dinners, formal invitations are often used. The invitation may be engraved, partially engraved, or handwritten. Typed formal invitations are not considered good etiquette. Formal invitations should follow this format:

Mr. and Mrs. Terence Jones
request the pleasure of
Mr. and Mrs. James Meilleur's
company at a dinner
in honour of
The Right Honourable Edward Schreyer
on Friday, the seventh of September
at half past eight o'clock
Safari Room, Deerfield Lodge
Charlottetown
R.S.V.P.   Black Tie

Printed or engraved invitation

Reply to an invitation promptly.

Acceptance

S7 This should contain virtually the same words as the invitation. It should be handwritten in the third person, as the illustration shows, on fine quality, double-fold stationery.

Mr. and Mrs. James Meilleur
accept with pleasure
the kind invitation
of
Mr. and Mrs. Jones
to attend a dinner
on Friday, the seventh of September
at half past eight o'clock.

Formal acceptance

Regrets

S8 To decline an invitation, it is polite to write a regrets note on good quality paper. The wording follows the same pattern as the acceptance.

Mr. and Mrs. James Meilleur
regret that they will
be unable to accept
the very kind invitation
of
Mr. and Mrs. Jones
to attend a dinner
on Friday, the seventh of September
as they have already accepted
an invitation for that evening.

Formal regret

Unit 16

Telephone and Other Tele-communications

The telecommunications services available in Canada form a complex communications network that permits users to exchange information of great diversity. Today's office worker must be aware of these services and know how to use them in the most effective and economical fashion.

T1
Telephone
T2
Telephone Technique

Identifying Yourself
T3
Suggested answering methods are:

- for a firm: "Campbell Company"
- your own phone: "Lister" or "Miss Levy"
- department phone: "Credit Department, Nicholls"
- another's phone: "Mr. McVean's office, Miss Spear"

Taking Calls
T4
- Answer promptly.
- Keep a note or message pad and pen near the phone.
- Check doubtful spellings with caller.
- Speak distinctly (do not smoke, chew, or conduct other conversations at the same time).
- If you must leave your desk, arrange for your phone to be answered.
- Avoid keeping callers on the line. Offer to call back if you need to obtain information. If you must leave the line, provide progress reports.

217

```
TELEPHONE CALL

To Mr. Mc Vean
Time 9.35    Date Nov. 8
From Mr. Nicholls
of Belfort Automotives
Phone No. 763-2911

| Please telephone | ✓ | Urgent |  |
| Returned your call |  | Was in to see you |  |
| Will call again |  | Wants to see you |  |

MESSAGE Your car will be
ready for you at 4.30
this afternoon.


Operator    J. Spear
BROWN & COLLETT LTD. P.T. 2
```

Telephone message form

Transferring Calls

T5
- Transfer only when it is essential and only if the caller agrees.
- If you *do not* know who should handle the call, note the caller's name and number and have the right person call back.
- If you *do* know who should handle the call, make sure that person is available and give a brief explanation of the call before you transfer it.

Making Calls

T6
- Keep an up-to-date directory of frequently called numbers (including area codes).
- Plan ahead: have questions ready, make notes if necessary, and/or have files available.
- Identify yourself and your affiliation.
- Use the most appropriate service and dial direct if possible.
- Consider time zones when making long-distance calls. (See Unit 19, U18.)
- Take advantage of any special rates or discounts (see the front section of your telephone directory).
- If a wrong long-distance number is contacted, call the operator (0) to have the charge cancelled.

Long-Distance Calls (Canada, United States, and Mexico)

T7
Direct dialling (from one number to another) is the most economical way of phoning long distance. Whenever the assistance of an operator is called upon, the cost of telephoning increases.

Long-distance enquiries: For long-distance enquiries, dial 1 + area code + 555-1212, and give the operator the name and address of the subscriber sought.

Dial Direct

T8

Station-to-station: a direct call with operator intervention only for particulars of billing. The charge begins when the called telephone is picked up.

To call *within the area* (between places with the same area code), dial 1 + the desired number.

St. John's and Corner Brook, Newfoundland, have the same area code (709); to call one location from the other, dial 1 + the desired number.

To call *another area* within North America, dial 1 + area code + number.

from Toronto to Deerfield Beach, Florida
dial 1   +   305   +   421-4353
access   area   Florida
code   code   number

Collect: the person receiving the call agrees to accept the charge for it.

Dial 0 + area code (if necessary) + number. When the operator responds, say "collect" and give your name.

Bill to a third number: a call is made from one number but billed to another.

Dial 0 + area code (if necessary) + number, When the operator responds, say "bill to" and give the area code and number to which the call should be charged.

Credit card: a useful device obtainable from the telephone company for a person who travels frequently and makes many calls. The person or company named on the card is billed monthly.

Dial 0 + area code (if necessary) + number. When the operator responds, say "credit card" and give the telephone credit card number.

Operator Assisted

T9

Person-to-person: this is useful when contact is required with a specific person or department. The charge begins when the specified contact is made. Person-to-person calls are more expensive than station-to-station calls.

Dial 0 + area code (if necessary) + number. When the operator responds, give the name of the person you wish to reach. *Collect, bill to third number,* and *credit card* services may be requested with person-to-person calls.

Overseas Calls

T10

The most economical overseas telephone call is made by dialling direct.

Overseas enquiries: to obtain the telephone number of an overseas party, dial 01 and ask the operator for the number.

Dial Direct (See Telephone Directory for Listing of Countries)

T11   **Station-to-station:** the cheapest type of overseas call.

Dial 011 + country code (2 or 3 digits) + routing code (1 to 5 digits) + local number (2 to 9 digits). The country code and routing code are obtainable from the telephone directory.

Collect, credit card, bill to third number, and **person-to-person** may be requested at an additional charge.

Dial 01 + country code + routing code + local number. When the operator answers, identify the kind of call you want and give the information shown above under **Dial Direct** (see this unit, T8.)

Operator Assisted

T12   Where direct dialling is not possible, dial 0 and the overseas operator will make the call for you.

T13 # Special Types of Calls

Appointment

T14   This is a call made for a particular time to guarantee reaching the desired person.

- The operator, on request, sets up the call by phoning ahead to the party and establishing the time of call.
- At the time arranged, the operator contacts both parties and connects them.

Conference

T15   This type of call is made when several people at different locations all wish to confer at the same time. Dial 0 for operator and ask for a conference call to be arranged. This service is now available across the world. Dial 01 and ask for the conference operator.

Marine

T16   This call is used for communicating with ships equipped for radio-telephone service. Dial 0 and ask for the marine operator.

Mobile

T17 This type of call is used to contact cars and trucks which have *manual* mobile telephone service. Dial 0 and ask for the mobile operator.

To call Access 450 customers, (those with direct dial mobile equipment) dial the 7-digit mobile number (preceded by the area code, if necessary).

WATS (Wide Area Transmission Service)

T18 • Inwats (Incoming WATS — Code 800): this is used by businesses and service companies to encourage customers to call long distance free of charge within a certain radius. Dial 1 + 800 + special Inwats number.
  • Outwats (Outgoing WATS): this service is available to companies that make many wide area calls. The charge is lower than for regular long-distance calls because customers usually pay on a flat-rate basis.

There are six WATS zones across Canada. The subscriber pays according to the zone coverage desired. In addition, a choice of rate structures based on hours of usage is possible.

Zenith

T19 This service is similar to Inwats (i.e., customers may call businesses long distance without charge) except that calls are possible only from specific locations. Dial 0 and place the call with the operator.

Telephone Directories

T20 The telephone company directory is in two parts: alphabetic (White Pages) and classified (Yellow Pages).

Alphabetic Directory (White Pages)

T21 Names, addresses, and telephone numbers of individuals and organizations are listed alphabetically by name. Names of subscribers are automatically listed free of charge, but a monthly charge is levied against subscribers wanting unlisted numbers.

The introductory pages list world-wide area codes, the types and rates of calls, telephone services available, and other useful facts.

For ease of reference, government department listings are placed together and printed on blue paper.

Classified Directory (Yellow Pages)

T22   Organizations wishing to be listed alphabetically by category and to advertise their service or product subscribe to the Yellow Pages. A charge is made for each listing and each advertisement.

Personal Directory

T23   Frequently used telephone numbers can be assembled in a personal directory for quick reference. These may be a list, a card index file, or an indexed container. The list should be organized alphabetically and should show the area code, the number, and the extension number, if appropriate.

T24
Business Telephone Equipment and Services

Centralized Answering

T25   The type of central answering service an organization has will be determined by the number of trunk (in/out) lines, extension lines, and services it requires. All calls coming into an organization are dealt with through some type of switchboard or telephone set.

PBX (Private Branch Exchange)

The switchboard operator using this type of equipment completes the connections for all incoming, outgoing, and interoffice calls.

PABX (Private Automatic Branch Exchange)

The switchboard operator using this type of equipment usually handles only incoming calls. Outgoing and interoffice calls are dealt with by employees directly.

Call Director (Desk-Top Switchboard)

This equipment is available with up to 10 trunk lines and up to 60 local lines, and can provide central answering services for a company or within a department. The operator handles only incoming calls.

Centrex

This is a large central switchboard in one location which has its own exchange number. Each employee has his/her own telephone and telephone number and can make and receive direct calls and interoffice calls.

Telephone Sets

These are equipped with a number of buttons which may be used in various ways. For example, a six-button set can be equipped with five incoming lines and a hold button; or four incoming lines, an intercom button and a hold button; or three trunk lines, one WATS line, a hold button and a buzzer. These sets can provide central answering services for the company or for a department within a company. Types available are: *6-button*, *10-button*, and *20-button*. The last two are modular units capable of accepting optional telephone units (e.g., automatic dialling unit, or handsfree speakerphone).

Hold	2139	2140	2141	2142	Intercom
◯	◯	◯	◯	◯	◯

Six-button telephone

How a Basic Telephone Set Works

- A call is signalled when a bell or buzzer rings and a button light flashes on and off.
- When the lighted button is depressed and the receiver lifted, the light stays on but the flashing stops.
- The *hold* button is depressed if a caller is asked to wait.
- The *intercom* button is depressed when connection to an inside-company extension must be made.

Computer-Based Telephone Systems

Computerized telephone systems are available for any size of installation. These can provide all the services of PABX or Centrex plus integrated voice and data communications, and many of the features listed under Additional Features. (See this unit, T26.) In addition, the telephone service now offers the Displayphone. This is an integrated voice and data telephone set. It consists of a telephone set, a screen, and a keyboard. It provides access to information from data bases, simultaneous voice and data communications, electronic mail capabilities, and interface with peripheral equipment. It features microprocessor-controlled software, call timing, clock, calculator, reminder service, auto dialling, handsfree capability, and last number redial.

Additional Features

T26
The equipment described under Centralized Answering usually includes both standard and optional features. These features are:

Automatic Dialling

This equipment can store up to 31 telephone numbers and automatically dial them by push button direction. If a line is busy, it can be redialled if the 32nd button is depressed.

Automatic Ring Again

When a busy station or outside line is free, the phone rings again.

Call Forwarding (Call Transfer)

Calls are automatically forwarded from one extension to another as instructed without attendant help.

Call Switching

If an extension is to be left unattended, incoming calls may be switched to another extension for answering.

Call Waiting

A person on a call gets a light *beep* tone periodically to warn of another call waiting.

Camp On

If a number called is busy, the caller can wait without hanging up and be automatically connected when the line is free.

Conference Calling

A third person — on some equipment, up to three additional people — can be brought in on a two-way conversation.

Data Transmission

(See this unit, T44.)

Dial Access to Central Dictating Systems

The caller can dial and dictate into the telephone. For more detail, see Unit 20, W16.

Group Listening

A speaker in the handset is switched on to enable those present to hear both sides of a telephone conversation.

Handsfree — Listen on Hold

If you are placed on hold, you may hang up and a built-in speaker will monitor the line for you.

Handsfree Speakerphone

This permits the user to move about the room and even hold conferences with several people present.

Interoffice Communications

This telephone system can provide a direct dial communication link between offices and departments. A *selective conference* feature is also possible that permits conferences using up to five lines at one time.

Last Number Redial

This feature automatically redials the last number the caller tried to reach.

Multiple-Line Conferencing (See Conference Calling)

On-Hook Dialling

Receiver may be left in place until dialling is complete.

Paging Access

This provides dial access to a loudspeaker paging system.

Saved Number Redial

This allows you to *store* a number while you make or receive other calls and then redial automatically.

Speed Calling

Numbers frequently called are stored and dialled automatically by push button command.

Tie-Trunks

These provide direct system-to-system links for multiple location businesses.

Video Conference Calls

By means of satellite hookup, participants can see as well as speak to each other (presently available in certain major Canadian cities).

The telephone service is constantly adding new developments to its range of services. A call to your telephone company will inform you about specific services or equipment to suit your company's needs.

Private Telephone Answering Services

T27   Organizations exist which will, for a fee, answer telephone calls on a subscriber's behalf. Such services are available on a 24-hour basis if needed. The telephone can be answered in the name of an individual, the name of a company, or any other identification requested. Some organizations simply take messages; others offer paging services. Consult the Yellow Pages of your telephone directory for a list of the answering service organizations in your area.

In addition, equipment may be purchased or rented that permits the telephone to be answered in the subscriber's absence. The subscriber makes a recording of his/her voice, which the caller will hear. The recording invites the caller to leave a message and his/her name and number so that the call may be returned.

Telegrams and Cables

T28   Where Telex is not suitable or available, and long-distance telephone is expensive, telegrams (in North America) and cables (overseas) are an effective means of dealing with rush orders or urgent messages. They may be sent prepaid or collect. Telegram and cable messages are generally delivered by phone and followed by a confirming copy.

Sending Telegrams and Cables

T29   • Plan the wording carefully for clarity and economy.
   • Prepare a written version in duplicate (forms available from CNCP).
   • Take the telegram or cable, or telephone it, to the nearest CNCP Telecommunications office. Telex subscribers who use the telegraph service frequently may contact CNCP direct via phone Tie-Line (a telephone wire connecting the subscriber to the CNCP office) or Tel-Tex. (See this unit, T43.)
   • Send out a confirmation letter the same day.

Telegram form

Confirmation letter for a telegram

Telegrams

Classes of Service (Canada, the United States, and Mexico)

T31 **Full Rate Telegram**

- receives immediate attention
- minimum charge for 15 words; additional words are charged extra
- delivery made as soon after transmission as possible

Night Letter

- minimum charge for 35 words, with an additional fee for every two additional words
- delivery made the next morning

Chargeable Words

T32 Telegrams may be written in plain language or in code. Charges are calculated on a per word basis, and the customer pays for the message only. The following are counted as one word: acceptable (dictionary) words, regardless of size; groups of five initials; each digit in a number; and less commonly used punctuation marks.

If telegrams are sent frequently, use the CNCP Telecommunications leaflet outlining acceptable code words and giving a detailed breakdown of chargeable words, numbers, symbols, and punctuation marks.

Telegraphic Money Orders

T33 This service may be used for sending money urgently almost anywhere in the world. Take the appropriate currency to a CNCP office and give the message and name and address of recipient. CNCP will transmit the message and instructions of payment to the destination telegraph office. The receiving office notifies the addressee, who must present identification before collecting the money.

T34 # Cables

Classes of Service (Overseas)

T35 **Urgent Message**

- receives top priority attention
- minimum charge for seven words; additional words are charged extra
- delivery is made as soon after transmission as possible

Full-Rate Cable

- minimum charge for seven words; additional words are charged extra
- delivery within hours of transmission

Letter Telegram

- minimum charge for 22 words; additional words are charged extra
- delivery made the next morning

Chargeable Words

T36 Since every word in a cable is charged, companies doing business internationally frequently adopt a cable address for economy. For example, "Canners," Hamilton, Ontario is the equivalent of Canadian Canners Limited, 44 Hughson Street South, Hamilton, Ontario—three words rather than eight. Such businesses also use code words when possible.

Code words are counted at the rate of 5 characters per word; plain language words are counted at the rate of 15 characters per word. A book listing acceptable code words is available from CNCP.

Teletype

T37 Teletype services are provided by two organizations. The Telex service is provided by CNCP Telecommunications, and TWX service by the Computer Communications Group (CCG) of the Trans Canada Telephone System. These services connect subscribers in Canada, the United States, and overseas.

How Telex and TWX Work

T38
- The sending operator prepares the information to be transmitted, dials the number of the receiving company, and gets a *go ahead* signal.
- The message is typed on a teleprinter (a special typewriter keyboard attached to a paper-feeding machine) and appears simultaneously on the recipient's teleprinter.
- The receiving machine prints the incoming message whether or not anyone is attending the equipment.
- Two operators can conduct a written conversation if necessary.

Teletype Directories

T39 These are provided by CNCP Telecommunications and CCG.

Other Telex Services

Telepost

T41   This service combines the CNCP Telecommunications network with the Canada Post service to provide same-day delivery of a letter. Telepost is cheaper than night letter telegrams.

How Telepost Works

T42
- The sender telephones a CNCP Public Message office and dictates the addressee's name, address (including postal code), and message.
- The information is electronically transmitted to the destination post office and delivered by letter carrier or directly onto the recipient's teleprinter.
- A Telex subscriber may send Telepost messages directly to destination post offices.

Tel-Tex

T43   A Telex subscriber can send telegrams to a non-subscriber by telexing the message to the CNCP Telecommunications office. CNCP transmits the message to its destination, where it is delivered by telephone and followed by a printed confirmation.

Data Transmission

T44   Large, highly computerized companies use telecommunications services for other than verbal or visual transmission. Data such as credit verification, inventory control, reservation requests, sales reporting, and financial transactions may be communicated by wire or microwave links provided by public companies such as CNCP through services known as Infoswitch, Datatelex, Infodat, Telenet, and Broadband and by private companies such as CCG through Datapac and Dataroute. The cost of transmission is dependent upon the type of service. Private networks are more costly because the user pays for the connecting line whether or not it is in use; shared networks (pay as you use) are more economical.

      Since this is an area of rapid and constant change in office technology, no attempt is made here to provide anything but an indication of data transmission possibilities. For detailed advice and assistance, contact the telephone company in your area, CNCP Telecommunications, or CCG.

Electronic Mail (Message Transmission)

T45   This is an expression used to describe the transmission of communications between compatible communicating word processors and between facsimile terminals.

Where compatibility does not exist between word processors, Infotex, a CNCP microwave network, is available. This service enables an organization to use its own terminal to access CNCP direct, and CNCP then transmits the communication to the addressee's terminal.

Facsimile Transmission

T46   This process permits the electronic transmission of an exact copy of any document from one location to another remote location over telephone lines. The material transmitted may be typed, handwritten, or drawn, and may include extremely detailed graphics and photographs. Two compatible units are needed — one for sending and one for receiving. An acoustic coupler is attached to the copier and the document is inserted. The sender dials a telephone number and is connected with a compatible telecopier. The hand set is plugged into the coupler, a switch is pushed, and the material is transmitted. Transmission cost is related to the speed of transmission. Facsimile transmission units are available with speed ranges from four minutes to 20 seconds per document and in varying degrees of automation. The equipment may be purchased or leased from the major copier equipment manufacturers.

For information on Intelpost, the facsimile transmission service provided by Canada Post, see Unit 13, PO15.

Unit 17

Travel Arrangements

Travel plans involve not only reserving the method of transportation but also can include reserving hotel accommodation, booking rental cars, obtaining international travel documents, and a host of other details. Some organizations have their own travel departments, but more frequently the office worker will either use a travel agency or do the work alone.

Using a Travel Agent

TA1   Travel agents are paid by carriers and hotels; there is no charge to the traveller. Travel agencies can offer excellent advice on accommodation, package tours, travel documents, car rentals, overseas travel, *etc.* In addition, they can be helpful about exchange rates, suitable clothing, customs arrangements, special events, and places of interest. However, an incompetent or unscrupulous agent can be a costly one, and it is recommended that before an agency is employed, its reputation be checked with the Better Business Bureau or the local chamber of commerce.

Air Travel

TA2   Reservations may be made either by phone or in person at the airport, at airline ticket offices, or at a travel agency. Tickets will be made up when payment has been made or credit has been established. (Some companies maintain monthly accounts with travel agencies; other companies provide key employees with credit cards for charging their travel bookings.)

The reservation information needed includes:
- name(s) of traveller(s)
- date of travel and destination
- class of service
- method of payment
- contact telephone number(s) of the traveller(s)

Fares

TA3

First Class and Economy

First class passengers can expect more room, more comfortable seats, a more extravagant meal, complimentary bar, and more personal services than can economy class passengers.

Some airlines have instituted special business class sections in their planes for travellers who have paid full economy fares. Passengers in this category generally can expect special check-in counters, complimentary bar service, first choice of meals and literature, an adjacent vacant seat, and quick exits.

Special Fares

APEX, Charter Class Fare, and *Excursion Fare:*These are individual round-trip fares which sell for less than two one-way tickets. These special bargain fares are offered by airlines on some flights at some times of the year. Purchasers must make bookings well in advance of the journey and cannot change the length of stay.

Group Fare: The purchaser travels on economy class on scheduled flights in groups and usually must purchase a land arrangement such as hotel or rental car.

Family Plan: The head of the family pays full fare: other members of the family receive discounts.

Types of Flights

TA4

Scheduled flight: the regular flight established by an airline which departs regardless of the number of seats sold.

Nonstop flight: no stops are made until the plane reaches its destination.

Direct flight: a stop or stops along the way will be made, but there will be no need to change planes.

Connecting flight: passengers must get off one plane along the route and board another.

Charter flight: a plane booked exclusively for group travel. This is among the cheaper forms of air travel, but you should anticipate full planes, a penalty for cancelling, and inflexibility in changing dates.

Baggage

TA5 Although international carriers sometimes base their free baggage allowance on mass, the usual practice is as follows: Each adult is permitted two articles to be checked (maximum dimensions of the first piece are 1.6 m length + height + width; and of the second piece, 1.35 m length + height + width); and cabin luggage (maximum dimensions 1.2 m length + height + width if it will fit under the seat). No single piece of baggage may exceed 31.8 kg. Luggage allowance for charter passengers varies with the carrier. Check with the airline if in doubt.

Airline liability for missing baggage is limited in accordance with its current tariffs. These can be checked at any ticket office. The airline accepts no liability for loss or damage to fragile or perishable items, money, jewellery, or negotiable securities.

Specially Chartered Planes

TA6 If all commercial flights are fully booked, the possibility of a specially chartered flight might be considered. Check with airports in the vicinity or private airline companies.

Getting To and From the Airport

TA7 Investigate the limousine, helicopter, and bus service schedules to and from all terminals. Compare costs and time involved. Consult the Yellow Pages under "Airport Transportation."

Train Travel

TA8 Reservations may be made directly with VIA Rail (a toll-free reservations number is provided in the local phone directory) or through a travel agent.

Reservations are required for sleeping accommodation, club car, and coach travel. Credit cards are accepted and phone reservations are honoured. Reservation information needed includes:

- destination
- desired arrival and return arrival times
- type of accommodation

Fares

TA9 Uniform fares operate all year round, although prices are slightly higher during summer and at Christmas and Easter. Special excursion fares are available for 1- to 3-day trips on short runs, and for 7- to 30-day trips on long runs at a savings of about 30 per cent.

Classes of Accommodation

TA10 *Coach*: slightly reclining seat only.

Daynighter: reclining seat with footrest.

The *Club 52* (between Toronto and Montreal only) offers a reclining seat with footrest. Meal and bar service can be purchased at seat.

The *Club Car* (between Toronto, Ottawa, Montreal) offers a reclining seat with footrest. A free meal is served and bar service is available.

Upper or lower berth: the upper berth is folded down from the side of the car to become a bed. During the day, with the upper berth in its folded position, passengers use the lower berth as seating accommodation.

Roomette*: private compartment with washroom. It sleeps one person.

Bedroom*: private compartment with washroom facilities. It sleeps two people. Chairs are provided during the day.

Ensuite*: two bedrooms separated by a collapsible wall. It sleeps up to four people.

Drawing Room*: three adjoining bedrooms.

*These passengers have priority for dining car service.

A snack bar with lounge facilities (often attached to the bar car) is available for all passengers and operates on trains between most major centres. On western trains, the Sceneramic Lounge Car is available to all passengers at no extra charge.

Cancellations

TA11 Cancellations must be made quickly. Refunds are made on straightforward fares, but excursion or high-season fares normally carry a penalty for cancellation. Consult your booking agent.

Luggage

TA12 Up to 70 kg per passenger is carried free in the baggage car (two suitcases is the maximum suggested for cabin luggage).

Arrangements may be made to transport animals in the baggage car only. (Feeding, *etc.*, is the responsibility of the owner.)

Auto Transporters

TA13　　Trans-Canada Auto will arrange to send your car by rail. This company has offices in all major centres. Consult the local telephone directory.

Bus Travel

TA14　　Buses provide economical, efficient, and reasonably comfortable travel. Most buses are air-conditioned and many have washrooms. The disadvantages of bus travel are that reservations cannot be made in advance, schedules are at the mercy of the weather, sleeping accommodation is not provided, and food is not served. This type of travel is most suitable for short trips and for travelling to centres not served by air or rail lines.

　　　　Passengers are permitted to carry 75 kg of luggage free in Canada and 60 kg to the U.S.A.

Sea Travel

TA15　　Once the major international carrier, ships tend now to be used mainly for holiday cruise travel. However, a few times a year passenger-carrying liners leave the west coast for stops in the Pacific and leave Montreal for Europe. Travel agents and the shipping lines will provide information and make arrangements.

Rental Cars

TA16　　Travellers wanting to rent cars can do so at airports, bus and train stations, hotels, through travel agents or airlines, or directly from the renting companies. Advance reservations are essential, and comparison shopping is recommended. Some companies quote unlimited distance rates and others a flat fee plus a charge per kilometre. Compare the insurance coverage provided in the rental arrangement, the amount of liability (deductible amount) in the event of an accident, and the amount to be paid if the car is dropped off at another location. A valid driver's license and proof of ability to pay (a credit card is suggested) are mandatory before a car may be rented.

Hotel/Motel Accommodation

TA17   There are many ways of reserving hotel or motel accommodation:

- through local offices of large hotel chains which have Telex or telephone tielines with their branches
- directly with the hotel by letter, telegram, telephone, or Telex
- through a travel agent (but possible room rate discounts might be forfeited)

In requesting accommodation, state the type and size of room required, the length of the occupancy, and the arrival and departure times. Rates are based on single occupancy of the room; a small additional charge is made for accommodating more people. Be sure to take advantage of any commercial room rate (corporate rate) discounts possible (e.g., to members of the Commercial Travellers Association, other registered associations, and travellers for large companies which give hotels regular business). Room rates do not include meals and taxes.

Hotels will generally not hold a reservation past 18:00 unless a guaranteed booking is requested. In this case, a bill will be sent whether or not the room is used.

Hotel and Restaurant Terms

TA18   If you are considering a package travel plan, the following definitions may be helpful:

- European Plan (EP): no meals included
- American Plan (AP): room and meals
- Modified American Plan (MAP): room, breakfast, and dinner
- Continental Plan: room and breakfast
- Table d'hôte: fixed charge for the meal
- Prix fixe: fixed charge for the meal
- à la carte: each dish on the menu is charged separately

The Itinerary

TA19   The itinerary is a detailed list of the travel arrangements, accommodation, appointments to be kept, and essential reminders. If arrangements are made through a travel agent, the agent will provide an itinerary as part of the service.

In establishing a workable itinerary, be sure that sufficient time is left for checking in at airports; that the traveller knows that arrival and departure times are *local* times; and that sufficient travel recovery time is allowed for before meetings are set up.

```
        ITINERARY AND RESERVATIONS FOR MRS. DANA McGRAW
                    April 24 - 29, 19--

        MONDAY, APRIL 24
  11:30  Depart Fredericton, N.B. on Eastern Provincial
        Flight 210
  12:20  Arrive Halifax, N.S.
  16:15  Depart Halifax on Air Canada Flight 618
  17:00  Arrive St. John's, Nfld.
  Stay   Hotel: The Landlubber (two nights)

        WEDNESDAY, APRIL 26
  16:25  Depart St. John's on Air Canada Flight 129
  17:55  Arrive Montreal, Quebec (Dorval Airport)
  Stay   Ritz Carlton Hotel (two nights)

        FRIDAY, APRIL 28
  12:15  Depart Montreal (Dorval Airport) on Air Canada
        Flight 618
  14:36  Arrive Halifax, N.S.
  Stay   Hotel Warwick

        SATURDAY, APRIL 29
  16:55  Depart Halifax on Eastern Provincial Flight 215
  17:55  Arrive Fredericton, N.B.
```

Itinerary

Travel Funds

TA20 To avoid the need for large sums of cash, funds may be taken in one of these forms:

- Credit cards: Bank credit cards and such travel and entertainment cards as American Express and Diners' Club are acceptable for most purchases in and out of Canada.
- Traveller's cheques: (See Unit 1, B36.) These are easily replaced and widely accepted. They are available in varying denominations. It is usually a good idea to get them in the currency of the country to be visited.
- Letters of credit: (See Unit 1, B30.) These permit the holder to obtain amounts of cash up to the stated limit in any branch of the bank which issued the letters.

If the need for an emergency supply of money arises, money can be telegraphed to the traveller. (See Unit 16, T33.)

Travel Insurance

TA21 Life and baggage insurance additional to that provided by carriers is obtainable from travel agents or insurance company booths at airports and railway stations. Additional health insurance for international travellers may be purchased directly through major insurance companies.

International Travel

TA22 Making arrangements for international travel is no different from making domestic bookings. You may prefer, however, to rely more on the travel agent's specialized knowledge.

Documents

TA23   **Passport**

This is required for travel to all overseas destinations. It is obtainable from the Passport Office, Department of External Affairs, Ottawa, or from regional offices in Toronto, Montreal, Vancouver, Edmonton, Halifax, or Winnipeg. The application form must be accompanied by a birth certificate or citizenship certificate plus two recent photographs, a list of the countries to be visited, and the appropriate fee. Allow sufficient time for processing of applications (anywhere from two weeks to two months, depending on the season).

Visa

This is a special permit required for visits to certain countries. Travel agents have information on these countries, the documents required when travelling to them, and the visa fee. Allow plenty of time for obtaining visas.

Health Requirements

TA24   Vaccinations and immunizations are required for some countries. Travel agents or local health officers can provide full details as to the requirements and the documentation needed. Do not leave this until the last minute because certain vaccinations consist of a series of injections given over a three-week period.

Customs

TA25   Travellers are allowed to bring duty-free purchases back into Canada under the following circumstances:

Absence	Goods to a value of
Less than 48 hours	—
More than 48 hours (once every calendar quarter)	$50
After 7 days (once every calendar year)	$150

Included in these allowances are liquor (1.1 L wine or liquor or 24 × 341 mL beer) and tobacco (200 cigarettes, or 50 cigars, or 1 kg tobacco).

Travellers may, of course, bring back additional items provided they are prepared to pay the duty. Some items, such as food and plants, may not be brought into Canada. Check with the local Canada Customs office if in doubt about a planned purchase.

It is wise to register any valuables (e.g., camera) being taken out of the country with the customs office so that there is no problem in bringing them back into Canada.

Unit 18

Typing Techniques

Users of typewriters and word processors share common needs. They both need to know how to operate their equipment to best advantage and how to produce typewritten work that meets the most exacting business and professional standards.

This unit attempts to satisfy the needs of both groups in the following five sections:

About Your Typewriter: covers basic typewriter settings for conventional typewriter users

Basic Typing Techniques: describes fundamental typewriter operations

Corrections and Revisions: offers assistance in making manual corrections

Style Practices: provides both typists and word processor operators with an up-to-date guide

Typed Communications: is a reference source for correct document set up

Typing Techniques ends with hints on typewriter care and typewriter selection.

About Your Typewriter

TT1   Most typewriters are available with either *elite* size type (12 pitch), which print 12 characters to the inch (2.54 cm) or *pica* size type (10 pitch), which print 10 characters to the inch (2.54 cm). Some typewriters have dual pitch capacity which allow for typing in either 10 or 12 pitch. Still other typewriters are equipped with proportional spacing which means that the space allowed for each letter is proportional to the space required by each letter. All typewriters, however, permit 6 horizontal lines to the inch (2.54 cm).

ELITE TYPE

PICA TYPE

Variable Pitch (Proportional Spacing)

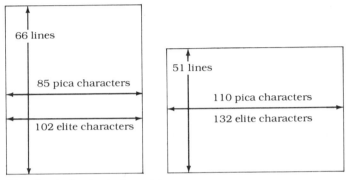

Standard-size typing paper

Read the manufacturer's manual that accompanies your typewriter so that you fully understand the scales, service keys, pressure settings, and special features of your particular machine.

To Find the Starting Line (Vertical Placement)

Single Spacing (SS)	now is the time) now is the time) now is the time)	line count is 3
Double Spacing (DS)	now is the time) ✓) now is the time) ✓) now is the time)	line count is 5
Triple Spacing (TS)	now is the time) ✓) ✓) now is the time) ✓) ✓) now is the time)	line count is 7

Determining line count with single, double, and triple spacing

TT2
1. Count the total number of lines to be typed plus any necessary spacing.
2. Subtract the total number of typing lines and spaces from the lines on the typing paper.
3. Divide the result by 2 and add 1 to obtain your starting line. (Ignore any fractions.)

To Find the Centre Point of the Paper

TT3
Most typewriters indicate the centre point for standard (letter) size paper by means of an arrowhead or round mark on the paper-guide scale of the machine. Other typewriters provide right and left hand markers against which to place the paper so that the centre of the paper lines up with the centre point indicated on the paper-guide scale.

When there is no paper-guide scale on your machine:
1. Fold a piece of regular typing paper in half down its length.
2. Open the sheet, insert it into your typewriter so that the left edge is against the paper guide, and note the point on the scale at which the fold appears.
3. If the number is a round one, such as 50 or 60, simply remember that number for future use.
4. If the number is not a convenient round number, pull forward the paper release, slide the paper over until the fold *is* on a round number, and adjust the paper guide so that it is tucked up tightly against the left edge of the paper. Leave the paper guide in that position permanently and remember the centre point number.

Note: This technique is designed to assist in establishing the centre point *only* when you *first* work with an unfamiliar typewriter.

To Set Margins

TT4
Divide the required line length by 2 and position your margin stops the resulting number of strokes on each side of the centre point. Add five extra strokes to the right-hand margin stop to act as a *bell allowance*. For example, a 70-stroke line would be set with 35 strokes to the left of the centre point and 40 strokes to the right of the centre point.

Basic Typing Techniques

TT5 Producing attractively typed material involves more than a knowledge of the keyboard. Correct centring and tabulation techniques, display devices, and useful heading styles all contribute to a first-class finished product. These fundamental elements of typewriting are outlined in the following pages.

Centring

TT6 **Regular Centring**

From the centre point of the paper, backspace once for every two characters and spaces in the line to be typed. Type the line.

HORIZONTAL CENTRING

(Backspace for each underscored character)

Extended (Spread) Centring

From the centre, backspace once for each character and space *except the last*. Type the line, leaving *one* space between characters and *three* spaces between words.

E X T E N D E D   C E N T R I N G

(Backspace for each underscored character and space)

Decorative Devices

TT7 Use these sparingly in business applications because of the amount of typing time involved.

Borders   HHHHHHHHH   VVVVVVVVV   ***********

Many letter combinations can be used with good effect.

Shadow   AGENDA

Ornamental

```
       A                          A
          G                    G
            E                E
              N            N
                D        D
                  A
```

Duplication Masters

TT8   For instructions in typing masters for duplication purposes, consult these pages:

Dittos: see Unit 14, R10.
Stencils: see Unit 14, R16 and R18.
Offset masters: see Unit 14, R24.

Enumerations

TT9   When information is to be typed in sections and subsections, use a consistent pattern of numbers, letters, and/or indentions so that the reader can easily identify the relative importance of the material.

```
(A)  ---------

     1.  -----------
         -----------

         A.  ------------
             ------------

         B.  ------------
             ------------

             (1)  --------------
                  --------------

                  (a)  ---------------
                       ---------------

                  (b)  ---------------
                       ---------------

             (2)  --------------
                  --------------

         C.  --------------
(B)  ------------
```

Heading Styles

TT10   Each of the following examples of heading styles may be centred, typed from the left margin, or backspaced (pivoted) from the right margin.

```
HEADING          Heading
HEADING          Heading

H E A D I N G    H e a d i n g
H E A D I N G    H e a d i n g
```

Justifying the Right Margin

TT11   In typing, justifying indicates that all lines end evenly with the right margin. To accomplish this, follow these steps.

1. Set your margins for the required line length.
2. Draw a vertical line at the right margin setting.
3. Type a rough draft, but do not type any characters beyond the line at the right margin setting.
4. For each line, count the number of spaces between the last letter and the line drawn at the right margin.
5. Spread the number of extra spaces for each line evenly between the words in the line so that there are no large gaps.
6. Type the final copy, inserting the extra spaces as you proceed. Each line will now end evenly with the right margin.

```
Dramatic changes are taking place  |✓✓
in business offices to solve the problem
of the rising costs of dealing with an  |✓✓
ever-increasing volume of paperwork.  |✓✓ ✓✓
Companies are turning more and more to  |✓✓
techniques such as word processing.  |✓✓✓
Word processing represents change:  in  |✓✓
the tools used to generate written com-  |✓
munications, in the role of the secre-  |✓✓
tary, and in procedures.
```

```
     Dramatic changes are taking place
in business offices to solve the problem
of the rising  costs of dealing with  an
ever-increasing    volume    of paperwork.
Companies are turning more  and  more to
techniques   such   as   word    processing.
Word processing represents   change:  in
the tools used to  generate written com-
munications, in the role  of the  secre-
tary, and in procedures.
```

Leaders

TT12   Leaders are intended to take the reader's eye from one piece of information to another.

Open . . . . open

Closed .... closed

Patterned .. .. patterned

Remember these points when you use leaders:

- Leave a space at each end of the line of leaders.
- With open and patterned leaders, be sure to align the dots vertically.

- If the right side is a figure column, end leaders three spaces before the column and line them up vertically.

```
Books ..............     $40.00

Pencils ............      5.00

Erasers ............      3.50
```

Pivoting

TT13 Use this technique when a typed line must end at a particular point or when succeeding lines must end at the same point.

1. Set the margins as usual, but set the right margin (or a tab stop) one space after the point at which you want the typing to end, e.g., set the right margin stop at 91 for typing to end at 90.
2. Type the required words at the left margin, and move the carriage to the right margin or tab.
3. Backspace from the right margin or tab stop once for every letter and space in the words to be pivoted.
4. Type the words. These will end exactly at the right margin or tab.
5. Continue until each line is completed.

```
Bloomsbury ................... Leon Edel

Blue Pages ............... Eleanor Perry

Chain Saw ............... Jackson Gillis

Competitive Tennis .... David A. Benjamin

Games End ................. Milton Dank

Helter Skelter .............. Ann Combs
```

Special Characters

TT14 Typewriters are not necessarily equipped with all the punctuation marks, symbols, or special characters you may need. Consult this list to allow you to create your own.

Special Character	Example	Method
Simple fraction	2/5	2 diagonal 5
Compound fraction	2 2/5	2 space 2 diagonal 5

Special Character	Example	Method
Multiplication sign	2 x 5	lower case x
Division sign	12 ÷ 3	colon over hyphen
Minus	12 - 3	hyphen
Addition	12 ≠ 3	oblique over hyphen
Equal	y = 3	two hyphens, one slightly above the other
Divide into (short)	2)12	right parenthesis and underscore
(long)	13)630	right parenthesis and underscore
Square root	√	v meeting oblique and underscore
Cents	¢	c over oblique
Dollars	$	S over oblique
Pounds sterling	£	f over L
Degrees	32^{0}C	o raised half line
Asterisk	note Å	A over v
Exponents	15^{6}	exponent raised half line
Chemical symbols	H_2SO_4	numbers lowered half line
Dash	--or -	two hyphens or space hyphen space
Exclamation mark	!	apostrophe over period
Square brackets	/sic/	diagonals and underscores
Feet and inches	5' 4"	apostrophe and quotation marks
Minutes and seconds	15' 52"	apostrophe and quotation marks
Ditto	"	quotation marks

Tabulation

TT15   To tabulate means to set up information in columns so that it is easy to read and attractive in format.

√N. Ontario [10]	Morris Kiu	√$ 72 468 [8]
Manitoba	Raj Kumar	100 650
Quebec	√Daniel Keith [12]	87 943

The first stage in tabulation is to find the longest item in each column.

Method 1 (Arithmetic)

TT16

Planning the Job

1. Locate the longest item in *each* column (key item). Sometimes the key item is the column heading.
2. Decide on the number of spaces to leave between columns. Six is standard for most work but anywhere from two to twelve is acceptable; three is standard for financial work, but two is acceptable.
3. Draw a plan showing columns and spaces, and note on it the character count of each key item and the amount of space to be left between columns.

42-stroke line needed
(10+6+12+6+8=42)

Setting the Machine

1. Clear any preset tab stops.
2. Clear any existing margin stops.
3. Set margins for the typing line needed for the table, i.e., add all the figures on your plan and set that line width. Only the left-hand margin stop is necessary.
4. Set tab stops for the start of the second and all succeeding columns by spacing forward from the left margin for the number of characters in the key item in the column plus the spaces in between and then depressing the tab set key.

Column Headings

Blocked: simply start typing the headings at the left margin and at all tab stops.

SALES

$1025.12

Centred: centre these headings over the columns.
A. *Short Heads*

SALES

$102 375.12

1. Follow instructions 1 to 4 for setting the machine.

2. Type the main table heading (title) and turn up a triple space.
3. Count the number of characters in the column heading. Subtract this number from the character count of the key item in the first column and divide the result by two. (Drop any fractions.) Space forward the resulting number from the left margin stop and type the column heading.
4. Depress the tab key. Repeat the procedure given in step 3 for the other column headings.
5. Turn up a double space and type the remainder of the tabulation.

B. *Long Heads*

Long column heads will be the key item (longest line) for your column count. Your stop will, in fact, be set for the column head.

SALES BUDGET

$17 000

1. Type the main table heading and turn up a triple space.
2. Type the column headings at the tab set points.
3. Centre the column *under* the head as follows:
    a. Find the longest item in the *column* and count the characters.
    b. Subtract this character count from the heading count.
    c. Divide the result by 2. (Ignore any fractions.)
    d. Clear the margin.
    e. Tap the space bar by the number found and reset the margin.
    f. Depress the tab key. Repeat steps a, b, and c.
    g. Clear the preset tab.
    h. Tap the space bar by the number found and reset the tab.
    i. Continue until all columns have been dealt with.
    j. Type the rest of the table.

Method 2 (Backspace)

TT17 To establish margins with this method, start at the centre point of the paper and backspace once for every two characters and spaces across the entire tabulation. To set tabs, space forward once for each key item character and column key and depress tab set key. Repeat for all necessary tab stops. Deal with column heads as previously instructed.

Ruled Tabulations

TT18
- Set up your tabulation as already described.
- Type in the horizontal rules as you proceed.
- Begin and end the horizontal rules at the left and right margins respectively.

- Note carefully the carriage returns needed to obtain the effect of a line of space above and below column headings, the body, and totals.

JANUARY TOTALS

		_DS_
		_DS_
N. Ontario	Manitoba	Quebec
		_SS_
		_DS_
72 468	100 650	67 943
9 005	20 725	6 319
37 291	5 432	18 250
		_SS_
		_DS_
118 764	126 807	92 512
		_SS_

Boxed Tabulations

TT19

- Type in the horizontal rules as you proceed and leave the vertical rules until you are finished the tabulation.
- Follow the points noted above for ruled tabulations.
- To insert the vertical rules either use the notch or hole in your cardholder and a sharp pencil *or* turn the paper sideways and use the underscore. The outside edges may be ruled but are better left open. Be sure to:

> Keep the rules *straight.*
> Place the rules in the centre of the available space.
> Begin and end the vertical rules at (not beyond) the bottom and top horizontal rules.

JANUARY TOTALS

N. Ontario	Manitoba	Quebec
72 468	100 650	67 943
9 005	20 725	6 319
37 291	5 432	18 250
118 764	126 807	92 512

Tabulation—Typing

TT20 In addition to the typing hints provided above, note the following:

Spacing

TT21

- Single or double spacing is acceptable. Use whichever will produce a tabulation that is attractive and easy to read.

- For any continuation (run on) lines, single space and indent two.
- Triple space under the main head and double space under the column heads.

```
Sales Report for Week Ending February 28, 19--
                          ✓
                         ✓
   Monday        Tuesday        Friday         Total
     ✓             ✓             ✓             ✓
    317           298           312           927
```

Headings

TT22 **Two-Line Headings**

Align single line headings with the *lower* line of two-line heads.

```
Sales
Department          Total

  7 162           14 865
```

Braced Headings

Braced headings are ones that are centred over a number of column headings. Set margins and tab stops for column headings and type the main heading. To type the braced heading:

1. Find the width over which the braced heading is to be centred, i.e., add the character count in the key items of the columns involved plus the spaces between.
2. Count the characters and spaces in the braced heading.
3. Subtract the two results from each other and divide the result by 2.
4. From the tab stop set for the first of the columns over which the braced heading is to be centred, space forward the number found in step 3 and type the braced heading. Repeat this procedure for each braced heading.
5. Type the rest of the tabulation.

```
     Report for Week Ending February 28, 19--
  ───────────────────────────────────────────────
       Western Provinces    │    Eastern Provinces
  ───────────────────────────┼─────────────────────
   B.C.   Alta.   Sask.   Man. │  Ont.   Que.   Maritimes
                              │
```

Space-Saver Headings

Income Tax Deductions	Pension Plan Payments	Workmen's Compensation Payment			

Note: Draw in the lines *before* you type the words.

Newfoundland	Nova Scotia	New Brunswick	Prince Edward Island				

Numbers

TT23

- *Whole numbers* are aligned from the right (units, tens, hundreds, *etc.*).

```
127
 32

159
```

Separate digits into groups of 3 by means of spaces.

12 141

- *Decimals* are aligned through the decimal marker, using a consistent style.

9.00	**Not**	9.		0.93	**Not**	.93
15.51		15.51		2.91		2.91

- *Dollar signs* are positioned to accommodate the longest line but are typed only at the beginnings and ends of columns.

```
$    37
1 021

$1 058
```

- *Per cent signs* are placed after the figure. Type after the first entry and on totals or sub totals only.

50%

Totals

Follow the spacing shown below unless space is at a premium.

$$\begin{array}{r} 127 \\ \underline{32} \\ 159 \end{array}$$ ←————Space

Tabulations With Long Edge of Paper Inserted First

TT24   Set up your tabulation as shown in this unit, TT15, but note this information: vertical line count is 51; number of possible strokes is 110 pica or 132 elite.

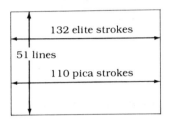

Production Tips for Tabulations

TT25
- Try to get your table to fit on one page.
- Develop your judgment so that you can estimate the margin and tab-stop positions and avoid the need for meticulous, time-consuming calculations.
- Block all headings.
- Make a note of the settings for tabulations that you do frequently, e.g., regular reports.
- Avoid vertical and horizontal rules.

Corrections and Revisions

TT26   Electronic typewriters, self-correcting typewriters, and word processing machines are equipped to handle changes in text and format. This section is directed to the typists who must resort to making corrections and revisions manually.

Making Corrections

TT27   Corrections can be made by means of a typing eraser, correction fluid, or correction tape. Choose the right material for the job. If you select a covering aid, try to erase the error first to avoid show-through problems.

Realigning

TT28

If you must make a typewritten change on a document *after* it is out of the typewriter, use this procedure.

1. Reinsert the paper.
2. Check a line of typing against the writing scale on the clear plastic cardholder for correct horizontal placement.
3. Pull forward the paper release.
4. Gently adjust the paper so that the horizontal alignment is correct and the printing point or the vertical alignment scale rests at the centre of a letter.

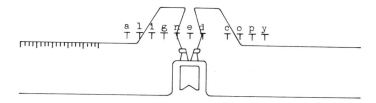

5. Push back the paper release.
6. If it is necessary to move the paper up or down, use the variable line spacer.
7. Check the alignment by putting the ribbon in the stencil position and typing a period. (Clean the key first.) You may have to adjust again.
8. Now type the correction.

Spreading

TT29

When a long word must be replaced by a shorter one, follow these steps:

- Erase the incorrect word.
- If the new word is one letter shorter, simply use the half spacer, or hold the carriage with one hand and type with the other to allow 1½ spaces at the beginning and end of the word.
- On machines with typing elements, make this adjustment by reaching under the cover with the fingers of the right hand and pressing against the ribbon cartridge while typing with the left hand.

If several letters are involved in the change, spread the correct letters evenly so that they occupy the space of the erased word.

```
That books is...          The incorrect story...

That book is...           The   correct  story...
```

Squeezing (Crowding)

TT30 When a short word must be replaced by a longer one, squeeze it in as follows:

- Erase the error.
- If there is only a one-character difference between the words to be changed, use the half spacer, or hold the carriage with one hand and type with the other to allow a half space at the beginning and end of the inserted word.
- On machines with typing elements, hold the ribbon cartridge as described in *Spreading* while you type the correction.

```
The salution is...              Now is the time...

The salutation is...            Now is that time...
```

If you need to make a correction close to the bottom of the page, roll the cylinder *backwards* rather than onwards. This will prevent the paper(s) from falling out and thus eliminate the need for realignment. This is a particularly useful tip when carbon copies are involved.

Proofreading Tips

TT31
- Proofread *before* you remove your work from the machine.
- Proofread with another person.
- Where lists of words, *etc.*, are concerned, count them to make sure nothing has been missed.

Proofreading (Correction) Marks

TT32 These are the symbols used in correcting communications produced as rough drafts.

Meaning	Symbol	Edited	Correctly Retyped
Change punctuation to a period	O	Stay there⊙	Stay there.
Change word	—	We ~~produce~~ *manufacture*	We manufacture
Close up	⊂	per‿cent	percent
Double space	ds ⊏	ds ⌈That should be / the way to work.	That should be the way to work.
Move number of spaces in direction shown	⑤]	⑤]By the time	By the time
Insert a hyphen	=	ready=made	ready-made
Insert letter or word	∧	pri︿ze and︿was	prize and it was

Meaning	Symbol	Edited	Correctly Retyped
Insert space	#	with it for the	with it for the
Leave in, do not omit (stet)	.....	This ~~service~~ will	This service will
Make all capitals	≡	Benjamin	BENJAMIN
Make capital letter small	/	at this Company	at this company
Make small letter a capital	≡	when she arrives	When she arrives
Move as shown	⌐	is available (to you)	is available
New paragraph	¶	¶During the last	During the last
Delete letter	\	letter writings	letter writing
Delete word	℮	offer you quality	offer quality
Raise above the line	V	according to Jones1	according to Jones[1]
Single space	SS	SS [payroll preparation / various employees	payroll preparation / various employees
Spell out, do not abbreviate	◯	Bring (4) books. / Third (Ave)	Bring four books. / Third Avenue
Transpose letters or words	～	recieve / receipts (cheques and)	receive / receipts and cheques
Underscore this	‗	Send it now.	Send it now.

Style Practices

TT33 Provided in this section is information on correct style practices as they relate to the typing of metric expressions and spacing after punctuation marks. For information on the current style practices used with the following, consult the sections indicated.

Abbreviations: see Unit 2, C25.
Capitalization: see Unit 2, C26.
Numbers: see Unit 2, C27.
Roman numerals: see Unit 19, U17.
Word division: see Unit 2, C29.

Typing Metric Expressions

TT34 *Note*: see Unit 19, U14 and U15 for a complete table of metric units, symbols, and conversions.

The style to be used in typing common metric terms, units of measure and their symbols is as follows:

Symbols

TT35

- Use only the symbols associated with the SI metric system. (See Unit 19, U11.)
- Use symbols rather than full metric terms with numbers.

  30 m

  Not   30 metres

- Use lower case, except when the symbol is derived from the name of an individual.

  mm for millimetre

  N for Newton

  C for Celsius

  Exception: Use capital L for litre.

  3 mL   2 L

- Leave a space between quantity and symbol.

  2.75 m

  The degree sign occupies the space in temperature expressions.

  32°C

- Do not start a sentence with a symbol.

  Distance is expressed in metres.

  Not   m is used to express distance.

- Do not pluralize metric symbols—both the singular and plural forms are the same.

  1 kg   75 kg

- Symbols are not abbreviations. Use a period only if the symbol occurs at the end of a sentence.

  He bought 0.75 kg of cherries.

  He bought 0.75 kg.

- Show square and cubic symbols by means of exponents (numerals typed a half line higher).

  16 m^2 32 cm^3

- Use the solidus (/) to represent *per.*

  He drove at 60 km/h.

Numbers

TT36
- Express fractions as decimals.

    2.75 kg

    Not $2\frac{3}{4}$ kg

- Use a zero in front of the decimal point when no whole number is shown.

    0.75 kg

- Use spaces to group figures into blocks of three. This applies to groupings on both sides of the decimal point. The space may be omitted in four digit numbers unless these numbers are listed in a column with other numbers of 5 digits or more.

    17 243.57 m

Numeric Times and Dates

TT37
Note: Numeric times and dates are not considered to be metric expressions but are related in the sense that they are methods of measurement.

- Type numeric dates in this sequence: year, month, day.

    19-- 04 12   (April 12, 19--)

    Year (four digits), space, month (two digits), space, day (two digits)
- When times are based on the 24-hour clock, use four digits and separate hours and minutes with a colon.

    04:30   16:22

Spacing Rules

TT38
Observe these spacing rules when you type punctuation marks and symbols.

Punctuation Mark	Spacing	Example
Apostrophe		
as possessive	no space	the boy's hat
as omission sign	no space	aren't you coming?

Punctuation Mark	Spacing	Example
Colon		
as punctuation	two after	He bought: a rabbit, a hen...
as time	none before or after	10:30 p.m.
as ratio	none before or after	3:6 is as 1:2
Comma	one after	An apple, a pear, and an orange.
Dash	either one space on each side of a hyphen *or* two hyphens without spaces	He can - he said. **OR** He can--he said.
Exclamation mark	two after	Good grief! What next?
Hyphen	no space	mother-in-law
Parentheses	one before the opening and one after the closing	Can you (as a friend) do this?
Period		
at sentence end	two spaces	Go home. It's time.
after abbreviations one abbreviation in caps	one space	Mr. J. Jones
two abbreviations or more in caps	no space	C.B.C.
any abbreviations in lower case	no space	b.c.c.
Question mark	two after	Can you? Will you?
Quotation marks	one before opening quote and one or two after completing quote (if a punctuation mark ends the closing quote, use the spacing required by that punctuation mark)	Mr. Winters asked, "Is the letter ready?"
Semi-colon	one after	She went east; he went west.

Symbol	Spacing	Example
Addition	one on each side	`3 + 2 = 5`
Ampersand (&)	one before and one after	`Smith & Wesson`
At (@) (each costing)	one on each side	`2 @ $15 = $30`
Cent sign	one after	`He paid 15¢ for it.`
Decimal	no space	`1.05`
Degree symbol	no space	`30°C`
Division	one on each side	`6 ÷ 2 = 3`
Dollar sign	one before	`He paid $15.`
Equality	one on each side	`6 x 2 = 12`
Feet	no space before, one after	`he was 6' tall`
Inches	no space before, one after	`he was 6' 2" tall`
Minutes and seconds	no space before, one after	`he ran in 5' 6"`
Multiplication	one on each side	`6 x 2 = 12`
Number (#)	one before, none after	`#3, 17 Avenue Rd.`
Oblique/Solidus	no space	`3 3/5; and/or; 31 km/h`
Percentage (%)	none before, one after	`5% plus 10%`
Subtraction	one on each side	`6 - 2 = 4`

See this unit, TT34 for spacing in metric expressions.

Typed Communications

TT39 This section contains information on how to produce typed documents quickly and easily.

Note: For typed examples of the following communications, consult the sections indicated.

Agendas: see Unit 11, MC4.
Itineraries: see Unit 17, TA19.
Meeting announcements: see Unit 11, MC3.
Minutes: see Unit 11, MC9.
Press releases: see Unit 2, C53.
Telegrams and *confirmation letters*: see Unit 16, T30.

Charts and Graphs

TT40
- Draw in pencil a very light outline of the chart to be completed. Draw this to scale if necessary.
- Use your typewriter for the outside horizontal and vertical lines and as much other data as you can. (A compass or any small, round object can be used for a pie chart.)
- Neatly insert any other necessary lines by hand.
- Erase whatever may remain of your light pencil outline.

Line Graph

TT41

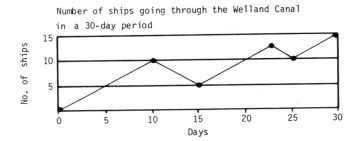

Vertical Bar Graph

TT42

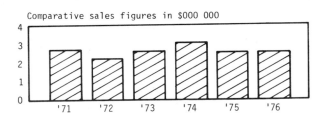

Horizontal Bar Graph

TT43

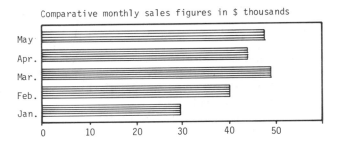

Pictogram (Picture Graphs)

TT44   Information is shown using symbols or illustrations.

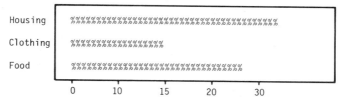

Pie Chart

TT45   Information is shown as sections of a circle.

Percentage amounts spent, out of income, by
the average Canadian family

Envelopes

TT46   If you are to benefit from the advantages offered by
mechanization in the post office, follow these rules for
envelope typing.

    Shown below are the two most frequently used sizes of
business envelopes (Nos. 10 and 8).

Return Address   Meter impression or stamp

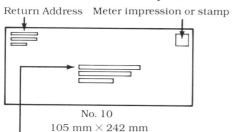

No. 10
105 mm × 242 mm

Mailing Address–line 14
(with exceptionally long addresses, start higher)
40 pica/50 elite characters from left edge

Special delivery instructions
or other notations—line 9

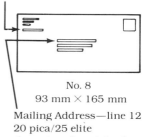

No. 8
93 mm × 165 mm

Mailing Address—line 12
20 pica/25 elite
characters from left edge

- Follow the style and punctuation pattern used in the letter
  to be contained in the envelope.
- Type carefully and spell accurately.
- Single space.

- Try to balance line lengths.
- Indent continuation lines by two spaces.
- Type delivery and any other special instructions (e.g., confidential, personal, registered, express, attention) at the left side on about line 9 lined up with the return address.
- The attention line may also be typed as the first line of the mailing address.
- See this unit, TT65 for additional typing details.
- *Always* include the postal code. (Find this on letterheads, return addresses on envelopes, or in postal code directories.) The postal code *must* be the last item typed. Try to position it on its own line. If this is not possible, separate it from the province with two spaces.
- Leave 19 mm of blank space at the foot of the envelope. The postal code must appear within a 26 mm band up from the blank space.
- Avoid abbreviations. Only the following are usually permissible:

Apartment	Apt.	Drive	Dr.
Avenue	Ave.	Heights	Hts.
Boulevard	Blvd.	Road	Rd.
Building	Bldg.	Rural Route	R.R.
Crescent	Cres.	Street	St.

See Unit 19, U3 and U4 for permissible provincial and state abbreviations.

Large Envelopes (Maximum 255 mm × 150 mm)

TT47
- Type the return address in the top left-hand corner.
- Centre the address on the envelope or use a label for the address and attach it to the centre of the envelope.

Addresses Typed on Continuous Form Labels

TT48
- Insert the first label in the typewriter (use the paper bail rollers to hold it firmly) with the remaining quantity still attached and stacked behind the typewriter.
- Type the required information. Move up to the next label, type the next address, and so on.
- Separate labels when all typing has been completed.

Note: Be sure the address is easy to read.

Chain Feeding Envelopes

TT49
This is a useful technique when many envelopes must be typed at one time. It permits a continuous supply of envelopes to be fed into your typewriter.

- Set a stack of envelopes on desk, flap side up and with open flap pointing away from you.

- Insert first envelope into typewriter.
- Type first envelope address.
- Insert next envelope immediately behind first one.
- One roll of the cylinder will remove the first envelope and position the second.

Folding Correspondence

TT50   Enclosures should fit envelopes as closely as possible.

Small envelope (No. 8)

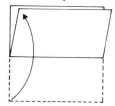

1. Place letter face *up* on desk. Fold in half.

2. Fold right third to left, making the fold slightly less than one-third of the way over.

3. Fold left third so that it extends 0.5 cm beyond the other two-thirds.

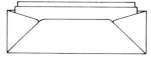

4. Insert last folded edge first.

Large envelope (No. 10)

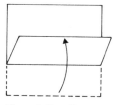

1. Place letter face up on desk. Fold slightly less than one-third up towards top.

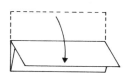

2. Fold down top of letterhead.

3. Insert so that second fold goes in first.

Window Envelopes

When you use window envelopes, be sure the enclosure fits the envelope snugly so that the address (including the postal code) cannot shift out of the window area.

Standard size specifications (with acceptable window positions) are available by contacting Canada Post.

Speedy Envelope Sealing and Stamping by Hand

TT51

Sealing

- Use a damp sponge or other moistener.
- Assemble ten envelopes one behind the other with flaps open and glued side up.
- Run the sponge over the first two or three envelopes. Seal them.
- Continue until all envelopes are sealed.

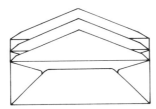

Stamping

- Assemble ten envelopes so that the stamp area is visible.
- Moisten a horizontal row of ten stamps.
- Quickly attach a stamp to each envelope.

Financial Statements

TT52

- Financial statements are reports prepared regularly for management that show the worth of the company and the operating results.
- Financial statements usually contain a descriptive column and money columns. Leave six to eight spaces after the first column. Leave two or three spaces between the money columns.
- Follow the techniques of tabulation. (See this unit, TT15.)

- Plan the job so that the final statement is both attractive and easy to read. (Use larger than normal paper or insert the long edge of the paper first, if necessary.)
- Use leaders if this will assist in reading.

```
                        MARTIN KOLCHETSKI
                        INCOME STATEMENT
                 FOR THE YEAR ENDED MARCH 31, 19-2


   Income
   Gross Sales ....................................    $92 206.45
        Less Returns and Allowances ...............        969.59

   Net Sales .....................................                  $91 236.86


   Cost of Goods Sold
   Merchandise Inventory, April 1, 19-1 ...........    $ 9 462.20
   Purchases ........................  $54 943.15
        Less Returns and Allowances ..    496.96
                                                        54 446.19

   Cost of Goods for Sale ..........................   63 908.39
        Less Mdse. Inv., March 31, 19-2 ...........    11 220.25
   Cost of Goods Sold ..............................                 52 688.14
   Gross Profit ....................................                $38 548.72


   Expenses
   Salaries Expense ................................   $13 731.24
   Delivery Expense ................................     1 560.60
   General Expense .................................       510.80
   Insurance Expense ...............................        62.00
   Supplies Expense ................................       440.80
   Depreciation Expense ............................       534.16

        Total Operating Expenses ...................                16 839.60

   Net Income ......................................               $21 709.12
```

Forms

TT53   See Unit 6, Forms, and also Legal Documents (this unit, TT54).

- When you type on lines, note that the descenders on longer characters should just touch the printed line.

grey

- Set tab stops for frequently recurring positions.
- Stay within the boundaries set by the preprinted form.

Legal Documents

TT54   There is nothing particularly difficult about typing legal documents. Simply apply normal rules of style (see Unit 2, C24) and, with minor modifications explained below, the rules of manuscript typing. (See this unit, TT85.)

- If you are employed by a legal firm, follow the *style guide* of your particular office.
- Corrections are permitted in most offices, but you must use either a correcting typewriter or an eraser. Liquid paper, correcting tape, or erasing.tape are not permitted.

Typing Preprinted Legal Forms

TT55
- When the available space is longer than necessary, centre the matter to be typed and fill any remaining space with ruled lines or hyphens.
- Fill in large spaces by ruling or typing a large Z.
- Keep your typed line within the margins set by the printing on the form.
- Use single spacing where space is limited.

Amended October, 1970   **OFFER TO PURCHASE**   Dye & Durham Limited Toronto
Printers to the Legal Profession
Form No. 116

I/WE, ... Shirley Boquist ....
of the ..... city ..... of ..... Toronto ....
.... Montford Properties .... (as purchaser), hereby agree to and with
(as vendor), through .... George Grindley, ...
to purchase all and singular the premises situate on the ..... west ..... side of ..... Wilfred Street ..... Agent
in the ..... County ..... of ..... Peel .... known as ..... 16 Wilfred
..... Street, Bramalea .... (herein called "the real property")
having frontage of about ..... 50 feet .... more or less, by a depth of about ..... 100 feet
being ..... the whole of ..... Lot No. ..... 4274 .... according to Plan No. 92
Registered in the Registry Office .... at Bramalea
at the price or sum of --- SIXTY-FOUR THOUSAND --- Dollars ($. 64,000...)
as follows: ..... TWENTY THOUSAND--- Dollars ($.20,000...)
cash or certified cheque to the said Agent/Vendor on this date as a deposit, and covenant, promise and agree to pay the--
balance of FORTY FOUR THOUSAND DOLLARS ($44,000) on the 30th day of September, 19--.

The following items, the property of the Vendor, shall be included in this sale for the price above mentioned:—

This Agreement shall be conditional upon the Vendor, at his own expense, complying with the provisions of the Planning Act and any amendments thereto.
PROVIDED the title is good and free from all encumbrances, except local rates, and except as aforesaid; said title to be examined by me at my own expense, and the Purchaser is not to call for the production of any title Deeds or Abstracts of Title, Proof or Evidence of Title, or to have furnished any copies thereof, other than those in Vendor's possession or under his control. Provided the same have been complied with, the Purchaser accepts the property subject to municipal requirements, including building and zoning by-laws, and to restrictions and covenants that run with the land. The Purchaser to be allowed
days from the date of acceptance hereof to investigate the title at his own expense, and if within that time he shall furnish the Vendor in writing with any valid objection to the title which the Vendor shall be unable or unwilling to remove, and which Purchaser will not waive, this agreement shall be null and void and the deposit money returned to the Purchaser without interest.
This offer to be accepted by   19   , otherwise void; and sale to be completed on or before the
day of   19   , on which date possession of the said premises is to be given to the
Purchaser, or he is to accept the present tenancies and to be entitled to the receipt of the rents and profits thereafter. This offer, when accepted, shall constitute a binding contract of purchase and sale and time in all respects shall be the essence of this agreement.
It is agreed that there is no representation, warranty, collateral agreement or condition affecting this agreement or the real property or supported hereby other than as expressed herein in writing.
Until completion of sale, all buildings and equipment on the property shall be and remain at the risk of the Vendor until closing and the Vendor will hold all policies of insurance effected on the property and the proceeds thereof in trust for the parties hereto, as their interests may appear. In the event of damage to the said buildings and equipment before the completion of this transaction, the Purchaser shall have the right to elect to take such proceeds and complete the purchase, or cancel this agreement, whereupon the Purchaser shall be entitled to the return without interest of all monies theretofore paid on account of this purchase.
Unearned Fire Insurance Premiums, Fuel, Taxes, Interest, Rentals and all Local Improvements and Water Rates to be proportioned and allowed to date of completion of sale; Deed or Transfer to contain covenant on part of the Purchaser to pay off any Mortgage that by the terms of this instrument is to be assumed and prepared at the expense of Vendor on form acceptable to the Purchaser's solicitor and if mortgage is to be given back, same to be prepared at the expense of the Purchaser on a form acceptable to Vendor and drawn pursuant to The Short Forms of Mortgages Act, Ontario.
Any tender of documents or money hereunder may be made upon the solicitor acting for the party on whom tender is desired and it shall be sufficient that a negotiable certified cheque may be tendered instead of cash.
Each party is to pay the costs for registration and taxes on his own documents.
Whenever the singular or masculine are used in this Offer, they shall mean and include the plural and feminine if the context or the parties hereto so require
Dated at   this   day of   19
SIGNED, SEALED AND DELIVERED   IN WITNESS whereof   have hereunto set   hand   and seal ,
in the presence of:

I/WE, hereby accept the above offer and its terms, and covenant, promise and agree to and with the said above-named purchaser to duly carry out the same on the terms and conditions above mentioned, and   hereby accept the deposit of $ out of which
the agent   hereby authorized to retain   commission of   per cent of an amount equal to
the above mentioned sale price.
Dated at   this
Witness:

T61   40%

Typing Entire Legal Documents

TT56

- Start approximately 10 lines down on the first page.
- Leave 12 pica spaces or 15 elite spaces for left margins and 10 pica spaces or 12 elite spaces for right margins if you use plain paper.
- Stay inside the ruled lines if you use ruled legal paper.
- Leave a 3 cm bottom margin.
- Number continuation pages on line 7. Continue typing on line 10.

```
                    I transfer the balance of the residue of my

              estate to my said husband, Michael David Revel, for his

              own use absolutely.

                    IN WITNESS WHEREOF I have to this my Last Will
              and Testament written upon this and two preceding pages
              of paper subscribed my name this 30th day of June, 19--.

              SIGNED, PUBLISHED AND DECLARED )
              by the above-named Janet Hazel )
              Revel, the Testatrix as and for )
              her Last Will and Testament, in )
              the presence of us both present )
              at the same time, who at her    )     _____
              request and in her presence and )      Janet Hazel Revel
              in the presence of each other   )
              have hereunto subscribed our    )
              names as witnesses.             )

              Name _____

              Address _____

              Name _____

              Address _____
```

- Double space. Indent paragraphs by 10.
- Note that the attestation section is single spaced.

Endorsements

TT57

The endorsement is typed on a separate page or on the outside fold of the document. It is the identification or title page of the document and shows the names of the people (parties) involved, document title, date, and name of legal firm, and in the case of litigation documents, the court where the case will be heard.

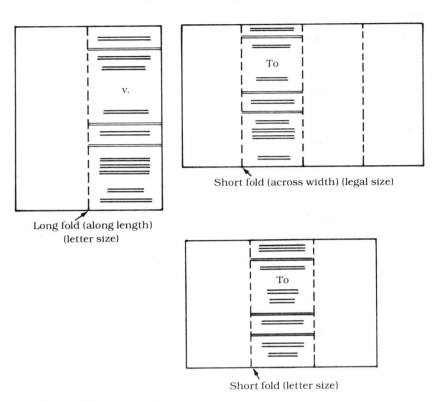

Litigation

Long fold (along length)
(letter size)

Other Documents

Short fold (across width) (legal size)

Short fold (letter size)

Once you have folded the document as suggested:

Litigation

- Type the name of the court beginning on line 6.
- Centre and type the title of the document halfway down the page between two horizontal lines.
- Centre the names of the parties between the court name and the title.
- Type the name and address of the law firm near the bottom. Leave a bottom margin of 3 cm.

Other Documents

- Centre and type the date on line 6.
- Centre and type the title of the document halfway down the page between two horizontal lines.
- Centre the names of the parties between the date and the title.
- Type the name and address of the law firm near the bottom. Leave a bottom margin of 3 cm.

Letters

TT58

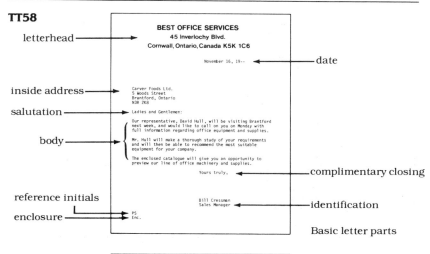

letterhead

date

inside address

salutation

body

complimentary closing

reference initials

enclosure

identification

Basic letter parts

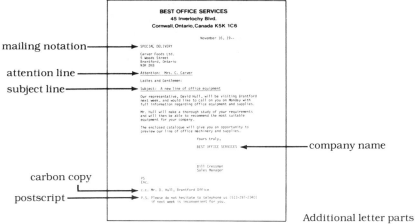

mailing notation

attention line

subject line

company name

carbon copy

postscript

Additional letter parts

Most business letters are typed in one of the three basic styles and in one of the three punctuation patterns illustrated below. (Additional styles are illustrated in this unit, TT79.)

TT59

TT60

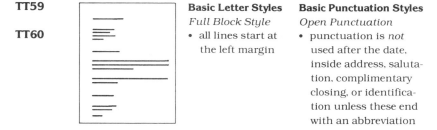

Basic Letter Styles

Full Block Style
- all lines start at the left margin

Basic Punctuation Styles

Open Punctuation
- punctuation is *not* used after the date, inside address, salutation, complimentary closing, or identification unless these end with an abbreviation

Block Style

- date and complimentary closing start at the centre
- all other lines start flush with the left margin

Mixed, Two-point, or Standard Punctuation

- a colon follows the salutation
- a comma follows the closing
- punctuation is *not* used after the date, inside address, company name, or identification unless these end with an abbreviation

Semi-block Style

- date and complimentary closing start at the centre
- paragraphs are indented

Closed Punctuation

- a period follows the date
- a comma follows all lines of the inside address except the last one* which is followed by a period
- a colon follows the salutation
- a comma follows the complimentary closing, the company name, and the individual writer's name
- a period follows the last word of the identification

Note:

- **Any one of the three punctuation styles illustrated may be used with any letter style.**
- Attention lines, subject lines, mailing notations, enclosures, reference initials, carbon copy notations have ending punctuation only if they end with an abbreviation.

*The postal code is *never* punctuated.

Letter Placement

TT61
- Letters should be typed on the page so that they are attractively framed by a balanced amount of white space.
- For speed and efficiency, use one margin setting for all your letters. Use either a 60-pica or 70-elite stroke line or set margin stops at the starting and ending points indicated by the letterhead design.

- Type the date a double or triple space below the printed letterhead. For a short letter, leave 8 to 10 lines between the date and inside address; for a long letter, leave only 4 lines. Allow 5 to 6 lines for the signature.

Where more precise placement than suggested above is needed, use the following guide.

Placement Guide

The date should be typed a double space or so below the printed letterhead.

Word count	Stroke line	From date to inside address
up to 100 (short letter)	40 pica/50 elite	8 lines
100 to 200 (medium letter)	50 pica/60 elite	6 lines
200 plus (long letter)	60 pica/70 elite	4 lines

This table is designed to provide guidance only. When attention and subject lines or any other displayed information is included, extra allowance must be made to the word count.

Mailing Notations

TT62
- Type mailing notations at the left margin midway between the date and inside address in solid capitals.
- Use only when a *special* mail service such as *express* or *registered* mail is used.

Special Notations

TT63
- Type special notations such as confidential, personal, *etc.*, at the left margin between the date and inside address.
- Use all capitals *or* initial caps and underscore.

Date

TT64
Either of these styles is acceptable:
- *Numeric*: 19-- 07 29
- *Standard*: July 29, 19--

Inside Address

TT65
- Use at least three typed lines.
- Attempt to keep line lengths approximately equal.
- Avoid abbreviations as much as possible. For acceptable street abbreviations see this unit, TT46.
- Indent any continuation lines by two strokes.

- *Always* include a *social* title—Mr., Mrs., Miss, Ms., Messrs. (plural male), Mesdames or Mmes (plural female).
- Professional titles and special titles such as Professor, Reverend, *etc.*, are not usually abbreviated, but Doctor (Dr.) may be.
- Do not show titles *and* degrees—use one or the other, but not both (B. Turcotte, Ph.D. or Dr. B. Turcotte).
- Check the proper form of address if you are writing to a prominent person in public life, politics, the clergy, or the military. (See Unit 2, C50.)
- Position in the company may be shown in these ways. (Note the use of the comma.)

```
Mr. F. Sharman, President
Buttonville Golf Club

Mr. F. Ciampaglia
President, B.I.B. Ltd.

Mrs. Jane Tobias
Director of Services
Collingwood Consultants Ltd.
```

- When street names are composed of numbers, use words for one to ten and use numbers for over ten.

```
160 Seventh Street

32 South 13th Street

43 - 13th Street
```

- Separate the town from the province with a comma.
- Provinces may be shown in full or in the abbreviated form. (See Unit 19, U3.)
- Type the postal code as the last item either on a line by itself or immediately after the province and separated from it by *two* spaces.

Attention Line

TT66
- Type the attention line two lines below the inside address, centred, or starting from the left margin.

Style Choices

```
Attention Mr. J. Dunn          ATTENTION MR. J. DUNN

Attention: Mrs. J. Crisp       ATTENTION: Miss M. Elliott

Attention: Mr. J. Dunn         Attention of the Traffic Dept.
```

Salutation

- Type the salutation two lines below the address (or attention line if there is one).
  Capitalize the first word and all nouns.

> Gentlemen   My dear Sir
> Dear Mr. Waugh   My dear Mrs. Bacchus

- See Unit 2, C51 for help in selecting the appropriate salutation.

Subject Line

TT68

- Type the subject line two lines below the salutation, centred, or starting from the left margin.

Style Choices

```
SUBJECT:  ANNUAL SALES CONVENTION

Subject:  Annual Sales Convention

Annual Sales Convention

Re:  Annual Sales Convention
```

Body

TT69

- Begin typing the body two lines below the salutation or subject line.
- Single space; double space between paragraphs. (In the case of an extremely short letter, double space the entire body.)

Complimentary Closing

TT70

- Type the complimentary closing a double space below the body.
- Capitalize the first word only:

> Yours truly
> Very sincerely yours

- See Unit 2, C51 for help in selecting the appropriate complimentary closing.

Company Name in Closing

TT71

- Avoid using this unless company preference demands it.
- Type the company name in capitals a double space below the complimentary closing.

```
Yours truly

GRANATO GRAIN CO.
```

- When the company name is long, it may be centred under the complimentary closing. Be consistent and centre the identification line(s) also.

Yours truly

GRANATO CANADIAN GRAIN COMPANY

Rosalie Granato

Identification Line

TT72
- Type the identification line anywhere from 4 to 7 lines below the closing or company name.
- Use it as a balancing line, i.e., if you have only a small amount of space left at the lower edge of the sheet, leave 4 lines; but stretch this to 7 lines if there is surplus space to be used.
- Show the name of the dictator/originator and/or the position that person holds.
- A male does not usually indicate his social title in the closing.

Grant Parker, President

(Miss) M. Chantrell
Vice Principal   **Or**

M. Chantrell (Miss)   **Or**

Mary Chantrell

- Type this on one or two lines. Do not let the identification extend beyond the longest line of the letter.
- If you are authorized to sign a letter in the dictator's absence, use one of these forms. (The dictator is Barbara Davison; the signer is Charmaine Reynolds):

Barb Davison
per
Charmaine Reynolds

Charmaine Reynolds
for
Barb Davison

Reference Initials

TT73
- Type reference initials at the left margin. Use the same line as the identification line *or* two lines below it.
- If the dictator/originator's name is typed in the identification, it is not necessary to show the initials.
- Show the dictator/originator's initials first, and the typist's initials second.

Style Choices

PHE:LF   **OR**   PHE:lf   (both dictator's and typist's initials shown)

LF   (only typist's initials shown)

LF 12   (typists are sometimes assigned numbers)

PHEllis:lf   (dictator's initials and last name shown if not in identification)

Enclosure Notation

TT74
- Use this notation when something is to be included with the letter.
- Type the notation one or two spaces below the reference initials.

Style Choices

Enc: Enclosure

Encl.   Enc. 3

Enc. Cheque $453.95

Carbon Copy Notation

TT75
- Use this notation when one or more people are to receive copies of the letter.
- Type the notation one or two spaces below the enclosure notation at the left margin.

Style Choices

c.c. Mr. D. Roswell   Copy to Mr. F. Rocca

cc Mr. D. Wilson   C.C. Mrs. M. Daniel

- When the distribution of the carbon copies is not to be shown on the original, a blind carbon copy notation should be used on the carbon copies only.

b.c.c. Mr. W. Roswell

bcc Mr. D. Wilson

- Either take out the carbon pack, remove the top sheet and first carbon and reinsert the remainder of the pack, *or* place a piece of scrap paper over the original and type.
- Some organizations favour the use of pc (photocopy) in place of c.c. where a facsimile is used instead of a carbon copy.

Postscript

TT76
- Use the postscript (p.s.) to add emphasis or to include something omitted in the body.
- Type it a double space below the last item.

Style Choices

```
P.S.  ------------        P.S.  ------------
-------------------       -----------
```

Headings on Multiple Page Letters

TT77
- When letters take up more than one page, on successive pages type a heading showing the addressee, the page number, and the date.

```
line 7 ──►Cooper Lumber Co.              2           19-- 08 12
```

```
        cheque will be received from you within the next few
        days.  If this cheque is not received, the matter
        will be ...
```

```
line 7 ──► Newfoundland Lumber Supply Company
           Page 2
           19-- 08 12
```

```
        cheque will be received from you within the ...
```

- Use the same quality stationery as used for page 1, but use a plain sheet (unless your firm has printed continuation-page stationery).
- Type the heading on line 7. Continue the body of the letter a triple space under the heading.
- The addressee's name is the first line of the inside address on page 1.
- Do *not* carry a divided word from one page to the next.
- Do *not* have fewer than two lines of a paragraph at the foot of one page or at the top of the continuation page.

Displayed Information

TT78   **Numbered Sentences**
- Leave a line of space above and below each numbered item.
- Single space each numbered item and double space between them.
- Either line up the numbers with the existing margin or indent five spaces from the left margin.
- Set a tab four places from the left margin and depress the tab for the second and succeeding lines.

```
                         April 19, 19--


Ms. A. R. Canning, President
Astrolite Limited
380 West Georgia Street
Vancouver, B.C.
V2P 1N7

Dear Ms. Canning:

Because of the rapidly growing number of contracts being
made from this office, it might be advisable for us to
consider enlarging the staff here.  May I suggest the
following plan for your consideration:

1.  The appointment of someone as Assistant to the Vice-
    President.  This person's major duties would be to
    take care of office administration.

2.  The appointment of a Sales Representative.  His or
    her duties would be to represent this company in
    follow-up contacts and to act as a technical consultant
    to potential customers.

Creation of these positions will release time to the Vice-
President so that additional attention can be given to the
mounting number of contacts in the central and northern
sections of the eastern coastal region.

                       Sincerely yours,



                       L. C. Horton
                       Vice-President
```

See this unit, TT23 for number alignment rules.

Quoted or Inset Information

- Leave a line of space above and below any information that has been quoted or that must be set off from the rest of the body.
- Indent five spaces from the left and right margins.
- Single space.

```
                         19-- 07 05



The Toronto Star
One Yonge Street
Toronto, Ontario
M2J 1P3

Gentlemen:

Please insert the following advertisement in the classified
advertising section of your paper in category 710, General
Help Wanted.

        Automotive parts manufacturing firm requires
        person to perform packaging and warehouse
        duties in the Toronto distribution centre.
        We offer a full benefits program, 5-day week,
        and good starting salary.
        Phone 232-3198.

Please make the advertisement a small one and arrange for it
to appear on Thursday and Friday, July 10 and 11.

                       Yours truly,



                       M. Sullivan
                       Personnel Manager

cb
```

Tabulated Information

- Follow the rules of tabulation. (See this unit, TT15.)
- Leave a line of space above and below the table.
- If the tabulation has a *short* line length (i.e., is narrower than the margins you would usually set for your letters) set up the tabulation normally.
- If the tabulation is a *long* one (i.e., is longer than the line length you would usually set for your letters), first calculate the tabulation and *then* set your margins for the rest of the letter. Set your margin stops five spaces to the right and to the left of the tabulation line length. This will guarantee that your tabulation stays within the line length of the letter.

```
Dear Mr. McMaster:

Please send us a quotation on each of the following
items:

        5 cm steel casing         SC4   5 sections

        1.5 cm Logan pump         LP1   4 sections

        3 cm twist steel cable    TS7   400 m

Please show f.o.b. point to Prince George, British
Columbia.
```

Additional Business Letter Styles

TT79   In addition to the basic business letter styles described in this unit, TT58, the following styles are used in some business situations. The body of each letter illustrated provides examples of occasions on which these letters might be useful.

```
April 6, 19--


Mrs. Edith Tait
Nursing Co-ordinator
North York General Hospital
Sheppard Avenue East
Willowdale, Ontario  M2J 1E1


SIMPLIFIED LETTER STYLE


You might select this letter, Mrs. Tait, for use in your
office if you are looking for a way of cutting letter
typing time to a minimum.  Notice that letters in the
Simplified Style have neither a salutation nor a
complimentary closing.  Note also that a subject line is
always included.

This letter is very similar to the full block style, and
should be set up in the same way.  The only typing detail
change to make is to the subject line.  Note that it is
typed a triple space below the inside address and a triple
space above the body.


Craig Elliott
Manager
```

April 6, 19--

Dear Mr. Denniston:

The letter style that is favoured by most government
departments, civil service offices, and by senior executives
for their personal correspondence is known as the official
style.

The official style is essentially a regular letter
that has the inside address typed as the last item. The
letter may have blocked or indented paragraphs and may be
typed in any one of the three punctuation styles.

If the letter includes a postscript, enclosure or
carbon copy notations, these are typed in their usual
positions.

Yours truly,

F. Benjamin

Mr. S. Denniston
247 Barrington Street
Halifax, N.S. B1L 2G5

April 6, 19--.

James, Kinney, and Kahn,
    Barristers and Solicitors,
        315 Main Street,
            Winnipeg, Manitoba. R3C 5N4

Gentlemen:

The letter style used here is known as "indented."
This is a very traditional style used occasionally by
legal firms and by some government departments.

To achieve the indented effect in the inside address
and closing section, a series of tab stops must be set
at five space intervals from the left margin and from the
centre point. It is standard practice to use closed
punctuation with the indented letter.

While the style may have an attractive appearance,
one has to ask if all that typing effort is really
justified.

Yours faithfully,

Robert Dow, Q.C.

```
                                          April 6, 19--


        Mr. G. Fleming
        Fleming & Sons
        372 Pender Street
        Vancouver, B.C.  V1K 2L3

        Dear Mr. Fleming:

        Have you been searching for a letter guaranteed to catch the
             attention of your customers through its eye appeal?
             Look no further!  The hanging indented (or suspended)
             style will do the job for you.

        Paragraphs in this letter style start normally, but the
             second and all succeeding lines are indented.  The
             indentation may be five or ten spaces depending on
             just how eye catching you want your letter to be.

        For the remaining set up details, simply follow the procedure
             for the block style letter.

                                 Yours sincerely,



                                 Maya Eby
                                 Circulation Manager
```

Form Letters

TT80
- When you must send the same basic letter with a few individual changes to many people, use a *form letter.*
- Type the original form letter as you would any letter, but leave space where the variable information is to be inserted, e.g., date, name, address, salutation, money amounts.
- Use a copying process that most clearly resembles original typing, e.g., offset.

```
        Dear Mr. and Mrs.

             Your recent application for a charge account has
        been approved, and your charge plate is enclosed.  Your
        credit limit has been set at          and your account will
        close on the          day of each month.

             We appreciate the opportunity to be of service to you
        and welcome you as a Lockwood charge account holder.

                                 Very truly yours,



                                 D. Kappelhoff
        Enc:                     Credit Manager
```

- Align the preprinted form letter in your typewriter very precisely so that even though you are typing only parts of the letter, the finished version looks like an individually typed letter.

Letters on Small Stationery

TT81
- The names given to stationery which is smaller than standard are Monarch and Baronial.

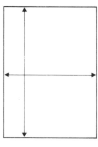   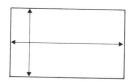

Monarch (18 cm × 27 cm)   Baronial (14 cm × 22 cm)

- They are used most frequently by senior business executives to add distinctiveness to their letters or when it is necessary to particularly catch a reader's attention.
- Set margins of 12 elite or 10 pica strokes from each side and follow all the other typing rules contained in this section.

Tips on Rapid Letter Production

TT82
- Remember that the full block style with open punctuation requires the least typing effort.
- Set one margin for *all* letter lengths and adjust the available space between date and inside address.
- Set tabs for all needed indentions in advance.
- *Block* attention and subject lines (i.e., start them at the left margin).
- Omit reference initials if they serve no real purpose.
- Do not type the company name if this is shown in the letterhead.
- Organize all the materials you need ahead of time.
- Proofread your work *before* you take it from the typewriter.
- Use a ruler or a line-a-time device for complicated work or small type.

Memorandums

TT83
Interoffice memorandums (memos) are used when written communication between company employees is necessary.

- Inside address, salutation, and complimentary closing are not used.

- Use block style and a consistent line length (60 pica, 70 elite).
- Do not repeat the originator's name in the signature area if it is given at the top. The initials may, however, be typed at the centre or left side a triple space below the body.
- Titles are not needed in the *To* and *From* sections but may, as a matter of courtesy, be used in the *To* section only.
- The set-up for carbon copies, enclosures, postscripts, and multiple pages is exactly the same as for letters.

```
                    M E M O R A N D U M


   To:      L. C. Horton, Calgary        Date:  June 4, 19--

   From:    J. E. Drury

   Subject:  Calgary Business Show

   We have been notified of the forthcoming Calgary Business
   Show.  We believe we should enter an exhibit.

   We shall contact Ms. Hosso, exhibit committee chairman,
   and keep you informed as plans develop for an entry in this
   show.

   If you have any suggestions as to the type of exhibit having
   the greatest impact, please get in touch with me.

   pt                        JED

   c.c.  T. Longmann
```

Post Cards

TT84 Post cards are useful for sending out brief notices, announcements, or messages. They usually measure 14 cm × 9 cm.

Line 3
5/6 spaces in

```
The ABC Company
48 Main Street
Toronto, Ontario
M3J 5L6
```

Line 10
20/24 spaces in

```
                         Ms. A. Navarra
                         57 Stone Street
                         Calgary, Alberta
                         W7N 4P2
```

Line 3
Line 5
5/6 spaces in

```
                              19-- 12 06

Dear Ms. Navarra:

Thank you for your subscription to our monthly news-
letter, "Economic Digest."

The yearly rate is $20.00, which covers the cost of
12 issues.  You may remit by personal cheque or postal
money order.

We appreciate your business.

                         Harold Mason
                         Circulation Manager
```

Reports, Essays, Manuscripts

TT85
- See Unit 2, C54 for guidance on *writing* reports and essays.
- Reports, essays, and manuscripts are so similar in their typed form that the instructions provided here apply to reports used in business, to formal academic essays, and to material being prepared for publication.
- Use a good-quality, *plain* white, letter-size, bond paper unpunched, and type on *one* side of the sheet only. Use onion skin for copies.
- Reports, essays, and manuscripts usually consist of a title page, contents page, body, and bibliography. Complex or very long documents may also contain a preface, appendixes, and an index.

Title Page (Cover Page)

TT86
The title page shows the company or institution name, document title (topic), name of author, name of person or company to whom submitted, and the submission date.

- Balance the layout so that the page is attractive and easy to follow.
- Use decorative borders if you wish, but a simple, conservative style is best.

Blocked title page
(attractive and easy to type)

Centred title page
(attractive but more
time-consuming to type)

Preface (also known as the Introduction, Abstract, Foreword, Synopsis, Summary, or Digest)

TT87   The preface outlines the purpose of the report, its scope and limitations, the methods of research employed, the major ideas in the report, the name of the person who authorized it, and any special observations or acknowledgements.

- Type the preface as a separate page and place it between the body and the title page.
- Use the same margins, placement, and spacing as for page 1 of the body but leave the page unnumbered.

```
                        PREFACE

        The results of research into the importance of the visual
effect of reports indicates that their appearance is indeed a
significant factor in their impact.
        It is hoped that this report will have the effect of
making report writers in the company aware of the importance
of devoting sufficient time and energy to illustrations,
reproduction means, and binding methods.

Acknowledgements
        In presenting this report, we wish to acknowledge the
assistance and co-operation received from the printing department
staff and the word processing centre staff.
```

Table of Contents (or Contents)

TT88   The contents page lists each major section (and sometimes subsections) of the document and appropriate page numbers. It is needed only in lengthy reports (ten or more pages) and should be prepared *after* the rest of the report has been typed so that accurate page numbers may be included.

- Use the same margin settings as in the body.
- If the contents list is a short one, centre the material vertically on the page. No page number is needed.
- If the contents list is a long one and likely to occupy more than one page, type the heading on line 13 and finish typing 6 lines up from the bottom edge. Start the continuation page on line 7. Use Roman numerals to number these contents pages.
- The contents page should follow the heading pattern and/or numbering system used in the report, essay, or manuscript itself.

```
┌─────────────────────────────────────────┐
│                                          │
│              TABLE OF CONTENTS           │
│                                          │
│    Illustrations . . . . . . . . . . . . . . . . .   1  │
│                                          │
│    Headings  . . . . . . . . . . . . . . . . . .   1  │
│                                          │
│    Reproduction  . . . . . . . . . . . . . . .   2  │
│                                          │
│    Binding . . . . . . . . . . . . . . . . . . .   2  │
│                                          │
│        Unbound . . . . . . . . . . . . . . . .   2  │
│        Top-bound . . . . . . . . . . . . . . .   2  │
│        Side-bound . . . . . . . . . . . . . .   2  │
│                                          │
│                                          │
│                                          │
│                                          │
│                                          │
│                                          │
│                                          │
│                                          │
└─────────────────────────────────────────┘
```

Placement (Margins and Starting Lines)

TT89

	Unbound	**Topbound**	**Sidebound**
Starting line, page 1	13	15	13
Starting line, page 2, *etc.*	7 (page number line 4, centre or right side)	10 (page number bottom right corner)	7 (page number line 4, centre or right side)
Left margin (strokes from left edge)	12 pica, 15 elite	12 pica, 15 elite	15 pica, 18 elite
Right margin (strokes from right edge)	12 pica, 15 elite	12 pica, 15 elite	12 pica, 15 elite
Bottom margin	3-4 cm (6-9 lines)	3-4 cm (6-9 lines)	3-4 cm (6-9 lines)

Spacing

TT90 Use double spacing and a five-space paragraph indention. (In business reports where there may be an important reason for saving space, single spacing is acceptable.) Use single spacing for displayed information (long quotations, numbered listings, footnotes, and bibliography).

THE BUSINESS REPORT: ITS FINISHED APPEARANCE

Research, organization, and writing skill are needed in the
preparation of an effective business report; but these ingredients
alone will not guarantee that the report will achieve the desired
effect. The final layout and appearance must be carefully considered
since they can greatly influence a reader.

ILLUSTRATIONS

The writer must not only try to make his report easy to read
but easy to understand as well. He must remember that words are not
the only tools he has available.

Quite often, words are not as dramatic in presenting
the data for a report as are graphic forms of communication.
Graphics are effective ways of sharing key statistics,
noteworthy trends or startling contrasts. Bar charts,
pie charts, trend lines: all these can help your reader
get key ideas better than words can--provided the data
has something significant to say.[1]

HEADINGS

"Headings and subheadings pinpoint and summarize ideas for easy
absorption by the reader."[2] Page after page of closely printed

---

[1]Laird, Dugan, Writing for Results: Principles and Practice,
Addison-Wesley Publishing Company, Reading, Mass., 1978, p. 201.

[2]Farmiloe, Dorothy, Creative Communication for Business
Students, Holt, Rinehart, & Winston, Toronto, 1977, p. 186.

- 2 -

material is boring to read. Break the text up into short units
topped with suitable headings or titles so that you keep your reader
on track and make his task easier.

REPRODUCTION

The type of report and its functions will influence the kind
of reproduction method used. Carbon copies may be appropriate for
copies to inter-company members; but reports to shareholders, for
example, should be reproduced by offset or some other process which
will produce good quality copies.

BINDING

Unbound

If the report is no more than ten pages long, staple it
at the top left-hand corner. Use a binding on a longer report.

Top-bound

Leave an extra top margin allowance so that none of the
typed matter is obliterated by the binding. Acco clips or
plastic covers are effective means of binding papers at the
top.

Side-bound

A wide left margin is required to allow for one of the
many choices of binding available: a 1 cm coloured paper strip
can be stapled at the left side; coloured board or clear plastic
binders to take 3-hole punched paper can be used; or a plastic

Headings

TT91

- Use headings, subheadings, and other subsection headings to organize the material, to show relationships, and to indicate the relative importance of the separate sections of the report.
- Decide in advance what your heading pattern is to be and stick to it.
- Suggested typing styles that will permit five categories (grades) of headings (not including the overall main heading) are:

  First category . . . . Capitals, centred
  Second category . . . . Capitals, side
  Third category . . . . Initial capitals, side, underscored
  Fourth category . . . . Initial capitals, side, indented 5, underscored
  Fifth category . . . . Initial capitals, side, run in

- To speed up your typing if you are working from a draft, decide on heading categories *before* you start typing and then code each heading in the job (e.g., number them from 1 to 5).
- Note that an extra line of space must be left *below* main heads and *above* all other headings.

```
                    HEADING REQUIREMENTS
                          ✓
                          ✓
        -------------------------------------------------

    -------------------------------------------------------
        ✓
        ✓
    IMPORTANT CONSIDERATIONS

        -------------------------------------------------

    -------------------------------------------------------
        ✓
        ✓
    Useful to Reader

        -------------------------------------------------

    -------------------------------------------------------
        ✓
        ✓
    Consistent Style

        ---------------------------------------------

    -------------------------------------------------------
        ✓
        ✓
    Pattern Followed   -----------------------------------

    -------------------------------------------------------
```

Numbering Systems

Some formal reports may need a numbering system to make the location of material easier. Use either one of the following two systems:

Decimal Style

1. A major topic.

   1.1 A section of the major topic.

      1.11 The next sub division.

      1.12 A second point at this level.

   1.2 A second section of the major topic.

2. The next major topic.

   2.1 A section of the next major topic.

Number/Letter Style

1. A major topic.

   A. A section of the major topic.

      1. The next sub division.

         a. Part of 1, above.

         b. Another part of 1, above.

2. The next major topic.

   A. A section of this major topic.

Ending the Pages

TT93 Each page should have a bottom margin of about 3 cm (6 lines). As a reminder, use a pencil to mark a point 4-6 cm from the end of the page *before* you begin typing *or* watch the paper-ending indicator on your machine *or* use a guide sheet (see this unit, TT101). Be sure to follow these rules:

- Type at least two lines of a paragraph at the foot of one page and always type at least two lines at the top of the next page.
- Do *not* divide the last (or first) word on a page.
- Do *not* type a heading on one page and the body on the next so that the heading is isolated.

Numbering the Pages

TT94 **Introduction (Table of Contents and Preface)**

- Leave these unnumbered unless many pages are involved.
- Use Roman numerals or letters of the alphabet if several pages are involved within each section.

Body

- Leave the first page unnumbered.
- Number second and succeeding pages either at the top (line 4) at the centre or right side, or bottom (4 lines up) at the right side.

Ending (Appendixes, Bibliography, Index)

- Leave these unnumbered unless several pages are involved.
- Use Roman numerals, Arabic numerals in parentheses, or letters of the alphabet if several pages are involved within each section.

Displayed Information

TT95 **Numbered Lists**

- Indent five spaces on each side or align with the margins.
- Single space, but double space between each item.

1. ------------------------------
   ----

2. ------------------------------

- Set a tab four places from the left so that alignment is simplified.

Tabulated Material

- Follow the rules given for tabulations. (See this unit, TT15.) Do *not* let your table extend beyond the margins of the body text.
- Single spacing is preferred.
- Leave a blank line above and below the table.
- Type footnotes related to a table below the table rather than at the foot of the page.

Illustrations

TT96
- For information on typing tables, charts, and graphs see this unit, TT40.
- If a list of illustrations is required, type this in numbered sentence format and insert it in the report after the body and before the bibliography.

Quoted Material

Short Quotations (Three or Fewer Typed Lines)

Type these within the body of the report and within quotation marks. End them with a raised numeral indicating a footnote reference.

Quoting Complete Sentences Use quotation marks, begin the quotation with a capital, and end it with a period.

Typists should be aware that, "Quotations of just

a few lines are double spaced and typed within

quotation marks."[2]

Quoting Parts of Sentences Use the ellipsis (3 periods) to indicate that not all of the sentence from which the quotation is taken has been used.

Typists should be aware that quotations and

paraphrases "...of just a few lines are double

spaced."[1]

Typists should be aware that quotations "...of just

a few lines..."[1] are double spaced and may be introduced

and ended by the ellipsis.

Note: Use *four* periods if the closing ellipsis comes at the end of the sentence.

Long Quotations (More Than Three Typed Lines)

- Leave a line of space above and below long quotations.
- Single space the quoted material.
- Indent five spaces on each side of the margins.
- Do *not* use quotation marks.
- Indent the first line an additional five spaces if you are quoting from the beginning of a paragraph.

Dorothy Farmiloe says on this subject:

An appendix is the place to put supplementary
material not essential to the report but which
may aid the reader's understanding of it in some
way.[2]

- If the quote opens part way through a sentence, use an ellipsis (...) to begin the quotation.
- If the quote closes with an incomplete sentence, use the ellipsis *plus* a period at the end.

Footnotes and Endnotes

Footnotes usually appear on the page on which quoted material appears. However, it is acceptable to type these notes on a separate sheet headed *Notes* and attach this to the end of the body. (See this unit, TT77.)

Footnotes and endnotes are used for two purposes:

- to provide additional useful information on a particular topic to that noted in the body of the report

```
6.  For more detailed information on Canada's
    population, consult the statistical data published
    regularly by Statistics Canada.
```

- to identify the source of information quoted exactly or paraphrased

```
11.  J.E. McCarthy and S.J. Shapiro, Basic Marketing,
     First Canadian Edition, Irwin-Dorsey, Georgetown,
     Ont., 1975, p. 157.
```

Numbering Footnotes and Endnotes

- Use Arabic numerals and number each quotation or reference consecutively throughout the report. Asterisks may be used when only a very few references are needed.
- In the body, type the reference numbers a half line above the regular typing line at the *end* of the quotation or reference and outside any punctuation.

```
. . . spacing is as you would expect."²
```

In the footnote or endnote itself, the numeral may or may not be raised.

Typing Footnotes

When footnotes must be typed on the page on which the reference appears, be sure you leave enough space at the bottom of the page. (To guarantee that you have sufficient room at the bottom edge for the footnotes *and* a 3 cm (6 line) bottom margin, raise the pencil line indicating page ending the equivalent of four typing lines (or 2 cm) each time you type the *end* of a footnote reference in the body.)

- When the typing is complete on a page, turn up *one* line under the body and type 20-24 underscores.
- Turn up a double space and begin typing the footnote references.
- Single space footnote references and double space between them.

- Follow the style and spacing illustrated below. This style will suit most applications, but some academic institutions may have particular requirements which must be followed.

    Show author(s) in the sequence of given name and family name.

    Underscore book names and type quotation marks around article titles.

    Punctuate footnotes as shown, i.e., use commas to separate each item and use a period at the end.

```
1.  G.A. Reid, Modern Office Procedures, 2nd Ed.,
    Copp Clark Pitman, Toronto, 1978, p. 358.
```


```
1.  G.A. Reid, Modern Office Procedures, 2nd Ed.,
Copp Clark Pitman, Toronto, 1978, p. 358.
```

Typing Endnotes

When quotation references (footnotes) are typed as a separate sheet, follow the style and typing set-up rules presented below.

- Start typing the page on line 13.
- Use the heading *Notes*.
- Single space each reference and double space between references.
- Place the sheet after the body of the document and in front of the bibliography.
- If continuation pages are required, start on line 7 and use a page numbering system that has not already been used (e.g., lower case Roman numerals).

NOTES


```
1.  Alice Munro, "The Time of Death," Canadian Short
    Stories, ed. Robert Weaver, Toronto, Oxford
    University Press, 1960, p. 97.

2.  Martin O'Malley, "Without Reservation," Canadian
    Business, Vol. 53, No. 4, April, 1980, p. 37.
```

References to Anthologies and Collections

Show the author and the work cited from the anthology, the anthology title (underscored) plus the name(s) of the editor(s), place of publication, publisher, and year of publication.

2. Alice Munro, "The Time of Death," <u>Canadian Short Stories</u>, ed. Robert Weaver, Toronto, Oxford University Press, 1960.

References to Books

Full Footnote   The standard footnote content includes footnote number, author, book title, publisher, place of publication, year of publication, and page number(s).

1. G.A. Reid, <u>Modern Office Procedures</u>, 2nd Ed., Copp Clark Pitman, Toronto, 1978, p. 358.

Short Footnote   When *full* reference to the work is made either in the text or in the bibliography, the footnote need include only footnote number, author (family name only), book title, and page number(s).

2. Reid, <u>Modern Office Procedures</u>, p. 356.

- For two authors, list their names in the order shown on the title page of the book.
- For more than two authors, show the first author and then *et al.*

5. F.C. Watkins et al., <u>Practical English Handbook</u>, 5th Ed., Houghton Mifflin, Boston, 1978, p. 89.

References to Periodicals and Newspapers

Show the author's name, article title (in quotes), periodical or newspaper name (underscored), volume number, month and year of publication, and page number(s).

3. Martin O'Malley, "Without Reservations," <u>Canadian Business</u>, Vol. 53, No. 4, April, 1980, p. 37.

Shortened and Recurring References

After a book or periodical has been footnoted in full once, or is to be shown in the bibliography, shortened references may be used following any of the styles below:

- the *short form* (author, title, page number)

- *ibid.* (short form of *ibidem*, meaning in the same place): this refers the reader back to the immediately preceding footnote
- *op. cit. (opere citato*, in the place cited): this refers the reader back to a previously cited work but a different page number
- *loc. cit.* (loco citato, in the place cited): this refers the reader back to the previously cited work

1. Reid, <u>Modern Office Procedures</u>, p. 228.

2. Ibid., p. 304.

3. Sharman, <u>The Business Bible</u>, p. 147.

4. Reid, op. cit., p. 326.

5. Sharman, loc. cit.

Note: Of these methods, the short form is the *preferred* form in business reports and academic papers. Very little additional typing effort is required to produce the short form and it is much easier to follow.

Bibliography

TT99   The bibliography is an alphabetical list of *all* the source material consulted by the author in the preparation of the report. Usually shown in each entry is the author(s), title, place of publication, publisher, and date of publication.

> Reid, G.A. <u>Modern Office Procedures</u>, 2nd Ed.
>   Toronto: Copp Clark Pitman, 1978.
>
> Watkins, F.C. et al.   <u>Practical English Handbook</u>,
>   5th Ed.   Boston: <u>Houghton Mifflin, 1978</u>.

- Type the bibliography on a separate page (or pages).
- Use the same margins as for the body. Start the first page on line 13 and succeeding pages on line 7.
- If a page numbering system is needed, use Roman numerals but leave the first page unnumbered.
- Centre and capitalize the main heading.

- Start the first line at the margin and indent the second line five or ten spaces.
- Single space each reference and leave a double space between them.
- Follow the punctuation shown in the illustration.
- Note that the first author is listed by family name first.
- When the work either does not have an author, or the author's name is not known, position the work in alphabetic order by the first word in the title, ignoring *A*, *An*, or *The*.

One author ⟶ Scherer, Avanell. Office Procedures: A Project Approach. Toronto: McGraw-Hill Ryerson, 1976.

Two authors ⟶ Smith, M.A. and Eileen Laker. Canadian Filing Practice, 2nd Ed. Toronto: Copp Clark Pitman, 1978.

Three or more authors ⟶ Forkner, Hamden L. et al. Correlated Dictation and Transcription, 2nd Ed. Toronto: Gage Educational Publishing Ltd., 1974.

Second book by same author(s) ⟶ ————. Forkner Shorthand. Toronto: Gage Educational Publishing Ltd., 1972.

Editor as author ⟶ Weaver, Robert, ed. Canadian Short Stories. Toronto: Oxford University Press, 1960.

Author unknown ⟶ Webster's New Collegiate Dictionary. Springfield: G. & C. Merriam Company, 1975.

Magazine article ⟶ Roberts, Wayne. "Control System Lets You Count All Copier Costs." Canadian Office, April, 1980, Vol. II, No. 4, p. 44.

Newspaper article ⟶ "West Urges Ottawa to Economic Summit." Toronto Star, April 24, 1980, Sec. A, p. A.1.

Institution as author and publisher ⟶ Council of Ministers of Education, Canada. Metric Guide. Toronto: The Council, 1977.

Government document ⟶ Ontario. Ministry of Education. The Formative Years. Toronto: The Ministry, 1975.

Index

TT100   An index is an alphabetic listing of all topics and their page numbers. It is often provided with very lengthy reports and academic papers.

Indexes will vary considerably with the nature of the material. However, use the same margins, and starting and finishing lines as the rest of the document, and plan your work so that the information is easy to follow.

Typing Guide Sheet for Reports and Manuscripts

TT101   • To simplify the layout task, rule a typing guide backing sheet with a broad felt-tip marking pen that shows top, bottom, and side margins. Type line numbers at the left side.

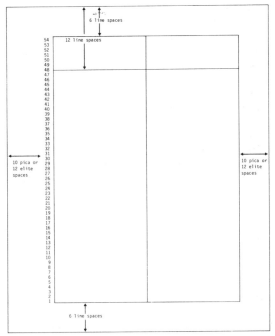

6 line spaces

12 line spaces

54
53
52
51
50
49
48
47
46
45
44
43
42
41
40
39
38
37
36
35
34
33
32
31
30
29
28
27
26
25
24
23
22
21
20
19
18
17
16
15
14
13
12
11
10
9
8
7
6
5
4
3
2
1

10 pica or
12 elite
spaces

10 pica or
12 elite
spaces

6 line spaces

Typing guide sheet

- Place this backing sheet behind the top copy and in front of the first sheet of carbon paper.
- Type just within the frame indicated on your guide.

TT102 Transcription Tips

Taking Dictation in Shorthand

TT103
- Date each page of your notebook.
- Start each day's dictation on a fresh page.
- Have several pens or pencils ready for dictation time.
- If you work for several dictators, use a different book (varied colours) for each.
- Number each piece of correspondence dictated.
- Develop a code for changes in your notes if the dictator is prone to making changes. (Leave a blank column on the left side of your page and write in the changes in the blank space. Start with an (A), continue with (B) and so on.)
- Write names, addresses, and unusual words in longhand.
- Leave some space after each dictated item in case special instructions are needed.
- Mark telegrams or other rush jobs with a fold-down on the page or some other quick method of identification.

- Underline your notes as follows:
  - one line under words to be underscored
  - two lines under words to be typed in capitals
- Do not interrupt the dictator in the midst of a letter unless you have fallen far behind in dictation. Wait for a convenient pause and check any doubtful point. Be prepared to read back the words preceding and following the section in question.
- Use interruptions in dictation time to read over your notes.

Transcribing

TT104   Whether you are preparing mailable transcripts from your own shorthand notes, a dictaphone, or someone's handwritten or typed rough draft:

- Get together all the supplies you need, e.g., paper, carbons, envelopes, correcting materials, dictionary, files.
- Look up information or do any mathematical calculations *before* you begin transcribing.
- Try to do the transcribing in one unit of time rather than several interrupted periods.

From Shorthand

- Check for urgent items and deal with those first.
- Read each letter through before you begin transcribing.
- Check for special instructions.
- Draw a diagonal line through each item when you have transcribed it.
- Place a rubber band around the last page transcribed so that you are ready for the next dictation session.

From Dictating Machines

- Check the indicator slip for instructions and corrections.
- Listen to the dictation all the way through.
- Listen to a phrase (up to 8 words), stop the machine, type the phrase.
- Check spellings before you start typing.

From Rough Draft

- Read a paragraph through before starting to transcribe it.
- Check spelling and punctuation.

TT105   Typewriter Care

Regular Care

TT106
- Each day, wipe all exposed parts with a soft, dry cloth.
- Clean out corners with a long-handled brush and use a stiff-bristle brush on the type. Brush toward yourself, never across the keys. Clean the brush as you work by wiping it on a paper towel. Dust under the machine too!

- Clean type bars daily.
- Cover your typewriter at the end of the day.
- If you use an eraser, move the carriage all the way to the left or right to prevent eraser dust from getting into the moving parts of the typewriter.
- *Don't* use force to get jammed keys apart. You may bend the type bars out of alignment and ruin the appearance of your typing.

Periodic Care

TT107
- Change the typewriter ribbon before it starts producing light copy.
- Check the tension and impression controls when you type letters and reports. These settings vary according to the number of carbon copies required.
- If your typing appears uneven (light and dark) check the following:
  dirt embedded in the type bars
  tension adjustment in the faulty type bars
  multiple copy control
  platen (cylinder)
- Leave repairs to the professional. Have your machine checked regularly for correct alignment of keys, oiling, *etc.* If you use your typewriter a great deal, you may be wise to buy a service contract from the manufacturer rather than pay a technician for each visit.

Typewriter Selection

TT108
Typewriters to meet every need are available for purchase. Your selection should be matched to the intended use of the equipment.

Carriage Length

TT109
The standard typewriter carriage length is 33 cm. Where greater length is frequently required, e.g., for complex financial statements, the purchase of a longer length carriage of 41 cm may be advantageous.

Type Size

TT110
Typewriters are available with a number of different type size possibilities.

- Pica typewriters produce 10 characters to the inch (10 pitch).

- Elite typewriters produce 12 characters to the inch (12 pitch).
- Proportional spacing typewriters produce type that occupies space in accordance with the amount required by each letter, e.g., the capital *M* occupies considerably more space than the lower case *i*. (*Note*: the appearance of work on these machines is most attractive but corrections are time consuming and difficult.)
- Pica/elite typewriters make it possible to produce material in either pica or elite pitch at the flick of a switch.

Type Faces

TT111 Where variation in type style is needed from time to time, consider purchasing a machine which can accept changeable type elements. Changeable type elements are available in a wide-ranging variety of styles and pitch sizes.

TT112 Self-Correcting Typewriters

Typewriters may be purchased which are capable of correcting errors involving single characters only and up to several lines of type. The increased cost involved is often outweighed by the savings in time.

Word Processors

TT113 Word processors (automated electronic typewriters) can produce error-free material automatically. Because the equipment is so complex, an entire unit of the book is devoted to it. (See Unit 20.)

Electronic Typewriters

TT114 The electronic typewriter bridges the gap between standard electric machines and the sophisticated word processors. The features available vary with the make and model, and may include some or all of the following: automatic character correction, quietness, fewer moving parts, changeable type element, variable pitch, automatic figure alignment, automatic centring and justifying, editing capability, memory capacity, and possibly mini-diskette storage. Some machines even have a partial display and/or communication capability.

Because the fear of making errors is not so great, typists tend to type faster on electronic typewriters than they do on conventional ones.

Unit 19

Useful Information

This unit contains business-related reference material which does not lie within the other topic areas covered in this handbook.

Abbreviations

U1   For standard business abbreviations, see Unit 2, C25.

U2   ### Places

Canadian Provinces and Territories

U3

Provinces and Territories	Abbreviations	
	Standard	**Two-letter**
Alberta	Alta.	AB
British Columbia	B.C.	BC
Labrador (part of Newfoundland)	Lab.	LB
Manitoba	Man.	MB
New Brunswick	N.B.	NB
Newfoundland	Nfld.	NF
Northwest Territories	N.W.T.	NT
Nova Scotia	N.S.	NS
Ontario	Ont.	ON
Prince Edward Island	P.E.I.	PE
Quebec	P.Q. or Que.	PQ
Saskatchewan	Sask.	SK
Yukon Territory	Yuk.	YT

United States, Districts, and Territories

The two-letter U.S. Postal Service abbreviations must appear on all envelope addresses.

States, Districts, and Territories	Abbreviations Standard	Two-letter
Alabama	Ala.	AL
Alaska	—	AK
Arizona	Ariz.	AZ
Arkansas	Ark.	AR
California	Calif.	CA
Colorado	Colo.	CO
Connecticut	Conn.	CT
Delaware	Del.	DE
District of Columbia	D.C.	DC
Florida	Fla.	FL
Georgia	Ga.	GA
Guam	—	GU
Hawaii	—	HI
Idaho	—	ID
Illinois	Ill.	IL
Indiana	Ind.	IN
Iowa	—	IA
Kansas	Kans.	KS
Kentucky	Ky.	KY
Louisiana	La.	LA
Maine	—	ME
Maryland	Md.	MD
Massachusetts	Mass.	MA
Michigan	Mich.	MI
Minnesota	Minn.	MN
Mississippi	Miss.	MS
Missouri	Mo.	MO
Montana	Mont.	MT
Nebraska	Nebr.	NE
Nevada	Nev.	NV
New Hampshire	N.H.	NH
New Jersey	N.J.	NJ
New Mexico	N. Mex.	NM
New York	N.Y.	NY
North Carolina	N.C.	NC
North Dakota	N. Dak.	ND
Ohio	—	OH
Oklahoma	Okla.	OK
Oregon	Oreg.	OR
Pennsylvania	Pa.	PA
Puerto Rico	P.R.	PR
Rhode Island	R.I.	RI
South Carolina	S.C.	SC

South Dakota	S. Dak.	SD
Tennessee	Tenn.	TN
Texas	Tex.	TX
Utah	—	UT
Vermont	Vt.	VT
Virgin Islands	V.I.	VI
Virginia	Va.	VA
Washington	Wash.	WA
West Virginia	W. Va.	WV
Wisconsin	Wis.	WI
Wyoming	Wyo.	WY

Foreign Countries, Capitals, Languages, and Currencies

U5 Current information as to countries, capitals, etc., may be found at public libraries, reference libraries, or by contacting the official representative of a foreign country in Canada. These foreign diplomats are usually located in major cities. A list of Canadian representatives abroad appears in the *Canadian Almanac and Directory.*

Foreign Words and Phrases Commonly Used

U6

ad hoc	temporary; for a specific purpose
ad infinitum	without limit or end
ad nauseam	to the point of disgust
ad valorem	according to value
bona fide	in good faith
caveat emptor	let the buyer beware
carte blanche	full discretionary powers
circa	about
coup d'état	a sudden and decisive political measure
cum laude	with honour, praise
deo volente	if God wills
dramatis personae	cast in a play; people in a dramatic situation
esprit de corps	team spirit, team work, co-operation
ex officio	by virtue of an office
fait accompli	something already done
faux pas	false step, error
incognito	in disguise
in toto	altogether, entirely
je ne sais quoi	indefinable quality
junta	administrative council usually formed as the result of a revolution

kudos	praise
laissez faire	the principle of letting people do as they please
modus operandi	method of operating
modus vivendi	way of life
ne plus ultra	the highest degree
nom de plume	pen name, pseudonym
non sequitur	does not follow, irrelevant
objet d'art	a work of art
per annum	each year
per capita	each person
per diem	each day
per se	itself
persona non grata	an unacceptable person
pièce de résistance	an outstanding item or event
pied-à-terre	temporary lodging
prix fixe	set price for a complete meal
pro forma	for the record, matter of form
pro rata	in proportion to
raison d'être	reason for being
répondez s'il vous plait	please reply
sine qua non	something essential
status quo	current state of affairs
tempus fugit	time flies
terra firma	solid earth, dry land
verbatim	word for word

U7   # Holidays

National

U8

New Year's Day	January 1
Good Friday	movable
Victoria Day	Monday prior and closest to May 24
Canada Day	July 1
Labour Day	first Monday in September
Thanksgiving Day	second Monday in October
Christmas Day	December 25

Government offices are also closed on Easter Monday and Remembrance Day (November 11).

Banks are also closed on Remembrance Day.

Provincial (in Addition to National Holidays)

U9

Alberta	Boxing Day	December 26
British Columbia	British Columbia Day	first Monday in August
	Boxing Day	December 26

Manitoba	Civic Holiday	first Monday in August
	Boxing Day	December 26
New Brunswick	Boxing Day	December 26
Newfoundland	St. Patrick's Day	March 17
	St. George's Day	April 23
	Commonwealth Day	May 24
	Discovery Day	June 26
	Memorial Day	July 1
	Orangeman's Day	July 12
	Boxing Day	December 26
Northwest Territories	Civic Holiday	first Monday in August
	Boxing Day	December 26
Nova Scotia	Boxing Day	December 26
Ontario	Civic Holiday (Simcoe day in Toronto and some other municipalities)	first Monday in August
	Boxing Day	December 26
Prince Edward Island	Boxing Day	December 26
Quebec	St. Jean Baptiste Day	June 24
Saskatchewan	Civic Holiday	first Monday in August
	Boxing Day	December 26
Yukon	Discovery Day	third Monday in August

U.S. National Holidays

ɑ10

New Year's Day	January 1
Washington's Birthday	third Monday in February
Good Friday	movable
Easter Monday	movable
Memorial Day	last Monday in May
Independence Day	July 4
Labor Day	first Monday in September
Columbus Day	second Monday in October
Veterans' Day	November 11
Thanksgiving Day	fourth Thursday in November
Christmas Day	December 25

Metric System

ɑ11   The metric system adopted by Canada is Le Système International D'Unités, referred to as SI. Because the system is an international one, it is essential that units, prefixes, and symbols be used properly. (Rules for typing metric expressions can be found in Unit 18, TT34.)

Metric Units

U12

Name	Unit of	Symbol
metre	length	m
litre	volume	L
gram	mass	g
second	time	s
degree Celsius	temperature	°C

Common Metric Prefixes

U13

Prefix	Meaning	Factor (Multiplier)	Symbol
mega	1 million	10^6 (1 000 000)	M
*kilo	1 thousand	10^3 (1 000)	k
hecto	1 hundred	10^2 (100)	h
deca	ten	10 (10)	da
deci	one tenth of a	10^{-1} (0.1)	d
*centi	one hundredth of a	10^{-2} (0.01)	c
*milli	one thousandth of a	10^{-3} (0.001)	m
micro	one millionth of a	10^{-6} (0.000 001)	μ

*most frequently used

Most Frequently Used Metric Measurements

U14

Quantity	Unit	Symbol
Length	millimetre	mm
	centimetre	cm
	metre	m
	kilometre	km
	(1 m = 100 cm or 1000 mm)	
Area	square centimetre	cm^2
	square metre	m^2
	square kilometre	km^2
	hectare	ha
Volume	cubic centimetre	cm^3
	cubic metre	m^3
	($1 m^3$ = 1 000 000 cm^3)	
	millilitre	mL
	litre	L (or small 1 when handwritten)
	(1 L = 1000 mL)	
Mass	milligram	mg
	gram	g
	kilogram	kg
	tonne	t
	(1 kg = 1000 g)	

Quantity	Unit	Symbol
Time	second	s
	minute	min
	hour	h
Speed	metres per second	m/s
	kilometres per hour	km/h
Temperature	degree Celsius	°C

Common Unit Conversion (to 3 decimal places)

U15

Length	1 inch	= 0.025 m (2.54 cm or 25.4 mm)
	1 foot	= 0.305 m (30.48 cm)
	1 yard	= 0.914 m
	1 mile	= 1.609 km
Area	1 square inch	= 6.452 cm²
	1 square foot	= 0.093 m²
	1 square yard	= 0.836 m²
	1 acre	= 0.405 ha (hectare)
	1 square mile	= 2.590 km² (259 ha)
Volume	1 fluid ounce	= 28.413 cm³ (28.4 mL)
	1 pint (imperial)	= 0.568 dm³ (0.57 L)
	1 quart	= 1.137 dm³ (1.14 L)
	1 gallon	= 4.546 dm³ (4.546 L)
	1 cubic inch	= 16.387 cm³
	1 cubic foot	= 28.317 dm³ (28.32L)
	1 cubic yard	= 0.765 m³
Mass	1 ounce	= 28.350 g
	1 pound	= 0.454 kg
	1 ton (short 2000 lb.)	= 907.185 kg
Speed	1 mile per hour	= 0.447 m/s
		= 1.609 km/h

Temperature $5/9 \times$ No. of degrees Fahrenheit – 32 = degrees Celsius

Some Easy to Remember Measurements

U16

- The standard doorway is about 2 m high and 0.75 m wide.
- An average chair is roughly 0.5 m high.
- A paper clip is about 3 cm long.
- There are about 200 mL in a cup of coffee.
- The width of a small fingernail is 1 cm.
- A coin is approximately 1 mm thick.

Note: The information provided above is based on *The Metric Guide, Second Edition*, 1976, published by the Council of Ministers of Education, Canada, distributed by O.I.S.E. Publications Sales. 252 Bloor Street West, Toronto, Ontario M5S 1V6.

Roman Numerals

- Use upper case numerals for major divisions in outlines and in literary publications (volumes, books, chapters, appendixes, *etc.*).
- Use lower case numerals for preliminary pages in reports and subsections.

Arabic	Roman	Arabic	Roman
1	I	30	XXX
2	II	40	XL
3	III	50	L
4	IV	60	LX
5	V	70	LXX
6	VI	80	LXXX
7	VII	90	XC
8	VIII	100	C
9	IX	300	CCC
10	C	400	CD
11	XI	XI	500
12	XII	600	DC
13	XIII	900	CM
14	XIV	1 000	M
15	XV	5 000	$\overline{V}$*
16	XV1	8 000	$\overline{VIII}$*
17	XVII	10 000	$\overline{X}$
18	XVIII	30 000	$\overline{XXX}$*
19	XIX	50 000	$\overline{L}$*
20	XX		

Note: A horizontal line placed over a number multiplies its value by 1000.

Build combinations of Roman numerals by prefixing or annexing letters. A letter prefixed to another is subtracted from it; a letter annexed is added.

$$49 = \overset{40}{\overbrace{L - X}} + IX = XLIX$$

$$62 = \overset{60}{\overbrace{L + X}} + II = LXII$$

Do not repeat a Roman numeral more than three times.

> 337 = CCCXXXVII
> (437 = CDXXXVII not CCCCXXXVII)
> 1984 = MCMLXXXIV

Time Zones

Canada

U19   Canada is divided into seven time zones. Note that there is one hour's difference between each zone as you move across the country. Newfoundland time, however, is only one-half hour different from Atlantic time.

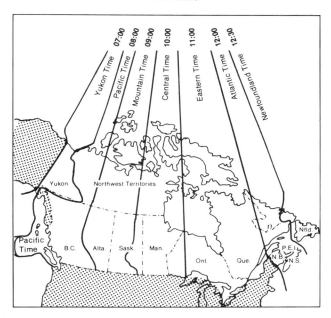

Subtract one hour from each zone from east to west.
Add one hour to each zone from west to east.

United States

U20   The United States is divided into four times zones with one hour's difference between adjacent zones.

Unit 20

Word Processing The Systems Approach to Office Management

Word processing is a concept that transforms information and ideas into business communications by using people, procedures, and equipment in the most efficient way. Essentially, what happens is that an operator, working from verbal or written instructions uses an automated electronic typewriter capable of producing error-free work at very high speeds and of storing the resulting input. This method produces typed communications in the fastest and most cost-efficient way.

Advantages of Word Processing

W1   Word processing can offer these advantages:

- improvement in the effectiveness and productivity of all office workers—from clerks to top management
- more cost-efficient typing support function
- elimination of tedious, time-consuming, repetitive typing tasks
- improvement in quality of typed work and speed of output
- greater career opportunities for secretaries
- availability of electronic mail capability, i.e., ability to transmit and receive messages
- fast storage and retrieval of records

Word Processing Equipment

W2   The major component of word processing equipment is the automated electronic typewriter which is more commonly known as a word processor or text editor. The equipment generally consists of a keyboard, a separate printer, a display device, and disk drives. It may be used on its own (standalone) or linked with a computer in either a shared logic or shared resource configuration.

Word Processors

W3   The capabilities of a word processor vary with the make and model but in general it can be expected to perform as follows:

- Information keystroked (typed) is video displayed (usually on a cathode ray tube—CRT) so that the operator can see what has been recorded before the text (material) is played back (produced in final form).
- Text editing (changes) may be achieved without the need for retyping the entire document and may range from altering a single character to inserting an entire paragraph.
- Once the material has been keystroked and edited, the playback is automatic and the machine can produce repetitively error-free documents at very high speeds.
- Storage capacity is provided. The equipment offers both internal and auxiliary electronic storage, i.e., the machine has a memory of its own and in addition permits what is in the internal memory to be transferred to an external device (a magnetic card, floppy disk/diskette, or disk cartridge) for filing. The material on the auxiliary device can be fed back into the word processor at any time for reuse and, if necessary, for changes without the need for a total retyping.
- Repetitive typing is eliminated and documents can be individualized. Material being keystroked can be coded to stop at particular points during playback so that such variable information as names, addresses, and numbers may be inserted.
- Formatting (setting up) is automatic, i.e., the machine will automatically centre, change margins, indent, justify, tabulate, and adjust line spacing.
- Material suitable for printing purposes can be produced. Text keystroked into a word processor and recorded on magnetic disk or tape can be processed through a photocomposer (phototypesetter) to produce fully justified typesetting for much less cost than is possible with commercial typesetting.

- Merging of stored material is possible, e.g., from among many stored form paragraphs just a few may be selected and merged automatically to produce a complete document; or mailing lists on one storage device may be merged with form letters on another device to produce automatically error-free individualized letters.
- Variety in appearance of the output is provided through pitch variations of pica and elite and the ability of the machines to accept interchangeable typing elements or wheels.

Other capabilities of the equipment may include sorting (the ability to arrange stored information in a desired sequence), searching (the ability to locate information, e.g., particular words), searching and replacing particular words or phrases, moving lines or paragraphs, presenting information in graphic format, the ability to accept typed documents through an optical character reader (thus eliminating re-keystroking), and data base enquiry.

Word processing is also available as a special program package on general purpose mainframe computers, minicomputers, and even personal computer systems.

Standalone Word Processors

W4

The *standalone* is an independent unit consisting of a keyboard, a printer, and usually a video display device. The unit contains its own internal electronic storage (memory) and intelligence and offers external storage via magnetic cards, floppy disks/diskettes, or disk cartridges. Some standalone word processors are capable of communicating with other word processors, i.e., what is keyed in on a unit in one place can be played out on a compatible unit in another place.

Computer-Based Word Processors

W5

Word processing systems may be set up in work stations so that they share the logic and storage of a central computer controller. In such *shared logic* systems, work stations cannot operate independently of the central controller. Some systems have a central disk drive and controller, and work stations that have their own intelligence and can operate independently of the central devices. These systems are known as *shared resource* systems.

Computer-based word processors all have communicating ability.

Software Programmable or Hardwired Equipment

Word processing equipment is either software programmable or hardwired.

Software programmable means that the capability of the equipment may be changed by means of programs available from the equipment manufacturer. This permits updating as new features become available. Present programs include general business accounting, inventory control, law office systems, hotel accounting, executive package (which includes calendar, appointment schedule, *tickler* system), spelling dictionary (which can verify the spelling of certain words), and a mathematics program (which permits addition, subtraction, multiplication, division, and percentages).

Hardwired means the equipment will remain for its life span with the same capabilities.

Word Processing Personnel

W6   In firms with centralized word processing set-ups, originators or authors (executives and managers) are supported by two kinds of specialized secretaries: *correspondence* (typing) secretaries and *administrative* (non-typing) secretaries. The correspondence secretary is a part of the word processing department; depending on the firm's organization, the administrative secretary may not be.

The terms used to describe correspondence secretaries may also include: word processing secretary, word processing operator, word processing specialist, or word processor.

Correspondence (Typing) Secretary

W7   The duties of the correspondence secretary usually include the production of letters, memos, reports, and statistics; proofing; taking dictation; and transcribing. The person employed in this capacity is familiar with document set-up, is a fast and accurate typist, and has excellent language skills. In addition, he or she can deal with hand-written or dictated material, is a good proofreader, is machine-oriented, enjoys deadline pressure, likes teamwork, has thinking and problem-solving ability, and can cope with quotas and measured work.

Administrative (Non-Typing) Secretary

W8   The work of an administrative secretary includes answering the telephone, handling the mail, composing correspondence; copying and collating; gathering information, filing, delivering messages, handling travel arrangements, and making calculations. The person employed in this position usually has a good knowledge of all business procedures, is capable of working independently, has particularly good human relations skills, can deal with constant interruptions, is flexible, has good verbal skills, and enjoys working for several people.

Career Paths in Word Processing Centres

W9 Suggested job descriptions and typical competencies for correspondence secretaries and administrative secretaries from entry level to supervisory level are shown in the following chart:

Typing (Correspondence Secretary)	Non-Typing (Administrative Secretary)
Word Processing Trainee	Junior Administrative Secretary
• requires 0-12 months word processing experience • responsible for typing and transcription • must be proficient in grammar, spelling, punctuation, proofing, editing, electronic keyboarding, time management, and use of reference sources • must be oriented toward machines and enjoy teamwork	• an entry level position • works as part of a team • responsible for filing, photocopying, handling appointments, keeping records and lists, handling mail, telephone duties, with little or no typing
Word Processing Operator or Specialist	Senior Administrative Secretary
• responsible for typing and transcription, including handling special documents and meeting high-quality typing standards • formats, produces, and revises difficult documents from any kind of input (e.g., technical and statistical reports) • must be skilled in all aspects of word processing equipment and procedures • must have full knowledge of secretarial procedures	• may act as supervisor of team of administrative secretaries • composes and edits documents for principals • undertakes research tasks

Typing **(Correspondence Secretary)**	**Non-Typing** **(Administrative Secretary)**
Word Processing Supervisor or Manager	Administrative Services Supervisor or Manager
• operates the word processing centre (or a section of it)	• co-ordinates work flow and administers work of team of administrative secretaries
• co-ordinates and assigns work, trains personnel, maintains standards, analyzes production data, and keeps records	• works with word processing manager or supervisor to ensure co-ordination of the two functions
• must have management skills and expertise in all processing functions	• may manage records retention (storage and retrieval of system input media) and filing

Word Processing Set-Ups (Configurations)

W10   The organization of the word processing facility in the office will vary with the size and needs of the firm. It may range from a large, self-contained, fully equipped (centralized) department down to a single, independent unit used by one operator (decentralized). Typical word processing set-ups are:

Centralized Word Processing Departments

W11   This is a separate department of the firm which has its own budget and which reports directly to management. Several organizational structures are possible. For example, the department may have responsibility for

- all the firm's typing and secretarial support services, with one manager responsible for *correspondence* (typing) services and one manager responsible for *administrative* (secretarial support) services

  or
- correspondence (typing) only, with administrative (secretarial support) staff being administered by the separate departments to which they belong

Decentralized Departments (Mini Centres)

W12   These are small word processing centres set up to serve individual departments under the direction of each department manager.

Satellite Centres

W13 These are set up like mini centres but occur only in firms that also have centralized word processing. The word processing department handles the bulk of the company's output; satellite centres deal with any special requirements of a department (e.g., confidential or rush jobs). In some firms, correspondence secretarial services may be centalized and the administrative secretarial support organized into satellite centres. In yet other firms, the reverse of this arrangement may exist.

Single Units

W14 These are used in traditional principal/secretary relationships.

Dictation Equipment

W15 Because of the high cost of word processing equipment, the machines must be kept working constantly if the greatest cost efficiency is to be achieved. Because in-person dictation is slow and deciphering handwriting is time consuming for the typist, machine dictation equipment is an essential component of a word processing system.

Dictation Equipment Choices

W16 Dictation machines are of two types:

- *independent portable or desk top units*, which are very similar to small tape recorders and consist of a recorder, a microphone, and a separate transcriber
- *centralized recording and transcribing units* with a telephone hookup to permit dictation

Centralized Recording Devices

Automatic changer (also known as discrete media recorder): This type of equipment permits continuous central recording without the need for someone to insert a new cassette, tape, *etc.*, when one is full because the recording medium is changed automatically. Long periods of dictation are possible, and transcription can be under way while dictation continues.

Endless loop: The recording tape is sealed into a tank and is not removed or touched. Such a system offers automatic, unattended use 24 hours a day. A supervisory console (or monitoring panel) enables dictation to be directed automatically to the secretary who can deal with it most rapidly. With this system, transcription can be going on just a very short time after the dictation.

Telephone Hookup

Telephone hookup to a central recording device may be made through a private and separate telephone system or through the regular telephone service. The telephone receiver is used for recording in both systems.

Private systems (purchased or rented) not supplied by the public telephone service: Three types are available:
- *nonselector* equipment: connected to one recorder only (if the recorder is in use, the dictator must wait)
- *manual selector*: dictator can select a vacant recorder
- *automatic selector*: dictator is automatically connected to first free recorder

Telephone company system: equipment provided by your local telephone service is connected with the centralized recording equipment. Access to the recording device is gained by dialling particular numbers, and dictation is possible from any extension telephone or from any outside telephone.

Note: Advice on efficient dictation techniques is provided in Unit 2, C60.

Compatible Technology in the Automated Office

W17   As the office becomes increasingly automated, more and more business activities are becoming integrated. Office automation already exists in many areas. Consult the index of this handbook for more information on the most recent developments in office automation, e.g., electronic mail, facsimile transmission, video conferencing, micrographics (particularly COM), and intelligent copiers (information distributors).

Word Processing Terms

W18   **Boilerplate:** a term used to describe what appear to be individually typed communications but are in fact form letters or form paragraphs combined with variables.

Codes: special instructions such as stop codes, underscore codes, backspace codes, tab codes, keystroked into the recording media. During playback the use of these codes results in the special instruction being carried out.

Communicating word processors: text can be automatically transmitted from one unit to another compatible unit via an internal network or over telephone lines.

Continuous loop: see endless loop recorders.

C.P.U.: the central processing unit of the computer.

CRT (Cathode Ray Tube): a video screen which displays the operator's input in electronic word processing systems prior to playback.

Cursor: a symbol on a CRT which indicates where the next character will be displayed.

Data base: see Unit 3, D18.

Disk drive: the device that makes possible the recording of text onto magnetic media.

Downtime: time when equipment is not operating correctly because of some malfunction.

Dumb terminal: a text-editing terminal of a computer-based system that relies on the computer for its intelligence.

Endless loop recorders: a continuous flow dictation system in which magnetic tape is sealed in a tank and loops around constantly.

Electronic mail: the use of electronic means (telephone lines, private networks, or satellite networks) to transmit printed information.

Floppy disk/diskette: a flexible magnetic storage medium.

Footer: page identification used at the foot of a page.

Formatting: setting margins, indents, *etc.*, for various typing set-ups, e.g., letters and reports.

Global search and replace: the capability of the word processor to locate a particular word or expression in stored information and replace it automatically with another word or expression.

Hard copy: a typed or printed document on paper.

Header: page identification used at the top of a page.

Infotex (CN/CP Telecommunication): permits national and international communication between word processors through the Telex network.

Input: the first stage in the processing of a typing job, e.g., the word originator's (author's) dictation.

Keyboarding or keystroking: inputting material into the system via an electronic keyboard.

Mag cards: magnetic cards which record text as it is being typed.

Menu: list of alternative operator actions supplied by the system.

Modems (modulator-demodulators): for using voice lines for data transmission (allows digital business machine signals to be converted to analog signals used with communications equipment).

MT/ST (magnetic tape Selectric typewriter): the first of the word processing machines—introduced by IBM in 1963.

Optical Character Recognition (OCR): units that can scan and enter typed material directly into the word processing system without the need for retyping.

Output: the completed job.

Peripherals: items of equipment that may be attached to the system, e.g., printers, photocomposers, telecommunications devices, or OCR.

Playback or playout: printing out of recorded material.

Prerecorded: material that has been put onto disk or tape for reuse, e.g., paragraphs for form letters, legal documents, collection letters.

Principal: person who initiates work and requires secretarial services.

Search: locating specific places in recorded material.

Scrolling: the movement of text on a visual display.

Shared logic systems: several operators at several keyboard terminals use the memory and processing powers of one computer or C.P.U. simultaneously.

Shared resource system: a system with a central disk drive and controller and work stations that have their own intelligence.

Smart terminal: text-editing terminal that has its own computer power but shares the printing and/or storage facilities of the computer.

Standalone: machines that operate independently, quite separate from any other machine (the machine has the ability to store, recall, and revise).

Text: printed or written matter.

Text editing: revising recorded information on electronic typing systems for automatic playback.

Throughput: the time involved in actually processing the job from initiation to completion.

Time sharing: several terminals from different organizations may be connected to a large computer system with the cost of the computer being shared.

Transcribing unit: playback component of a dictation machine.

Turnaround time: the time taken between the beginning and the completion of a job once it has been given to the word processing operator.

Video display: see CRT.

Wraparound: the automatic process of carrying an incomplete word from one line to the next.

INDEX

The boldface numbers in this index refer to page numbers; the lightface letter and number combinations are the locator codes on the pages.

Please note the following points as you use this index:
1. The references shown indicate the points at which information **starts** in each case.
2. Use the code letters which identify each unit to help you quickly locate the **kind** of information you want. For example, if you want information on **typing** letters, use the TT (Typing Techniques) references rather than C (Communications) references. On the other hand, if you want information on **writing** letters, then use the C references.

322   Index

Key punch, **85**-D10

Labels
  envelopes, **262**-TT48
  file folder, **105**-F21
Language skills, **21**-C1
Last number redial, **225**-T26
Lateral records cabinets,
  118-F39
Leaders, **244**-TT12
Ledger, **18**-B56
Legal documents, **265**-TT54
Legal forms, **133**-FO25
Letter mail, overseas,
  196-PO33
Letter parts, **271**-TT62
Letter placement, **270**-TT61
Letter samples, **54**-C32
  acknowledgement,
    apology, collection,
    complaint,
    congratulatory, enquiry,
    form, introduction,
    order, payment,
    recommendation,
    reservations, sales,
    sympathy, thank you
Letter styles
  block, **270**-TT60
  full (extreme) block,
    269-TT60
  hanging indented
    (suspended), **280**-TT99
  indented, **279**-TT99
  modified block, **270**-TT60
  official, **279**-TT99
  semi-block, **270**-TT60
  simplified, **278**-TT99
Letter telegram, **228**-T35
Letters of credit, **9**-B30;
  237-TA20
Letters, production of,
  281-TT82
Letters
  typing, **269**-TT58
  writing, **54**-C32
Library use, **149**-I10
Lighting, **98**-E17
Line graph typing,
  260-TT41
Listening skills, **93**-E5
Literary references,
  291-TT98; **294**-TT99
Loans, **10**-B31
Long distance
  calls, **218**-T7
  enquiries, **218**-T7
Long edge tabulations,
  252-TT24
Luggage. *see* Baggage.

MICR, **81**-D3
Magnetic
  disk, **81**-D3; **85**-D10
  tape, **81**-D3; **85**-D10
Mail services, **189**-PO1

Mailing notations,
  271-TT62
Main guides, **105**-F20
Manual selector equipment,
  318-W16
Manuscript
  typing, **283**-TT85
  writing, **69**-C54
Margin, **167**-M15
Margin setting, **241**-TT4
Marine calls, **220**-T16
Markdown, **167**-M15
Markup, **167**-M15
Master Charge, **9**-B26
Math sign typing, **246**-TT14
Mathematics in business,
  159-M1
Mean averages, **168**-M19
Measurements
  metric, **305**-U11
  possessives in, **35**-C12
Median, **169**-M19
Meetings
  agenda, **173**-MC4
  announcing, **172**-MC3
  conducting, **174**-MC6
  minutes, **175**-MC9
  planning, **171**-MC1
Memorandum
  typing, **281**-TT83
  writing, **68**-C52
Memory unit, computer,
  82-D5
Metric
  expressions, **255**-TT34
  system, **305**-U11
Microfiche, **121**-F47
Microfilm, **120**-F45; **85**-D10
  storage devices, **120**-F47
  types, **120**-F46
Microforms, **120**-F47
Micrographic storage,
  120-F45
Minutes, recording,
  176-MC9
Mixed punctuation,
  270-TT60
Mobile calls, **221**-T17
Mobile carriage filing
  systems, **119**-F41
Mode, **169**-M19
Monarch stationery,
  281-TT81
Money orders
  bank, **10**-B32
  postal, **194**-PO17
  telegraphic, **227**-T33
Money packets, **194**-PO18
Mood, def. of, **76**-C61
Motel accommodation,
  236-TA17
Motions, **175**-MC7
Multiple line conferencing,
  225-T26
Multiple page letters,
  276-TT77

N.S.F. cheques, **7**-B19
National holidays, **304**-U8
News release, **68**-C53
Night letter, **227**-T31
Noise control, **98**-E17
Non-restrictive clauses,
  comma with, **37**-C14
Nonselector equipment,
  318-W16
Notice of meeting, **172**-MC3
Nouns
  caps. of, **45**-C26
  def. of, **76**-C61
  plurals of, **49**-C28
  possessives of, **34**-C12
Number alignment,
  251-TT23
Number, def. of, **76**-C61
No. 8 envelope, typing,
  261-TT46
No. 10 envelope, typing,
  261-TT46
Numbered sentences in
  letters, **276**-TT78
Numbering systems in
  reports, **288**-TT92
Numbers
  in alpha. sequencing,
    103-F13
  hyphens in, **40**-C18
  in listed items, **243**-TT9
  in metric expressions,
    257-TT36
  roman numerals, **308**-U17
  rules for expressing,
    48-C27
  in tabs, **251**-TT23
  as words or figures,
    48-C27
Numeric
  dates, **257**-TT37
  times, **257**-TT37
Numeric filing, **109**-F27

OCR, **81**-D3
OMR, **81**-D3
Object, def. of, **76**-C61
Office layout, **97**-E16
Official letter, **279**-TT79
Offset
  duplicating, **200**-R1;
    209-R23
  master typing, **209**-R24
On-hook dialling, **225**-T26
Open punctuation,
  269-TT59
Operation of
  spirit duplicator, **205**-R12
  stencil duplicator,
    208-R20
Operator assisted calls,
  219-T9
  overseas calls, **220**-T12
Optical character
  recognition, **81**-D3
Optical mark reading, **81**-D3
Order bill of lading, **138**-G3